Justices William J. Brennan, Jr. and Thurgood Marshall on Capital Punishment

Its Constitutionality, Morality, Deterrent Effect, and Interpretation by the Court

Alan I. Bigel

University Press of America, Inc.
Lanham • New York • London

Copyright © 1997 by
University Press of America,® Inc.
4720 Boston Way
Lanham, Maryland 20706

12 Hid's Copse Rd.
Cummor Hill, Oxford OX2 9JJ

ISBN 0-7618-0614-8 (cloth: alk. ppr.)

This book is dedicated in loving memory of Uncle Kelly, who passed away on November 16, 1995. A man who shared love, intellect and compassion in equal proportion, he possessed a measure of class and character which will always inspire me and which I don't expect to encounter again.

Introduction

The death penalty will likely remain among the handful of controversial political and social issues most fervently debated into the indefinite future. The extensive literature on its legality and morality, and the myriad arguments which essentially derive from these criteria, will both enlighten and inflame public opinion. Justices William J. Brennan, Jr. (1956-1990) and Thurgood Marshall (1967-1991), who will deservedly be ranked among the handful of great civil libertarians of the 20th century, unwaveringly maintained that the death penalty is unconstitutional and a barbaric form of punishment which has been arbitrarily inflicted based on racial and ethnic bias. This study carefully examines their opinions and seeks to integrate their objections to the larger public debate on capital punishment. Their sentiments on the death penalty are an invaluable contribution to our understanding of this complex and emotionally charged subject.

I wish to express profound gratitude to the *Notre Dame Journal of Law, Ethics & Public Policy* for permission to reprint this article, which appeared in Volume 8, Issue #1 (1994). None of the text has been changed. As always, my everlasting thanks is reserved for my mother, whose love and encouragement have made my career success possible, and my late father, who left way too soon but lives on ever so strongly in my heart.

ARTICLES

JUSTICES WILLIAM J. BRENNAN, JR. AND THURGOOD MARSHALL ON CAPITAL PUNISHMENT: ITS CONSTITUTIONALITY, MORALITY, DETERRENT EFFECT, AND INTERPRETATION BY THE COURT

ALAN I. BIGEL

JUSTICES WILLIAM J. BRENNAN, JR. AND THURGOOD MARSHALL ON CAPITAL PUNISHMENT: ITS CONSTITUTIONALITY, MORALITY, DETERRENT EFFECT, AND INTERPRETATION BY THE COURT

ALAN I. BIGEL*

Of the 106 individuals who have served on the United States Supreme Court up to the end of the October, 1992 Term, only two — Justices William J. Brennan, Jr., and Thurgood Marshall — were categorically opposed to capital punishment for the duration of their tenure. Brennan, who announced his retirement on July 20, 1990, served on the Court thirty-four years, a tenure equaled by just four other members,[1] and exceeded only by Justice William O. Douglas (1939-1975). Marshall, who retired immediately after the end of the October, 1990 Term, and died on January 24, 1993, at the age of eighty-four, served for twenty-four years. Both men were widely praised for their contributions to American legal jurisprudence.[2]

---

* B.A. 1976, Brooklyn College; M.A. 1978, and Ph.D. 1984, The New School for Social Research. Professor of Political Science, University of Wisconsin-La Crosse. I wish to thank Tammy Hass for her patience and diligence in typing this material. I also wish to express profound gratitude to Justice Brennan for his willingness to read this article.

1. Chief Justice John Marshall (1801-1835) and Justices Stephen J. Field (1863-1897), John Marshall Harlan (1877-1911), and Hugo L. Black (1937-1971) each were on the Court thirty-four years.

2. Brennan's stature had been acknowledged throughout his tenure. In 1966, Chief Justice Earl Warren stated that, "[i]n the entire history of the Court, it would be difficult to name another Justice who wrote more important opinions in his first ten years than [Brennan]." Earl Warren, *Mr. Justice Brennan*, 80 HARV. L. REV. 1, 2 (1966). In 1974, Leonard W. Levy wrote that Brennan "[w]ith each passing year [ ] has grown in stature and attainments." LEONARD W. LEVY, AGAINST THE LAW: THE NIXON COURT AND CRIMINAL JUSTICE 39 (1974). Immediately following his retirement, Brennan was characterized as one of the most influential members ever to have served on the Court. On July 23, 1990, three days after Brennan announced his decision to step down, several guests on the PBS broadcast of MacNeil-Lehrer Newshour assessed his impact. Though he strongly disagreed with Brennan's judicial philosophy, Robert Bork, unsuccessfully nominated to the Court by President Ronald Reagan in 1987, stated that Brennan was "the most powerful justice in this century on the Supreme Court." Nina Totenberg, law correspondent for National Public Radio, declared that there is not "an area of the law in which there is not a landmark opinion written by William Brennan." Also appearing on the aforementioned telecast, former Representative Barbara Jordan labeled Brennan "an institution within an institution." *MacNeil-Lehrer Newshour* (PBS

While it remains for history to definitively record their most significant contributions,[3] the jurisprudence of Brennan and Marshall on capital punishment has conspicuously carved a unique niche. Their opposition to the death penalty was fundamentally rooted in their conception of judicial power and the role of the Court in American society. This article will examine their opinions on the death penalty and will seek to understand whether a range of issues connected with its infliction can be reconciled with constitutional protections. Beyond the wording of applicable provisions of the Constitution, Brennan and Marshall's positions also touched on a number of social and political questions invariably raised in consideration of capital punish-

---

television broadcast, July 23, 1990), *quoted in* W. WAT HOPKINS, MR. JUSTICE BRENNAN AND FREEDOM OF EXPRESSION 3 (1991). New York University School of Law Professor Norman Dorsen, reflecting on Brennan's decision to retire, noted that "a titanic figure had passed from the public scene." Norman Dorsen, *A Tribute to Justice William J. Brennan, Jr.* (pt. 4), 104 HARV. L. REV. 15 (1990).

Unlike Brennan, whose opinions were admired as cogent and carefully crafted pieces of intellectual scholarship, Marshall was paid tribute for his symbolic role in dramatizing lingering abridgment of civil rights and individual liberty. Praise for Marshall as a formidable figure on the Court was widespread. Retired Justice Brennan declared that Marshall "is one of our century's legal giants." William J. Brennan, Jr., *A Tribute to Justice Thurgood Marshall* (pt. 1), 105 HARV. L. REV. 23 (1991). William Coleman, Jr., Chairman of the NAACP Legal Defense and Educational Fund, stated that Marshall "is among the very few Americans who have made a significant difference in the quality of life of our nation." William T. Coleman, Jr., *A Tribute to Justice Thurgood Marshall* (pt. 3), 105 HARV. L. REV. 42 (1991). Also reflecting on Marshall's significance at the time of his retirement, Federal District Judge Robert L. Carter for the Southern District of New York wrote:

> Marshall's steadfast belief in the Constitution as the pillar of democratic and egalitarian principles and in law generally as the protector of the poor and the powerless — and his efforts toward the realization of these ideals — reminds the American people as a whole of their vast potential for social progress.

Robert L. Carter, *A Tribute to Justice Thurgood Marshall* (pt. 2), 105 HARV. L. REV. 33, 42 (1991).

3. Both Brennan and Marshall had many years of service on the Court; however, while longevity is helpful in enabling a justice to build a reputation, this alone does not — as demonstrated in the case of Justice Benjamin Cardozo, who served but six years (1932-1938) and is generally regarded as among the "great" members in the history of the Court — ensure high stature. Depth of intellectual reasoning, philosophical consistency, number of occasions in which a dissenting position is ultimately adopted by the majority, total number of opinions written, and perception by colleagues as an obstructionist or consensus builder when seeking to forge a majority coalition, among other considerations, affect historical assessments of a justice. The passage of time will enable scholars to more fully perceive the contributions of Brennan and Marshall in these and other areas.

ment. Is the death penalty a statistically demonstrable deterrent to the commission of murder? Is capital punishment more cost effective than life imprisonment without parole? Is it morally justifiable for government to execute individuals? Has the death penalty been arbitrarily imposed? To what extent should public opinion affect a state's willingness to legalize capital punishment, and should the Court challenge this preference? The morality, legality, and practicality of capital punishment permeated Brennan and Marshall's opinions, and their impact on public discourse will also be addressed.

I.   WILLIAM J. BRENNAN, JR., AND THURGOOD MARSHALL JOIN THE COURT

A.   *Brennan's Appointment and Constitutional Jurisprudence*

1.   Brennan's Nomination and Confirmation Hearings

William J. Brennan, Jr., was born on April 25, 1906, in Newark, New Jersey.[4] The second of eight children, Brennan characterized his childhood as "comfortable."[5] His father, who came to the United States from Ireland in 1893, shoveled coal and became active in local labor unions; he later became City Commissioner and Newark's Director of Public Safety.[6] Brennan enormously admired his father's work ethic and integrity, and declared that no individual has had a greater influence on him.[7]

Brennan attended public school in Newark, and enrolled in the Wharton School of the University of Pennsylvania, where he earned a bachelor's degree, cum laude, in economics in 1928.[8] Three years later, he graduated from Harvard Law School "among the top 10 students in the class."[9] Brennan joined the Newark firm of Pitney, Hardin & Skinner, where he specialized

---

4. Tim O'Brien, *William J. Brennan, Jr.*, *in* EIGHT MEN AND A LADY: PROFILES OF THE JUSTICES OF THE SUPREME COURT 52 (National Press 1990). For additional biographical material on Brennan, see STEPHEN J. FRIEDMAN, WILLIAM J. BRENNAN, JR.: AN AFFAIR WITH FREEDOM (1967); Stanley H. Friedelbaum, *Justice William J. Brennan, Jr.: Policy-Making in the Judicial Thicket, in* THE BURGER COURT: POLITICAL AND JUDICIAL PROFILES 101-05 (Charles Lamb & Stephen Halpern eds., 1991); Jeffrey T. Leeds, *A Life on the Court: A Conversation with Justice Brennan*, NEW YORK TIMES MAGAZINE, October 5, 1986, at 24-27; HOPKINS, *supra* note 2, at 4-6.
5. O'Brien, *supra* note 4, at 53.
6. HOPKINS, *supra* note 2, at 4-5; Friedelbaum, *supra* note 4, at 101.
7. O'Brien, *supra* note 4, at 53.
8. Linda Greenhouse, *Vacancy on the Court; Brennan, Key Liberal, Quits Supreme Court; Battle for Seat Likely*, N.Y. TIMES, July 21, 1990, at 7A, col. 4-5.
9. *Id.*

in labor relations.[10] In 1949, Brennan left the firm upon accepting an appointment from Governor Alfred Driscoll to the New Jersey Superior Court.[11] Brennan was subsequently elevated to the Appellate Division of the Superior Court, and, in 1952, he became an Associate Justice of the New Jersey Supreme Court.[12]

Frustrated with the perceived inability of state courts to expeditiously process cases, Brennan became a prominent advocate of trial reform. His proposals were supported by his colleague, nationally renowned New Jersey Chief Justice Arthur T. Vanderbilt, who asked Brennan to deliver a speech on his behalf to a gathering of judges and court administrators in Washington, DC, in 1956.[13] United States Attorney General Herbert Brownell, impressed with Brennan's comments, recommended him to President Eisenhower as a possible replacement for Justice Sherman Minton, who announced his intention to retire for health reasons at the end of the October, 1955 Term.[14] On September 28, 1956, Brownell telephoned Brennan to arrange a meeting at the White House the next day, when Brennan learned that he was going to be chosen as the next Justice.[15] Brennan, given a recess appointment, joined the Court on October 15, 1956, and the Senate Judiciary Committee held confirmation hearings on February 26 and 27, 1957.[16]

The questions presented to Brennan focused on three areas. On the first day, Senator Joseph McCarthy of Wisconsin, who was not a member of the Committee but was granted permission to

---

10. O'Brien, *supra* note 4, at 53.

11. HOPKINS, *supra* note 2, at 5.

12. *Id.*

13. *Id.* at 5-6.

14. *Id.* at 6.

15. Accounts differ as to why Eisenhower chose Brennan to replace Minton. Clearly, Chief Justice Vanderbilt's praise of Brennan to Eisenhower as "possess[ing] the finest judicial mind that he had known" enormously influenced the President, as revealed in his memoirs. DWIGHT D. EISENHOWER, THE WHITE HOUSE YEARS: MANDATE FOR CHANGE, 1953-1956, at 226-27 (1963), *quoted in* HENRY J. ABRAHAM, JUSTICES AND PRESIDENTS: A POLITICAL HISTORY OF APPOINTMENTS TO THE SUPREME COURT 262 (1985). However, at the time of the appointment it was alleged that Vanderbilt himself expressed displeasure with Brennan's selection, and that he was Eisenhower's first choice. O'Brien, *supra* note 4, at 53-55. *See also* BERNARD SCHWARTZ, SUPER CHIEF: EARL WARREN AND HIS SUPREME COURT — A JUDICIAL BIOGRAPHY 205 (1983). Political considerations likely played a major role in Brennan's selection. "The Eisenhower campaign," said one scholar, "apparently believed that a Roman Catholic Democrat from the Northeast would help win some extra support for the president's reelection bid." HOPKINS, *supra* note 2, at 6. *See also* ABRAHAM, *supra* at 263.

16. N.Y. TIMES, Feb. 27, 1957, at 15, col 3-6; N.Y. TIMES, Feb. 28, 1957, at 16, col 3-4.

appear, sought to elicit Brennan's position on the allegedly sub-
versive objectives of Communist Party activities in the United
States, and congressional efforts to investigate this subject.[17]
Brennan agreed that there is no "more vital function of the Congress than the investigatory function of its committees," and
stated that he "can't think of a more important or vital objective
of any committee investigation than that of rooting out subver-
sives in Government;"[18] however, he refused to speculate on the
goals of the Communist Party, claiming that this would be inappropriate given the number of cases touching on this subject
which are pending before the Court.[19]

Brennan was also questioned about his belief on separation
of church and state. Responding to Senator Joseph C.
O'Mahoney of Wyoming, also a Roman Catholic, as to whether
he felt bound to follow the edicts of the Pope in questions concerning freedom of religion, Brennan emphasized that the oath
he took for every public office he has held to support the Constitution shall be "unreservedly"[20] paramount over any other
obligation.

Concerning his judicial philosophy, Brennan refrained from
expressing support for a specific mode of constitutional interpre-

---

17. During the 1940s and 1950s, the House Un-American Activities
Committee and the Senate Internal Security Subcommittee and Permanent
Investigations Subcommittee had been conducting investigations into alleged
Communist Party activities in the United States. This subject, investigated
intermittently by Congress since the end of World War I, had aroused intense
controversy and often acrimonious debates on the proper exercise of
congressional inquisitorial power at the time of Brennan's nomination. *See
generally* CARL BECK, CONTEMPT OF CONGRESS: A STUDY OF THE PROSECUTIONS
INITIATED BY THE HOUSE UN-AMERICAN ACTIVITIES COMMITTEE (2d ed. 1974);
RONALD GOLDFARB, THE CONTEMPT POWER (1963); WALTER GOODMAN, THE
COMMITTEE: THE EXTRAORDINARY CAREER OF THE HOUSE COMMITTEE ON UN-
AMERICAN ACTIVITIES (1968).

18. *Nomination of William J. Brennan, Jr., to the United States Supreme Court:
Hearings before the Senate Judiciary Committee*, 85th Cong., 1st Sess., 1957
(hereinafter *Hearings.*). For an account of Senator McCarthy's questions, see
Hopkins, *supra* note 2, at 9-11.

19. For a discussion of cases concerning alleged Communist Party
activities which had been on the Court's docket at the time of Brennan's
appointment, see WALTER F. MURPHY, CONGRESS AND THE COURT: A CASE STUDY
IN THE AMERICAN POLITICAL PROCESS (1962). For a comprehensive analysis of
the entire array of cases coming to the Court on congressional investigations
into the associations and conduct of alleged Communist Party members, see
Alan I. Bigel, *The First Amendment and National Security: The Court Responds to
Governmental Harassment of Alleged Communist Sympathizers*, 19 OHIO N.U. L. REV.
885 (1993).

20. *Brennan Stands on Judicial Oath, supra* note 16, at 16.

tation.[21] Asked by Senator James O. Eastland of Mississippi whether the meaning of the Constitution was fixed or adaptable to evolving contemporary needs, Brennan initially responded that this would depend on the circumstances of a case.[22] Pressed by Eastland to be more specific, Brennan declared that "it is part of the judicial process to consult a lot of things which may bear upon the particular case."[23] Brennan did not elaborate; he added that he has always endeavored "to apply the law whether the applicable law is constitutional, legislative, or common law or otherwise to the facts of the given case that is before us."[24] He seemed to eschew a mechanical interpretation of the Constitution, and agreed with statements of Senator Arthur J. Watkins of Utah that it would be preposterous to rigidly follow precedent since fallible human beings may not share the same views as to what its provisions mean.[25] The members of the Judiciary Committee did not press Brennan for his views on the Court's potential for shaping social policy and its role within the framework of separation of powers and federalism.

On March 19, 1957, the Judiciary Committee voted 11-0 (four members were not present) to recommend confirmation, which was immediately endorsed by a voice vote of the full Senate later that day.[26] Brennan took his oath on March 22, 1957.

2.   Brennan's Judicial Philosophy

In recent years, there has been a proliferation of literature examining various modes of constitutional interpretation.[27] Is

---

21.   *Hearings, supra* note 18, at 34.
22.   *Id.* at 36, *quoted in* HOPKINS, *supra* note 2, at 1.
23.   *Hearings, supra* note 18, at 38, *quoted in* HOPKINS, *supra* note 2, at 1.
24.   *Hearings, supra* note 18, at 38, *quoted in* HOPKINS, *supra* note 2, at 8.
25.   *Hearings, supra* note 18, at 39, *quoted in* HOPKINS, *supra* note 2, at 8.
26.   *Senate Votes 11 to 0 for Brennan*, N.Y. TIMES, March 20, 1957, at 23; *Senate Confirms 2 for High Court*, N.Y. TIMES, March 20, 1957, at 38.
27.   *See, e.g.*, JOHN AGRESTO, THE SUPREME COURT AND CONSTITUTIONAL DEMOCRACY (1984); HADLEY ARKES, BEYOND THE CONSTITUTION (1990); SOTIRIOS A. BARBER, ON WHAT THE CONSTITUTION MEANS (1986); PHILIP BOBBITT, CONSTITUTIONAL FATE: THEORY OF THE CONSTITUTION (1982); JOHN H. ELY, DEMOCRACY AND DISTRUST: A THEORY OF JUDICIAL REVIEW (1980); SUPREME COURT ACTIVISM AND RESTRAINT (Stephen C. Halpern & Charles M. Lamb eds., 1982); GARY L. MCDOWELL, CURBING THE COURTS: THE CONSTITUTION AND THE LIMITS OF JUDICIAL POWER (1988); MICHAEL J. PERRY, THE CONSTITUTION, THE COURTS, AND HUMAN RIGHTS: AN INQUIRY INTO THE LEGITIMACY OF CONSTITUTIONAL POLICY MAKING BY THE JUDICIARY (1982); LAURENCE H. TRIBE & MICHAEL C. DORF, ON READING THE CONSTITUTION (1991); HARRY H. WELLINGTON, INTERPRETING THE CONSTITUTION: THE SUPREME COURT AND THE PROCESS OF ADJUDICATION (1990); CHRISTOPHER WOLFE, JUDICIAL ACTIVISM: BULWARK OF FREEDOM OR PRECARIOUS SECURITY? (1991).

the Constitution to be read as an enumeration of explicit commands and prohibitions, or as a body of general guidelines to be reexamined by each generation? If the meaning of the Constitution changes over time, what role should the Court play in assessing the applicability of provisions to contemporary priorities? Is the Court bound to interpret the Constitution as it was construed by the founding fathers, or is it appropriate for the justices to seek to affect the direction of social policy? Addressing these questions, Thomas Grey asked whether justices must "confine themselves" to "norms derived from the written Constitution" or whether they "may . . . also enforce principles of liberty and justice when the normative content of those principles is not to be found within the four corners of our founding document?"[28] Both positions present formidable challenges.

A justice who endeavors to adjudicate cases based on "norms derived from the written Constitution"[29] may seek to decipher and apply the original intention of a provision or adopt a literal interpretation of the text.[30] Both of these approaches present obstacles. The foremost difficulty with a jurisprudence relying on original intention is definitional. Does "original intention" refer to the Philadelphia debates in 1787, historical events ante-

---

28. Thomas Grey, *Do We Have An Unwritten Constitution?*, 27 STAN. L. REV. 703, 703 (1975). Two other influential scholars presented comparable depictions of judicial power. John Hart Ely identified two types of judicial review: "Interpretivism," where justices "deciding constitutional issues . . . confine themselves to enforcing norms that are stated or clearly implicit in the written Constitution," and "noninterpretivism," the "contrary view that courts should go beyond that set of references and enforce norms that cannot be discovered within the four corners of the document." ELY, *supra* note 27, at 1. Similarly, Michael J. Perry discussed two perspectives: "[I]nterpretive," where a justice" ascertains the constitutionality of a given policy choice by reference to one of the value judgments of which the Constitution consists — that is, by reference to a value judgment embodied, though not necessarily explicitly, either in some particular provisions of the text of the Constitution or in the overall structure of government ordained by the Constitution"; and "noninterpretive," where a justice "makes the determination of constitutionality by reference to a value judgment other than one constitutionalized by the framers." PERRY, *supra* note 27, at 10-11.

29. Grey, *supra* note 28, at 703.

30. On occasion, a justice may base adjudication on both the wording and perceived original intention of a provision. *See, e.g.,* Richmond Newspapers, Inc. v. Virginia, 448 U.S. 555 (1980) (Burger, C.J., for the majority); New York Times v. United States, 403 U.S. 713 (1971) (Black, J., concurring). Two modern scholars have argued that these criteria are compatible — and the only legitimate — methods of constitutional interpretation. *See* RAOUL BERGER, FEDERALISM: THE FOUNDERS' DESIGN (1987); ROBERT BORK, THE TEMPTING OF AMERICA: THE POLITICAL SEDUCTION OF THE LAW (1989).

cedent to the convening of the Constitutional Convention, the debates in the state ratifying conventions, the sentiments of the First Congress, Court opinions issued during the framers' generation, the letters and correspondence of the framers, or other sources? Focusing on the discussions at the Philadelphia Convention, is emphasis to be placed only on those proposals voted on or on any statement made by the framers? Can the sense of the founders be determined by the silence of members on issues raised during the debates, or is original intention to be based only on the spoken words? The elusiveness of this task is compounded by the uneven participation of the framers. It has been estimated that only twenty-nine of the fifty-five delegates were present for every session and that almost one-third of the members "missed long and critical portions" of the deliberations.[31] Moreover, Madison's notes,[32] though helpful, are by necessity incomplete; one scholar has estimated that Madison probably was able to record "at best . . . only one-fifth of what was said."[33]

Adopting a strict interpretation of the wording similarly may not simplify the task of constitutional adjudication. Many provisions written into the Constitution were not the product of painstaking debate but rather were worded to accommodate differences in opinion. Gouverneur Morris, draftsman of the Constitution, declared that he endeavored "to select phrases which, expressing my own notions, would not alarm the others or shock their self love."[34] Even if the wording is unambiguous, how does one reconcile language of the Constitution which makes possible an interpretation contrary to the express intentions of the framers? Justice Oliver Wendell Holmes, Jr. cautioned that, when reading the words of the Constitution, "we must realize that they have called into life a being the development of which could not have been foreseen completely by the most gifted of its begetters."[35] Holmes emphasized that constitu-

---

31. CLINTON ROSSITER, SEVENTEEN EIGHTY-SEVEN: THE GRAND CONVENTION 178 (1966).

32. MAX FARRAND, THE RECORDS OF THE FEDERAL CONVENTION OF 1787 (1937).

33. LEONARD W. LEVY, ORIGINAL INTENT AND THE FRAMERS' CONSTITUTION 288 (1988). Other records of the Philadelphia debates are also fragmentary. See James H. Hutson, Riddles of the Federal Constitutional Convention, 44 WM. & MARY Q. (3d ser.) 411 (1987); James H. Hutson, The Creation of the Constitution: The Integrity of the Documentary Record, 65 TEX. L. REV. 1 (1986).

34. C. HERMAN PRITCHETT, THE AMERICAN CONSTITUTION 45 (1968) (quoting Gouverneur Morris).

35. Missouri v. Holland, 252 U.S. 416, 433 (1920) (Holmes, J., for the majority).

tionality must be based "in the light of our whole experience and not merely in that of what was said a hundred years ago."[36]

Arguably, then, neither originalism nor textualism may definitively be employed to establish constitutionality. It is also necessary to examine the role of the Court within the framework of separation of powers and federalism. Is the Court obligated to uphold legislation, irrespective of its perceived reasonableness or necessity,[37] once it has determined that a particular branch — at the federal or state level — is not precluded from exercising contemplated power, or may the justices take the initiative in embarking the country on a political or social vision?[38] The wording of the Constitution and the Court's position within the overall framework of government may furnish sufficient maneuverability to the justices to institute policy preferences.

Brennan's judicial philosophy recognized that provisions of the Constitution are to be flexibly construed to accommodate perceived contemporary needs. He neither exclusively embraced nor rejected original intent and textualism; indeed, both were integral components of Brennan's justification for an adjudicatory function which compelled the Court to assess the substance of legislation.

Brennan's belief in the organic meaning of the Constitution was apparent from his statements on the significance of original intent. His position was dramatized on July 9, 1985, when Attorney General Edwin Meese III, in a speech before the American Bar Association, extolled the virtues of a jurisprudence based on original intent, and criticized Brennan's alleged judicial activism.[39] On October 12, Brennan, speaking at Georgetown Uni-

---

36. *Id.* Along similar lines, Chief Justice Earl Warren wrote that, in assessing school segregation, "we cannot turn the clock back to 1868 when the [Fourteenth] Amendment was adopted . . . [w]e must consider public education in the light of its full development and its present place in American life throughout the Nation." Brown v. Board of Education, 347 U.S. 483, 492-93 (1954) (Warren, C. J., for the majority).

37. On the Court, the most vigorous present supporters of this position are Chief Justice William Rehnquist and Justices Antonin Scalia and Clarence Thomas. Most recently, *see, e.g.*, Hudson v. McMillian, 112 S. Ct. 995 (1992) (Thomas, J., dissenting) (cruel and unusual punishments); Planned Parenthood of Southeastern Pennsylvania v. Casey, 112 S. Ct. 2791 (1992) (Scalia, J., concurring in part and dissenting in part) (abortion); Payne v. Tennessee, 111 S. Ct. 2597 (1991) (Rehnquist, C.J., for the majority) (capital punishment).

38. For several variations of this position, see *supra* note 27.

39. Edwin Meese, III, Speech Before the American Bar Association (July 9, 1985), *in* THE FEDERALIST SOCIETY, THE GREAT DEBATE: INTERPRETING OUR WRITTEN CONSTITUTION (1986).

versity, responded in a lengthy address on the meaning of the Constitution and the intent of the framers.[40]

Praising the meticulous work of the founders, Brennan declared that they created "a blueprint for government"[41] intended to be adaptable to changing needs. Each generation, "in response to both transformations of social condition and evolution of our concepts of human dignity,"[42] must reexamine provisions of the Constitution, and Brennan believed that the framers purposely adopted ambiguous wording to facilitate this undertaking. While denying that justices are "platonic guardians appointed to wield authority according to their personal moral predilections,"[43] Brennan maintained that the framers intended the federal judiciary to play a role in applying constitutional provisions to new circumstances. The founders, he emphasized, bequeathed to posterity not a rigid code of conduct but rather a body of principles, and adjudication aimed toward the "ceaseless pursuit of the constitutional ideal of human dignity"[44] fulfilled original intention by validating the aspirations of the document.

Clearly, Brennan did not repudiate reliance on original intention. He maintained that faithfulness to originalism depended not on mechanically adopting the policies in effect at the time of the Philadelphia Convention; rather, to the extent that each generation reduces arbitrariness in the application of its laws, enhances procedural protections in the courtroom for the accused, and eliminates discriminatory exercise of governmental power, the ideals of the founders are fulfilled.

Brennan believed that the Constitution, as envisioned by the framers, was an aspirational projection on the evolving relationship between government and the citizenry, and that each generation, building upon the work of its predecessors, must strive for a more enlightened sense of justice. The Court, as a coequal branch of government, must play a role in this ongoing endeavor, and Brennan's belief that the Constitution "places certain values beyond the power of any legislature"[45] affected his conception of federalism.

On August 7, 1964, after only eight years on the Court, Brennan, in a speech to a Conference of Chief Justices in New York,

---

40. Justice William Brennan, Jr., *The Constitution of the United States: Contemporary Ratification*, Address at Georgetown University (October 12, 1985), *in* 27 S. TEX. L.J. 433 (1986).
41. *Id.* at 438.
42. *Id.* at 439.
43. *Id.* at 434-35.
44. *Id.* at 445.
45. *Id.* at 437.

expounded on his understanding of federalism.[46] Brennan did
not read the Constitution as a document which merely conferred
spheres of sovereignty on two separate and exclusive jurisdictions;[47] rather, he believed that states, empowered to exercise
"the widest latitude to deal with the dynamics of social and economic change in seeking to satisfy their needs and further their
progress,"[48] and the central authority, share a common goal to
protect individual rights. However, the geometric growth of governmental power beginning in the New Deal period has created
numerous opportunities for intrusion into citizens' lives, thereby
enhancing the judiciary's obligation to protect individual freedom. Brennan did not attach great importance to the kind of
jurisdiction federal or state judges might exercise in discharging
this duty; the judicial function compelled judges, regardless of
what governmental level encroachments on individual liberty
transpired, to prevent potentially repressive governmental
action. The federal judiciary, Brennan believed, will inevitably
play a more extensive role as the proliferation of governmental
regulation diminishes divergence among states and makes us "a
more united nation."[49]

Brennan's commitment to preserving individual rights from
possible governmental abridgment with vigorous exercise of judicial power envisaged an active role for the Court. Brennan did
not believe that the Court must defer to state practices alleged to
abridge liberty until the political process successfully implemented remedial action; rather, he envisioned "individuals and
governments confront[ing] each other, with courts mediating
between the two."[50] As he made clear in a highly influential[51]
article published in 1977,[52] state judges, within their respective
jurisdiction, are to be no less vigilant in protecting their citizens
from violations of state constitutional provisions than federal

---

46. William J. Brennan, Jr., *Some Aspects of Federalism*, 39 N.Y.U. L. Rev. 945
(1964).

47. For a discussion claiming that this dual relationship is mandated by
both the text of the Constitution and the intent of the framers, see BERGER,
supra note 30, at 48-76.

48. Brennan, *supra* note 46, at 954.

49. *Id.* at 960.

50. Robert C. Post, *Justice Brennan and Federalism*, 7 Cons. Comm. 227, 233
(1990).

51. It has been determined that Brennan's article is "the nineteenth most
frequently cited law review article of those published within the past forty
years." Fred Shapiro, *The Most-Cited Law Review Articles*, 73 Cal. L. Rev. 1540,
1550 (1985).

52. William J. Brennan, Jr., *State Constitutions and the Protection of
Individual Rights*, 90 Harv. L. Rev. 489 (1977).

judges in safeguarding the guarantees of the Constitution. Where "state courts can be trusted to safeguard individual rights," the Court has confined "the protective role of the federal judiciary;"[53] however, Brennan emphasized, "our federal system . . . provides a double source of protection for the rights of our citizens"[54] when state judges do not shield their citizens against abridgment of liberty. Thus, Brennan recognized a degree of state autonomy not to enable local legislatures to independently establish modes of interaction among its citizens, but rather to devise policies which do not fall outside the parameters of federal protection of liberty. Brennan elaborated on this dichotomy in a 1986 address on the Bill of Rights and the states.[55]

Brennan believed that the Bill of Rights placed certain powers beyond the reach of government to abridge. Initially, their provisions were considered binding only on federal power;[56] however, with the ratification in 1868 of the Fourteenth Amendment,[57] the federal government, by Section 5,[58] acquired jurisdiction over state protection of individual liberty. The degree of potential federal supervision was clarified in the 1960s, when many of the procedural protections of the Bill of Rights were held to be binding on the states.[59] Expressing his belief that this

---

53.   *Id.* at 502-03.

54.   *Id.* at 503.

55.   William J. Brennan, Jr., *The Bill of Rights and the States: The Revival of State Constitutions as Guardians of Individual Rights*, 61 N.Y.U. L. REV. 535 (1986).

56.   Barron v. Baltimore, 7 Peters 243 (1833).

57.   Section 1 of the Fourteenth Amendment provides:

All persons born or naturalized in the United States and subject to the jurisdiction thereof, are citizens of the United States and of the State wherein they reside. No state shall make or enforce any law which shall abridge the privileges or immunities of citizens of the United States; nor shall any State deprive any person of life, liberty, or property, without due process of law; nor deny to any person within its jurisdiction the equal protection of the laws.

U.S. CONST. amend. XIV, § 1.

58.   Section 5 of the Fourteenth Amendment states: "The Congress shall have power to enforce, by appropriate legislation, the provisions of this article." U.S. CONST. amend. XIV, § 1.

59.   Benton v. Maryland, 395 U.S. 784 (1969) (double jeopardy); Duncan v. Louisiana, 391 U.S. 145 (1968) (trial by jury); Washington v. Texas, 388 U.S. 14 (1967) (compulsory process for obtaining witnesses); Klopfer v. North Carolina, 386 U.S. 213 (1967) (speedy trial); Parker v. Gladden, 385 U.S. 363 (1966) (impartial jury); Pointer v. Texas, 380 U.S. 400 (1965) (confrontation of witnesses); Malloy v. Hogan, 378 U.S. 1 (1964) (protection against self-incrimination); Gideon v. Wainwright, 372 U.S. 335 (1963) (right to counsel); Robinson v. California, 370 U.S. 660 (1962) (cruel and unusual punishments); Mapp v. Ohio, 367 U.S. 643 (1961) (exclusionary rule).

was one of the Warren Court's greatest accomplishments,[60] Brennan declared that the Fourteenth Amendment acknowledged a minimum level of human liberty and dignity which was beyond the power of government to abridge. Incorporation of the Bill of Rights, Brennan maintained, underscored that states "could [not] be trusted to nurture individual rights,"[61] and, since the Fourteenth Amendment contained ambiguous wording,[62] it would ultimately befall to the federal judiciary to establish evolving conceptions of justice to guide them.

In short, Brennan did not view the Constitution as containing a set of fixed principles; rather, it embodied an ongoing aspiration of the citizenry to achieve an enlightened state of justice. While the Constitution conferred power to two different levels of government, its vision transcended jurisdictional boundaries and obligated public officials and the citizenry to engage in an ongoing effort to enhance individual liberty. Because state legislatures have historically been unsuccessful in fulfilling this objective, the judicial branch will be compelled to play a pivotal role in protecting individuals against governmental encroachments on freedom. And the ambiguous wording of constitutional provisions will require federal judges to formulate evolving standards of justice and human dignity by which to measure state enactments, the legality of which will be based not on degree of popular support within a state or how widespread a practice may be.

The literature on this ongoing controversy is increasingly vast. *See generally* JUDITH BAER, EQUALITY UNDER LAW: RECLAIMING THE FOURTEENTH AMENDMENT (1983); RAOUL BERGER, GOVERNMENT BY JUDICIARY: THE TRANSFORMATION OF THE FOURTEENTH AMENDMENT (1977); RICHARD C. CORTNER, THE SUPREME COURT AND THE SECOND BILL OF RIGHTS: THE FOURTEENTH AMENDMENT AND THE NATIONALIZATION OF CIVIL LIBERTIES (1981); MICHAEL K. CURTIS, NO STATE SHALL ABRIDGE: THE FOURTEENTH AMENDMENT AND THE BILL OF RIGHTS (1986); HORACE FLACK, THE ADOPTION OF THE FOURTEENTH AMENDMENT (1908); HOWARD J. GRAHAM, EVERYONE'S CONSTITUTION: HISTORICAL ESSAYS ON THE FOURTEENTH AMENDMENT, THE "CONSPIRACY THEORY," AND AMERICAN CONSTITUTIONALISM (1968); WILLIAM E. NELSON, THE FOURTEENTH AMENDMENT, FROM POLITICAL PRINCIPLE TO JUDICIAL DOCTRINE (1988); JACOBUS TENBROEK, THE ANTISLAVERY ORIGINS OF THE FOURTEENTH AMENDMENT (1951); Akhil R. Amar, *The Bill of Rights and the Fourteenth Amendment,* 101 YALE L.J. 1193 (1992); Charles Fairman, *Does The Fourteenth Amendment Incorporate the Bill of Rights? The Original Understanding,* 2 STAN. L. REV. 5 (1949); Stanley Morrison, *Does the Fourteenth Amendment Incorporate the Bill of Rights?,* 2 STAN. L. REV. 140 (1949); Michael P. Zuckert, *Congressional Power Under the Fourteenth Amendment — The Original Understanding of Section Five,* 3 CONS. COMM. 123 (1986).

60. Brennan, *supra* note 55, at 536.

61. *Id.* at 537.

62. *See supra* note 57.

During Brennan's tenure, no individual was more in accord with this judicial philosophy than Justice Thurgood Marshall.[63]

B. *Marshall's Confirmation and Understanding of the Constitution*

1.   Marshall's Selection as the First African-American Justice

Thurgood Marshall was born on July 2, 1908, in Baltimore, Maryland, "with scarcely better prospects than thousands of other Negroes who ended up as high-school dropouts."[64] Segregation permeated every phase of his life;[65] however, as a youngster, Marshall, perhaps due to his relatively comfortable upbringing[66] and father's attitude,[67] was not sensitive to racial

---

63.   In the October, 1989 Term, the last in which Brennan and Marshall sat together, both voted identically 94.2% of the time. Note, *The Supreme Court, 1989 Term: Leading Cases: IV. The Statistics*, 104 HARV. L. REV. 360 (1990). For a tabulation of the voting alignments of the justices, see the annual November issue of *Harvard Law Review* which focuses on the Court's most recent Term.

64.   *High Court Appointee Thurgood Marshall*, N.Y. TIMES, June 14, 1967, at 32.

65.   The neighborhood in which Marshall grew up was described as follows:

> Baltimore was a town where blacks attended 'colored school' run by a white superintendent who said he wouldn't build a swimming pool for students because 'Negroes don't deserve swimming pools.' It was a town where the parochial schools let students out ten minutes earlier than the black public schools to minimize fights between the two groups. Not a single department store in Baltimore was open to blacks, not a single restroom that blacks could use was to be found downtown.

Juan Williams, *Marshall's Law*, in ROGER GOLDMAN WITH DAVID GALLEN, THURGOOD MARSHALL: JUSTICE FOR ALL 143 (1992). For an elaboration of racial and social conditions in Marshall's childhood, see MICHAEL D. DAVIS & HUNTER R. CLARK, THURGOOD MARSHALL, WARRIOR AT THE BAR, REBEL ON THE BENCH 30-46 (1992); CARL T. ROWAN, DREAM MAKERS, DREAM BREAKERS: THE WORLD OF JUSTICE THURGOOD MARSHALL 33-49 (1993).

66.   ROWAN, *supra* note 65, at 33-34.

67.   With no formal education, William Marshall held a number of jobs, and, given the social climate of his time, was subjected to ongoing racial taunts. ROWAN, *supra* note 65, at 37-39. Likely overwhelmed by frustration and pride, William "encouraged. . .[his son] to adjust to segregation, not to fight it." Williams, *supra* note 65, at 143. At the same time, Marshall's father had a keen mind and took an interest in court cases by both attending local trials and reading about them in the newspaper. When Thurgood was thirteen his father, after briefly explaining treatment of blacks in the former Confederate states following the end of the Civil War, told him that "the Constitution was the Founding Fathers' blueprint for the way things should be, not a description of the way things were." DAVIS & CLARK, *supra* note 65, at 38. *See also*, LEWIS H. FENDERSON, THURGOOD MARSHALL: FIGHTER FOR JUSTICE 29 (1969). Marshall himself declared that his father's teaching encouraged him to become a lawyer, suggesting that William imparted to his son not to accept injustice passively and

stratification.[68]   His   teen   years   furnished   opportunities   to
become acquainted with the law.   The high school Marshall
attended was located next to the police station, where he often
overheard officers coercing suspects,[69] and his father occasion-
ally took him to the courthouse.[70] Often disciplined in school,
Marshall's high school principal punished him by sending him to
the basement to memorize sections of the Constitution. Years
later, Marshall declared that, "[b]efore I left that school I knew
the entire Constitution by heart."[71] In 1925, he entered Lincoln
University in Pennsylvania, known as "the oldest American educational institution for blacks."[72] Graduating cum laude in 1930,
he decided to attend law school, and, after being rejected by the
University of Maryland because of race, Marshall enrolled at
Howard University.[73]

Marshall had the good fortune to be at Howard when its
President, Mordecai Johnson, had been enhancing the rigorous-
ness of the curriculum and recruiting first rate faculty. During
Marshall's years as a law student, Howard had become "a labora-
tory where civil rights law was invented, where students and
faculty developed the legal arguments that would propel the
courts and the nation towards change."[74] After graduating in
1933 at the top of his class,[75] Marshall briefly entered private
practice in Baltimore, where he worked on civil rights cases and
became affiliated with the local branch of the NAACP.[76] In 1936,
Marshall became special assistant legal counsel in charge of litigation.[77] Personally enduring racial insults,[78] Marshall passion-
ately practiced civil rights litigation, acquiring a reputation as a
vigorous and extremely able attorney.[79] In 1950, he was named

---

to be willing to work patiently but persistently to improve the human condition.
DAVIS & CLARK, *supra* note 65, at 38.

68.   Williams, *supra* note 65, at 143.
69.   *Id.* at 144.
70.   *Id.*
71.   DAVIS & CLARK, *supra* note 65, at 37.
72.   William Daniels, *Justice Thurgood Marshall: The Race for Equal Justice, in*
THE BURGER COURT: POLITICAL AND JUDICIAL PROFILES, *supra* note 4, at 213.
73.   *Id.*
74.   *Id.* at 214. For a discussion of Howard University's tradition and
curriculum at the time of Marshall's enrollment, see DAVIS & CLARK, *supra* note
65, at 47-58.
75.   Williams, *supra* note 65, at 145.
76.   Daniels, *supra* note 72, at 214.
77.   *Id.*
78.   DAVIS & CLARK, *supra* note 65, at 105-19.
79.   ROWAN, *supra* note 65, at 50-97, 124-29. *See generally* RICHARD KLUGER,
SIMPLE JUSTICE: THE HISTORY OF BROWN v. BOARD OF EDUCATION AND BLACK
AMERICA'S STRUGGLE FOR EQUALITY (1975).

director and chief counsel of the Legal Defense and Educational Fund.[80]

While Marshall's crowning achievement was his successful argument before the U.S. Supreme Court, in the landmark 1954 case of *Brown v. Board of Education*,[81] to declare segregation in public schools unconstitutional, he had amassed an extremely impressive record; while with the NAACP Marshall "won twenty-nine out of thirty-two cases before the Supreme Court and numerous victories in the lower courts."[82] Indeed, one scholar noted, Marshall "masterminded the litigation of the civil-rights movement for almost a quarter of a century."[83] In 1961, President John F. Kennedy successfully nominated Marshall to the United States Court of Appeals, where he acquired a reputation as a skillful and meticulous legal writer. Four years later, President Lyndon B. Johnson appointed him Solicitor General, and, in 1967, Marshall was nominated to fill the vacancy created by the retirement of Justice Tom C. Clark.

Aside from reservations expressed by some Southern senators, Marshall's nomination was generally greeted with enthusiastic support. Stating that Marshall "has already earned his place in history," the President, noting that he would be the first black to sit on the Court, declared: "I believe it is the right thing to do, the right time to do it, the right man and the right place."[84] On July 13, 1967, one month to the day after Johnson spoke with Marshall about filling the upcoming Court vacancy, the Senate Judiciary Committee commenced hearings, which continued to the 14th, 18th, 19th, and 24th.[85]

Unsurprisingly, Marshall was asked to discuss his judicial philosophy, but refused to respond to specific issues which he believed might come to the Court. Senator John L. McClellan, Democrat of Arkansas, opened the hearings by attacking various Warren Court rulings which allegedly undermined the ability of police to perform law enforcement, and asked Marshall for his views on wiretapping,[86] right to counsel,[87] obtaining confes-

---

80. Daniels, *supra* note 72, at 214.
81. 347 U.S. 483 (1954). For an examination of Marshall's role in bringing and arguing this case before the Court, see generally KLUGER, *supra* note 79; ROWAN, *supra* note 65, at 143-219; DAVIS & CLARK, *supra* note 65, at 136-78.
82. LEVY, *supra* note 2, at 42.
83. *Id.*
84. Roy Reed, *Marshall Named For High Court, Its First Negro*, N.Y. TIMES, June 14, 1967, at 1.
85. DAVIS & CLARK, *supra* note 65, at 273.
86. *See, e.g.*, Berger v. New York, 388 U.S. 41 (1967).

sions,[88] and the exclusionary rule,[89] among other areas. Marshall refrained from specifically addressing these issues, and responded with a broad generalization: "I'm worried as anybody about the mounting rate of crime. But I am equally determined that whatever is to be done must be done within the United States Constitution."[90]

During the other four days of hearings, no major attempt was made to learn Marshall's judicial philosophy. To be sure, he was asked his opinion on original intention, which elicited a brief statement that the Constitution must be construed as a "living document"[91] applicable to circumstances unforeseen by the framers, and on the importance of legislative history, to which Marshall responded that it was "relevant but not controlling;"[92] however, much of the questioning dealt with "the kind of esoterica found in a law school exam."[93] For example, Senator Strom Thurmond, Republican of South Carolina, asked, seeking to embarass Marshall, to state who drafted the Thirteenth Amendment,[94] to discuss the origins of the Fourteenth Amendment's privileges or immunities clause,[95] and to name the number of "provisions of the Bill of Rights . . . held by the Supreme Court to be binding on the states."[96] Marshall alternately responded with the answer, when he knew it, and with "folksy directness"[97] when irritated with the pointlessness of the questioning. Marshall was also asked whether his years of civil rights litigation "had

---

87. *See, e.g.,* Miranda v. Arizona, 384 U.S. 436 (1966); Gideon v. Wainwright, 372 U.S. 335 (1963).

88. *See, e.g.,* Escobedo v. Illinois, 378 U.S. 478 (1964).

89. *See, e.g.,* Mapp v. Ohio, 367 U.S. 643 (1961).

90. Fred P. Graham, *Senate Confirmation of Marshall Delaying by McClellan Questions,* N.Y. TIMES, July 14, 1967, at 12.

91. Fred P. Graham, *Marshall is Questioned on Fine Points of the Law,* N.Y. TIMES, July 20, 1967, at 17.

92. *Id.*

93. DAVIS & CLARK, *supra* note 65, at 273.

94. N.Y. TIMES, *supra* note 91, at 17. The Thirteenth Amendment states in Section 1: "Neither slavery nor involuntary servitude, except as a punishment for crime whereof the party shall have been duly convicted, shall exist within the United States, or any place subject to their jurisdiction." U.S. CONST. amend. XIII, § 1.

95. N.Y. TIMES, *supra* note 91, at 17. For the text of the Fourteenth Amendment's privileges or immunities clause, see *supra* note 57.

96. N.Y. TIMES, *supra* note 91, at 17.

97. *Id.* For example, when asked, "What provisions of the slave codes in existence in the eighteen-hundreds was Congress desirous of eliminating in the Civil Rights Act of 1866?," Marshall responded: "There were many of the so-called black codes and I don't know about all of them, but one was a statute in my own state of Maryland that prevented Negroes from flying kites."

prejudiced him against the white people of the South,"[98] to which he responded that he would interpret the law "without any personal predilection."[99]

On August 30, 1967, the Senate, by a vote of 69-11, confirmed Marshall's nomination.[100] He took his seat on October 1.

2. Marshall's Understanding of the Constitution

Unlike Brennan, who articulated the subtle points of his constitutional philosophy in a number of law review articles,[101] Marshall did not employ this forum to explain his position on such subjects as original intention, federalism, judicial activism and self-restraint, and the implications of ambiguous phrases in the Constitution.[102] While Marshall's jurisprudence can be deciphered from his opinions,[103] his understanding of the Constitution most fully emerges within the context of events which shaped his life, as well as his legal activities prior to taking his seat on the Court.[104] Whether Marshall's greatest accomplishments to the life of the law came during his years of litigation on behalf of the NAACP or during his period of service on the Court will, over time, be examined; nevertheless, Marshall's judicial philosophy, perhaps uniquely in the twentieth century, is, noted one scholar, "linked to the larger social context that permeated his personal and professional life," and what he "witnessed in this context . . . [—] racism, oppression, segregation, discrimination, and the denial of equal protection of the laws [—]"[105] is an integral component of his constitutional approach.

Marshall's most revealing insight into his view of the Constitution may have come in an address delivered in 1987 to com-

---

98.   *Id.*
99.   *Id.*
100.   Fred P. Graham, *Senate Confirms Marshall As the First Negro Justice,* N.Y. TIMES, August 31, 1967, at 1.
101.   *See, e.g., supra* notes 40, 46, 52, and 55. *See also* William J. Brennan, Jr., *Constitutional Adjudication,* 40 NOTRE DAME LAW. 559 (1965); William J. Brennan, Jr., *Fundamentals of Judicial Review,* Address to the Student Legal Forum at the University of Virginia Law School (February 17, 1959), *in* ALAN F. WESTIN, AN AUTOBIOGRAPHY OF THE SUPREME COURT 258-66 (1963).
102.   The only two law journal articles published by Marshall prior to 1986 touched on his general conception of the Constitution as a vehicle to effect social change. *See* Thurgood Marshall, *Group Action in the Pursuit of Justice,* 44 N.Y.U. L. REV. 661 (1969); Thurgood Marshall, *The Continuing Challenge of the Fourteenth Amendment,* 3 GA. L. REV. 1 (1968).
103.   *See* Daniels, *supra* note 72, at 213.
104.   William J. Brennan, Jr., *A Tribute to Justice Thurgood Marshall* pt.1, 105 HARV. L. REV. 23 (1991).
105.   Daniels, *supra* note 72, at 234.

memorate its bicentennial.[106] Concerning the enduring permanence of the intentions of the framers, Marshall declared:

> I do not believe that the meaning of the Constitution was forever 'fixed' at the Philadelphia Convention. Nor do I find the wisdom, foresight, and the sense of justice exhibited by the framers particularly profound. To the contrary, the government they devised was defective from the start, requiring several amendments, a civil war, and momentous social transformation to attain the system of constitutional government, and its respect for the individual freedoms and human rights, that we hold as fundamental today.[107]

Marshall suggested not that the writing of the Constitution has been insignificant, but that the work of the framers should not be viewed in isolation. The pathways of history, transformation of the human condition, and the evolution of political, social, and economic patterns, have all — as the abolition of slavery and the movement for civil rights have dramatically illustrated — redefined the meaning of the Constitution far beyond the vision of the founders. The work of the Philadelphia Convention must be viewed with its "inherent defects"[108] and subsequent "suffering, struggle, and sacrifice that has triumphed over much of what was wrong with the original document,"[109] to fully comprehend the promise of the Constitution. Each generation, to achieve evolving aspirations, will need to devise "new constitutional principles . . . to meet the challenges of a changing society."[110]

Marshall's understanding of the Constitution was virtually identical to Brennan's. While neither was willing to repudiate original intention — indeed, in racial discrimination and civil liberties cases Marshall frequently discussed the framers and practices of their time — both Justices emphasized that constitutional provisions evolve in meaning as conditions and priorities change. Marshall, no less than Brennan, believed that the judiciary must play an active role in shaping an evolving vision of justice, and must vigorously serve to protect the rights of minorities, and those who are outside the political and socioeconomic mainstream, from possible governmental oppression. Both acutely realized that the federal courts may be the last opportunity for

---

106. Thurgood Marshall, *Commentary: Reflections on the Bicentennial of the Constitution*, 101 HARV. L. REV. 1 (1987).

107. *Id.* at 2.

108. *Id.* at 5.

109. *Id.*

110. *Id.* at 4.

aggrieved individuals to obtain redress, and their efforts to establish minimum judicial standards, and hopefully prevent excessive or arbitrary exercise of power by federal and state officials, fulfilled Brennan and Marshall's conception of the role of the Court in American society.

These considerations permeated the opinions of Brennan and Marshall on capital punishment. They consulted but refused to rigidly adhere to views of the death penalty prevalent in the founding generation; this issue, both emphasized, must be perceived in light of modern conceptions of human dignity. Believing in the pivotal — though not omnipotent — role of the federal judiciary in shaping modes of interaction between government and the citizenry, Brennan and Marshall did not hesitate to formulate minimum standards to guide states in their treatment of those accused of murder. Their position on capital punishment envisioned an enlightened plane of justice which they believed society aspired toward, and this, Brennan and Marshall were convinced, was the most fundamental component of constitutional adjudication, and a fulfillment of the vision and promise of the founders and the document itself.

II.   THE EIGHTH AMENDMENT'S PROHIBITION AGAINST INFLICTION OF "CRUEL AND UNUSUAL PUNISHMENTS"

A.   The Original Understanding of Capital Punishment

The Eighth Amendment states: "Excessive bail shall not be required, nor excessive fines imposed, nor cruel and unusual punishments inflicted."[111] The phrase "cruel and unusual punishments" first appeared in the English Bill of Rights of 1689, though the concept was expressed in the Magna Carta. Chapter 14 of that document provided in pertinent part that "[a] free man shall not be amerced for a trivial offence, except in accordance with the degree of the offence; and for a serious offence he shall be amerced according to its gravity. . . ."[112] Parliament, by this clause, did not seek to ban specific types of punishment, but rather to prohibit judges from imposing penalties not legally sanctioned, and from exceeding statutory guidelines in sentenc-

---

111.   U.S. CONST. amend. VIII.

112.   *Quoted in* Anthony F. Granucci, *'Nor Cruel and Unusual Punishments Inflicted': The Original Meaning*, 57 CAL. L. REV. 839, 846 (1969). Concern for fixing penalties proportionate to the offense committed predates the writing of the Magna Carta; according to Granucci, statutory provisions assigning monetary compensation for various types of bodily injury appeared prior to the Norman Conquest of 1066. *Id.* at 844-45.

ing.[113] The death penalty, which in England dated back to the reign of King Alfred (871-901 A.D.),[114] was not prohibited in Magna Carta; Chapter 39, which provided that no person shall be deprived of his life, liberty, or property, but "by the judgment of his peers or by the law of the land,"[115] indicated that capital punishment may be imposed provided that statutory guidelines are followed. There is also no evidence suggesting that England sought to abolish the death penalty prior to the writing of the Bill of Rights in 1689; indeed, for the period beginning with the reign of King Henry VIII in 1509 and proceeding into the 1600s the annual number of executions remained high.[116]

The death penalty was imposed in the American colonies for a wide range of offenses.[117] The first known infliction of the death penalty took place in Jamestown Colony in 1608, and, during the seventeenth century, there were 162 documented executions in the colonies.[118] There was little debate on the death penalty by statesmen of the Revolutionary period; however, evidence indicates that its infliction was widely accepted. Of the eleven states which wrote new constitutions after 1776 (Rhode Island and Connecticut retained their colonial charters), nine, to be sure, prohibited infliction of cruel and unusual punishments;

---

113. For an analysis of events prior to the writing of the Magna Carta concerning assessment of penalties, see Granucci, *supra* note 112, at 844-45. *See* RAOUL BERGER, DEATH PENALTIES 30-31 (1982).

114. 3 JAMES STEPHEN, HISTORY OF CRIMINAL LAW IN ENGLAND 24 (1883), *quoted in* Note, Furman v. Georgia: *Deathknell For Capital Punishment?*, 47 ST. JOHN'S L. REV. 107, 108 (1972).

115. MAGNA CARTA ch. 39, *quoted in* Murray v. The Hoboken Land and Improvement Co., 18 How. 272, 276 (1856).

116. According to one scholar, a 1948 study revealed that the annual rate of executions averaged 140 during the reign of King Henry VIII (1509-47); 560 during the tenure of King Edward VI (1547-53); following a decline in frequency, 90 per year during the occupation of Charles I (1625-49); and "990 more during the ten years of the Commonwealth under Oliver Cromwell (1649-58)." 1 LEON RADZINOWICZ, A HISTORY OF ENGLISH CRIMINAL LAW, 140-42 (1948), *quoted in* RAYMOND PATERNOSTER, CAPITAL PUNISHMENT IN AMERICA 5 (1991).

117. The range of offenses punishable by death in colonial America included, in addition to murder, rape, burglary, sodomy, arson, treason, adultery, witchcraft, blasphemy, sexual immorality, horse stealing, counterfeiting and forgery, and, in some Southern states, stealing, concealing with intent to emancipate, and inciting to insurrection, slaves. *See* WILLIAM J. BOWERS, LEGAL HOMICIDE 133-34 (1984); HUGO BEDAU, THE DEATH PENALTY IN AMERICA 7-8 (3rd ed. 1982), *quoted in* PATERNOSTER, *supra* note 116, at 5.

118. Victoria Schinader & John O. Smykla, *A Summary Analysis of Executions in the United States 1608-1987: The Espy File, in* THE DEATH PENALTY IN AMERICA: CURRENT RESEARCH 6 (Robert M. Bohm, ed., 1991), *quoted in* PATERNOSTER, *supra* note 116, at 4.

however, during the 1700s, the total number of executions was 1391,[119] almost nine times as many as those carried out in the 1600s.[120]

No reference to the death penalty was made at the Philadelphia Convention of 1787 or at the state ratifying conventions, and little discussion took place in the First Congress on Madison's proposed amendment.[121] Only a few minutes' time was devoted to the phrase "cruel and unusual punishments." The only discussion on this subject came from Congressman William Smith of South Carolina, who declared that the wording of the Eighth Amendment was "too indefinite," and Congressman Samuel Livermore of New Hampshire, who stated: "It is sometimes necessary to hang a man, . . . villains often deserve whipping, and perhaps having their ears cut off; but are we in the future to be prevented from inflicting these punishments because they are cruel?"[122] Livermore's concern that this clause might limit Congress' discretion to punish offenses as capital did not indicate that the First Congress wished to restrict capital punishment or curb legislative discretion in its mode of infliction. Indeed, the death penalty was legal in all thirteen states in 1789, and, one year later, the First Congress itself enacted legislation which punished by death the crimes of murder, robbery, rape, and forgery of public securities.[123]

Capital punishment, extensively employed for centuries in England, was also widely adopted both during the colonial period and the generation of the founding fathers. However, during the early 1800s there had been abolitionist agitation, and, in the years leading up to the Civil War, "most of the Northern and Eastern states"[124] had significantly reduced the number of crimes punishable by death, and revised capital proceedings to

---

119. *See id.*

120. *See supra* text accompanying note 118.

121. *See generally* HELEN E. VEIT ET AL., CREATING THE BILL OF RIGHTS, THE DOCUMENTARY RECORD FROM THE FIRST FEDERAL CONGRESS (1991). The prohibition against "cruel and unusual punishments" was the tenth of twelve Amendments submitted by the First Congress to the states, but the first two were not ratified, numerically changing the original Tenth Amendment to the Eighth.

122. 1 ANNALS OF CONG. 782-83 (1789).

123. Act of Apr. 30, 1790, 1 Stat. 115, *quoted in* Berger, *supra* note 113, at 47.

124. JAN GORECKI, CAPITAL PUNISHMENT: CRIMINAL LAW AND SOCIAL EVOLUTION 86 (1983).

confine the discretion of jurors and sentencing authorities.[125] In 1846, Michigan became the first state to abolish capital punishment, to be followed, in the period prior to the Civil War, by Rhode Island in 1852, and Wisconsin in 1853.[126] Thus, while capital punishment was widespread in our formative years, it had generated debate concerning its morality and necessity.[127]

The original understanding of the prohibition against "cruel and unusual punishments" cannot be definitively determined, in part because seeking to define initial conceptions is elusive.[128] To be sure, both the death penalty and barbaric forms of punishment, prevalent in British history,[129] continued in early American experience.[130] Conceivably, the phrase "cruel and unusual" referred not to the type of punishment imposed but rather to the

---

125. *See generally* LOUIS P. MASUR, RITES OF EXECUTION, CAPITAL PUNISHMENT AND THE TRANSFORMATION OF AMERICAN CULTURE, 1776-1865 50-92 (1989); PATERNOSTER, *supra* note 116, at 6-9; GORECKI, *supra* note 124, at 83-87.

126. GORECKI, *supra* note 124, at 86.

127. *See infra* text accompanying notes 175-88.

128. *See supra* text accompanying notes 29-36.

129. *See generally* Granucci, *supra* note 112. Sir William Blackstone noted that one hundred sixty nonclergyable capital crimes were statutorily enacted in the 1760s. 4 WILLIAM BLACKSTONE, COMMENTARIES 18 (1768), *cited in* GORECKI, *supra* note 124, at 60 n.118. Concerning noncapital offenses, Blackstone emphasized that punishment should be consistent with statutory guidelines rather than arbitrarily imposed by the biases of the judge. Among the types of punishment discussed by Blackstone are the pillory, the stocks, the duckingstool, whipping, splitting the nostrils, branding, and cutting off the hand or ear. *Id.* at 369-72, *quoted in* Granucci, *supra* note 112, at 862-63.

130. For example, the North Carolina legislature passed a law in 1786 requiring horse thieves, for a first offense, to "stand in the pillory one hour, and [be] publicly whipped on his, or her or their bare backs with thirty-nine lashes well laid on, and at the same time [to] have his, her, or their ears nailed to the pillory and cut off, and [to] be branded on the right cheek with the letter H of the length of three-quarters of an inch, and on the left cheek with the letter T of the same dimensions as the letter H, in a plain and visible manner." The death penalty was to be imposed for a second offense. State Records of NC (Holdsboro, 1905) xxiv, 795. In 1785, Pennsylvania enacted a law providing that an individual filing for bankruptcy who committed perjury at the time assets were examined, which "tend[ed] to the damage of the creditors twenty pounds," shall be required to "stand in the pillory in some public place two hours and have one of his ears nailed to the pillory and cut off." 12 Pa. Stat. at L., 76-77. In Virginia, a statute in effect in the 1780s, and reenacted in 1792, punished, for a first offense, the stealing of hogs, by inflicting, "twenty-five lashes, well laid on, at the public whipping post of the county;" for a second offense, one was required to "stand two hours in the pillory, on a court day, at the court house of the county, . . . and have both ears nailed thereto, and, at the end of two hours, have the ears cut loose from the nails." A third offense was punishable by death. 6 Hening, Va. Stat. at L., 121-23, *quoted in* 1 WILLIAM W. CROSSKEY, POLITICS AND THE CONSTITUTION IN THE HISTORY OF THE UNITED STATES 474-75 (1953).

duration and degree of suffering inflicted.[131] In short, it is unclear whether the framers wished to uphold or proscribe capital punishment by the "cruel and unusual punishments" clause, and uncertain as to what types of offenses or modes of punishment might have been acceptable to them. The original understanding of this phrase may be more fully understood by examining provisions of the Constitution applicable to the death penalty.

B.   *The Constitutionality and Morality of the Death Penalty*

1.   Is Capital Punishment Constitutional?

The Eighth Amendment's prohibition of "cruel and unusual punishments" does not, by itself, sanction or proscribe the death penalty. The language of the Bill of Rights, however, suggests that its infliction in certain circumstances was constitutionally recognized. The Fifth Amendment states that no one shall be "deprived of life, liberty, or property, without due process of law," and that no person shall "be twice put in jeopardy of life or limb" for the same offense or be compelled "to answer for a capital, or otherwise infamous crime."[132] This suggests that persons may, consistent with "due process of law," be deprived of life. In 1868, seventy-nine years after the Bill of Rights was written, the Fourteenth Amendment, providing in pertinent part that "no State shall . . . deprive any person of life, liberty, or property, without due process of law,"[133] indicates that legislatures, provided that "due process" is furnished, may impose the death penalty.

The wording of these phrases would appear to make the death penalty legal; indeed, one scholar contended that the First Congress "was not outlawing by the eighth amendment the right to impose death penalties it simultaneously recognized in the

---

131.   *See, e.g.,* Hugo Bedau, who wrote: "An unbroken line of interpreters has held that it was the original understanding and the intent of the framers of the Eighth Amendment to proscribe as 'cruel and unusual' only such modes of execution as compound the simple infliction of death with added cruelties," such as "burning at the stake, [and] crucifixion." HUGO A. BEDAU, THE DEATH PENALTY IN AMERICA 14, 35 (rev. ed. 1967), *quoted in* BERGER, *supra* note 113, at 49. Raoul Berger argued that the "cruel and unusual punishments" clause was originally "concerned solely with the *nature* of the punishment — barbarous, torturous — not with the *process* whereby the sentence was handed down." BERGER, *id.* at 131 (emphasis in original).

132.   U.S. CONST. amend. V.

133.   U.S. CONST. amend. XIV, § 1. *See supra* note 57.

fifth."[134] However, unaccompanied by careful debate, it is uncertain whether capital punishment is sanctioned by the Fifth and Eighth Amendments. Leonard Levy pointed out that the drafting of the Bill of Rights was "imitative, deficient, and irrationally selective" and that, rather than addressing specific issues, the authors wrote a random catalogue of rights that seemed to satisfy their urge for a statement of first principles — or for some of them."[135] During debates in the 39th Congress (1866-68) on the Fourteenth Amendment, not a single statement was made concerning whether inclusion of the word "life" as being prohibited from deprivation without "due process of law" might, contrary to the intentions of the authors, authorize the states to retain or institute capital punishment.[136]

A literal reading of pertinent provisions in the Fifth, Eighth, and Fourteenth Amendments indicates that the death penalty is not precluded if states choose to adopt it. However, the phrases "cruel and unusual punishments" and "due process of law" do not specify the types of offenses which may be categorized as capital or the modes of proceeding to be followed if it is litigated. Perhaps states are free to sanction the death penalty for any offenses desired, and, provided that defendants are accorded all due process of law protections statutorily enacted, no constitutional challenge is presented.[137] In other words, are statutes which do not violate any express provision of the Constitution presumed valid? Could a state, for example, punish jaywalking as a capital offense, and claim that there is nothing in the Constitution which specifically prohibited such a measure? Would this punishment become acceptable if elaborate due process safeguards were instituted to ensure that a defendant facing this penalty had every opportunity to challenge prosecutorial allegations? Laurence Tribe emphasized that it would be improper to "lift

---

134. BERGER, *supra* note 113, at 46. For a critical analysis of Berger's position, see David A.J. Richards, *Constitutional Interpretation, History, and the Death Penalty: A Book Review*, 71 CAL. L. REV. 1372 (1983) and Hugo A. Bedau, *Thinking of the Death Penalty as a Cruel and Unusual Punishment*, 18 U.C. DAVIS L. REV. 873 (1985).

135. LEONARD W. LEVY, ORIGINS OF THE FIFTH AMENDMENT 411 (1968).

136. For an examination of the topics discussed while drafting the Fourteenth Amendment, see *supra* note 59.

137. This has been the position of Chief Justice William Rehnquist. *See* Alan I. Bigel, *William H. Rehnquist on Capital Punishment*, 17 OHIO N.U. L. REV. 729 (1991). On the death penalty, Justice Scalia has unwaveringly voted with Rehnquist. *Id.* at 762. While it is premature to assess Justice Thomas' philosophy, it is likely that he will follow this position on the Eighth Amendment. *See* Hudson v. McMillian, 112 S. Ct. 995 (1992) (Thomas, J., dissenting).

one [constitutional] provision out, hold it up to the light, and give it its broadest possible interpretation, while ignoring the fact that it is immersed in a larger whole."[138]

If the wording of the Constitution is "only a framework" and "not a blueprint,"[139] it may not be possible to conclude that the death penalty is constitutional based on recognition of this punishment in the Fifth and Fourteenth Amendments. What types of punishments are "cruel and unusual," and how might this prohibition in the Eighth Amendment be reconciled with provisions in the Bill of Rights? The Court has applied most of the procedural safeguards of the Bill of Rights as binding on the states,[140] which would make a capital offense in violation of the Constitution if it does not conform with its provisions; hence, a punishment may be "cruel and unusual" in a due process context. Yet, given its ambiguous wording, it is not clear as to what procedures do not meet stipulations in the Bill of Rights. How can it be ascertained, for example, whether evidence against a capital defendant was obtained by an "unreasonable search[ ] and seizure[ ];"[141] whether an accused is being "twice put in jeopardy of life and limb;"[142] whether one has been tried "by an impartial jury" with a satisfactory opportunity to "be confronted with the witnesses against him" and to "have compulsory process for obtaining witnesses in his favor;"[143] and whether effective "assistance of counsel"[144] was available? Arguably, it is not possible to state whether capital punishment is constitutionally sanctioned since this will be based on uneven trial proceedings.

It is uncertain whether the words "cruel and unusual" apply to the content of legislation as well as the process by which a defendant is tried. The Eighth Amendment prohibits infliction of punishments which are "cruel *and* unusual;" by refraining from employing the word "or" it would appear that, to be unconstitutional, a penalty must be measured by its severity and frequency with which it is carried out. There are no objective standards to assess degree of cruelty, which may be both physical and psychological, and a punishment thought to be cruel in the sense that, among other factors, it is disproportionate to the offense allegedly committed, may or may not be unusual,

---

138. LAURENCE TRIBE & MICHAEL C. DORF, ON READING THE CONSTITUTION 22 (1991).
139. *Id.* at 6.
140. *See supra* note 59 and text accompanying notes 56-62.
141. U.S. CONST. amend. IV.
142. U.S. CONST. amend. V.
143. *Id.*
144. U.S. CONST. amend. VI.

depending on how often a state is able to carry out a sentence. In short, capital punishment may only be constitutional if the Court believes that this penalty is both appropriate, given the heinous nature of a crime, and consistent with the pattern in which a state has charged, tried, convicted, and sentenced similarly situated defendants.

How is the Court to make this assessment? Is perception of "cruel and unusual" to be based on attitudes toward punishment prevalent at the time the Eighth Amendment was written, or is it necessary for the Court to apply this standard in light of evolving notions of justice? Should trends in public opinion affect the Court's position, and does the overwhelming adoption of capital punishment by state legislatures affect its constitutionality? Is it appropriate for the Court to establish procedural standards to be followed by states which choose to sanction the death penalty, or may the justices, based on their conceptions of morality, seek to affect philosophical attitudes on capital punishment? Clearly, the prohibition against infliction of "cruel and unusual punishments" must be examined from a number of perspectives which may affect perceptions as to whether the death penalty is constitutional.

2. Abolitionist and Retentionist Positions on the Death Penalty

Though capital punishment was widely practiced at the time the Eighth Amendment was adopted,[145] vigorous debate on the morality of the death penalty, already widespread during the Revolutionary period,[146] persisted after the Constitution was written. The most prominent and elaborate discussion opposing the death penalty in the 1790s was put forward by Benjamin Rush, "the most influential physician in America, a signer of the Declaration of Independence, and a prolific essayist."[147] In a series of essays written in the late 1780s and early 1790s,[148] Rush maintained that capital punishment is antithetical to the "mild and

---

145.   *See supra* text accompanying note 123.

146.   *See* MASUR, *supra* note 125, at 50-70.

147.   *Id.* at 62.

148.   *See*, BENJAMIN RUSH, CONSIDERATIONS ON THE INJUSTICE AND IMPOLICY OF PUNISHING MURDER BY DEATH (1792) [hereinafter CONSIDERATIONS ON INJUSTICE]; BENJAMIN RUSH, AN ENQUIRY INTO THE EFFECTS OF PUBLIC PUNISHMENTS UPON CRIMINALS AND UPON SOCIETY (1787); Benjamin Rush, *Rejoinder to a Reply to the Enquiry into the Justice and Policy of Punishing Murder by Death*, 5 AM. MUSEUM 63, 121 (1789); Benjamin Rush, *An Enquiry Into the Justice and Policy of Punishing Murder by Death*, 4 AM. MUSEUM 78 (1788).

benevolent principles"[149] of republican government, a repudiation of the Lord's vision that humankind display forgiveness and compassion,[150] and insensitive to society's need to (seek to) rehabilitate offenders.[151] While the death penalty was not abolished in Rush's lifetime, a few state legislatures, in the 1780s and 1790s, revised statutes reducing the number of capital crimes[152] and more strictly codifying procedures for its infliction,[153] giving rise to further debate,[154] which has continued unabated, on the appropriateness of capital punishment.

Essentially, supporters and opponents of capital punishment have raised the following questions in seeking to justify their position: Is the death penalty a deterrent to the commission of murder? Is it offensive to human dignity, and to evolving notions of justice, for government to sanction capital punishment? Is life imprisonment without parole a more cost effective alternative to the death penalty? Is retribution an appropriate objective of punishment? Is the death penalty arbitrarily imposed? Is the discretion exercised by juries and judges resulting in more frequent death sentences for defendants who are minorities and socioeconomically disadvantaged? Does public opinion support or reject capital punishment? Can convicted murderers be rehabilitated, and is society obligated to make this effort? A number of studies on capital punishment may illuminate the arguments put forward by abolitionists and retentionists.

3. The Deterrent Effect of Capital Punishment

Perhaps the most extensively examined aspect of capital punishment has been its alleged deterrent effect. Does enact-

---

149. CONSIDERATIONS ON THE INJUSTICE, *supra* note 148, at 19, *quoted in* MASUR, *supra* note 125, at 65.

150. Rush, *An Enquiry into the Justice and Policy of Punishing Murder by Death*, *supra* note 148, at 16.

151. RUSH, CONSIDERATIONS ON THE INJUSTICE, *supra* note 148, at 13.

152. *See* MASUR, *supra* note 125, at 71-81.

153. *Id. See also* PATERNOSTER, *supra* note 116, at 6-7.

154. Though no prominent statesman in Rush's time favored abolition of capital punishment, a few addressed mitigating the severity of criminal sanctions. In the 1770s, Thomas Jefferson, in a bill proposal to the Virginia legislature, wrote that "if the punishment were only proportional to the injury, men would feel it their inclination, as well as their duty, to see the laws observed," and supported the death penalty only for murder and treason. Thomas Jefferson, *A Bill for Proportioning Crimes and Punishments*, *in* MERRILL D. PETERSON, JEFFERSON: WRITINGS 349-52 (Library of America ed. 1984). Benjamin Franklin, also reflecting on the proportionality between an offense and its punishment, asked: "Is it not murder . . . to put a man to death for an offence which does not deserve death?," 2 JARED SPARKS, THE WORKS OF BENJAMIN FRANKLIN 479 (1840), *quoted in* MASUR, *supra* note 125, at 62.

ment of capital punishment statutes discourage potential murderers from committing homicide? This may be examined by comparing homicide figures in contiguous states which retain and do not statutorily impose the death penalty; by analyzing murder statistics in a state which has abolished capital punishment compared with the period during which the death penalty was legal; by noting the frequency with which those convicted of murder are executed; and by observing whether there has been a decrease in the homicide rate for a specific period following a highly publicized execution. An early study, published in 1925, declared that evidence on the deterrent effect of capital punishment is inconclusive,[155] and, in 1952, an examination of homicide rates in the abolitionist states of Michigan, Wisconsin, Rhode Island, and Minnesota during the period 1931-1946 indicated that they were statistically comparable to figures in neighboring states which retained the death penalty.[156] The most extensive examination of the possible deterrent effect of capital punishment has been undertaken by Thorsten Sellin, beginning with his landmark 1959 work titled *The Death Penalty*,[157] and followed by revised studies in the 1960s and 1980s.[158]

Sellin examined the annual homicide rates for contiguous retentionist and abolitionist states, as well as changes in murder statistics when a state had abolished or reinstated the death penalty. Covering the period from 1920 to 1955, Sellin examined homicide rates for five sets of contiguous states,[159] and concluded that there was no statistically significant difference in the number of murders committed between neighboring states

---

155. Edwin H. Sutherland, *Murder and the Death Penalty*, 15 J. AM. INST. CRIM. L. & CRIMINOLOGY 522 (1925).

156. Karl F. Schuessler, *The Deterrent Influence of the Death Penalty*, 284 ANNALS AM. ACAD. POL. & SOC. SCI. 54 (1952).

157. THORSTEN SELLIN, THE DEATH PENALTY (1959).

158. THORSTEN SELLIN, THE DEATH PENALTY (1982); THORSTEN SELLIN, THE PENALTY OF DEATH (1980); CAPITAL PUNISHMENT (Thorsten Sellin ed., 1967).

159. In the Midwest, Sellin considered three groups (those which have the death penalty are indicated with the word "capital," and states which mandate a maximum punishment of life imprisonment are designated "noncapital"): Michigan (noncapital), Indiana (capital), Ohio (capital) — Minnesota (noncapital), Wisconsin (noncapital), Iowa (capital) — North Dakota (noncapital), South Dakota (capital), Nebraska (capital) — and, in the New England area, two groups were studied: Maine (noncapital), New Hampshire (capital), Vermont (capital) — Rhode Island (noncapital), Massachusetts (capital), Connecticut (capital). PATERNOSTER, *supra* note 116, at 222.

which punish by death and life imprisonment,[160] or within states during the period before and after a capital punishment statute is repealed or adopted.[161] Sellin's findings, which suggest that capital punishment cannot statistically be shown to deter criminals from committing murder, gave rise to other major studies which claimed to examine a wider range of socioeconomic factors in assessing the significance of numerical variations. Three major studies of this issue were published in the 1970s by Isaac Ehrlich.[162]

Covering the period 1933-1969, Ehrlich argued that geographical proximity, by itself, presented an incomplete comparison of homicide statistics; since no two states have an identical population density and urban and rural configuration, similar rates of unemployment in particular racial and age groups, and comparable methods of law enforcement, a multidimensional perspective on the possible deterrent effect of capital punishment can best be ascertained by examining nationwide annual murder figures. Comparing the number of convictions for murder with executions, Ehrlich, arguing that deterrence is evident when death penalty statutes are vigorously enforced, concluded that , "[a]n additional execution per year over the period in question [1933-1969] may have resulted, on average, in 7 or 8 fewer murders."[163]

Ehrlich's contention that capital punishment is a deterrent to the commission of murder brought forth additional studies, in part challenging the variables which he employed in reaching his conclusion,[164] and, simultaneously, inquiring into whether a

---

160. Examining the rate of homicide for every 100,000 inhabitants, Sellin concluded that, for each of his five groups, see supra note 159, the numerical difference between states with the highest and lowest homicide rates was between 1.3 and 0.4. See PATERNOSTER, supra note 116, at 222.

161. In 1967, Sellin published data from eleven states — Arizona, Colorado, Delaware, Iowa, Kansas, Maine, Missouri, Oregon, South Dakota, Tennessee, and Washington — and concluded that the rates of homicide, per 100,000 inhabitants, remained constant. SELLIN, supra note 158, at 122-24.

162. Isaac Ehrlich, Capital Punishment and Deterrence: Some Further Thoughts and Additional Evidence, 85 J. POL. ECON. 741 (1977); Isaac Ehrlich & Joel C. Gibbons, On the Measurement of the Deterrent Effect of Capital Punishment and the Theory of Deterrence, 6 J. LEGAL STUD. 35 (1977); Isaac Ehrlich, The Deterrent Effect of Capital Punishment: A Question of Life and Death, 65 AM. ECON. REV. 397 (1975).

163. Ehrlich, The Deterrent Effect of Capital Punishment: A Question of Life and Death, supra note 162, at 414. For a criticism of the position that the death penalty is a deterrent to the commission of murder, see James A. Fox & Michael L. Radelet, Persistent Flaws in Econometric Studies of the Deterrent Effect of the Death Penalty, 23 LOY. L.A. L. REV. 29 (1989).

164. For an extensive critique of Ehrlich's findings, see JACK P. GIBBS, CRIME, PUNISHMENT AND DETERRENCE (1975); FRANKLIN ZIMRING & GORDON

deterrent effect was present after the early 1970s, when many states revised their capital statutes. A study published in 1988,[165] comparing murder rates in abolitionist and retentionist states from 1973 to 1984, concluded that states which had the death penalty had higher rates of homicide than both states which imposed a maximum punishment of life imprisonment and the national average.[166] Comparing contiguous states which had, and refused to impose, the death penalty, it was also found that the homicide rate for the period 1973-1984 was either comparable in capital and noncapital states, or, in some instances, slightly higher in states which retained the death penalty.[167] Other studies concluded that there is no lower incidence of murder of law enforcement officers in capital as opposed to noncapital states;[168] that publicity accompanying an execution has not resulted in a short term lower homicide rate in the state;[169] and that the rate of homicide had not appreciably changed in the

---

HAWKINS, DETERRENCE (1973); FRANKLIN E. ZIMRING & GORDON HAWKINS, CAPITAL PUNISHMENT AND THE AMERICAN AGENDA (1986); David C. Baldus & James Cole, *A Comparison of the Work of Thorsten Sellin and Isaac Ehrlich on the Deterrent Effect of Capital Punishment*, 85 YALE L.J. 170 (1975); Arnold Barnett, *Crime and Capital Punishment: Some Recent Studies*, 6 J. CRIM. JUST. 291 (1978); Theodore Black & Thomas Orsagh, *New Evidence on the Efficacy of Sanctions as a Deterrent to Homicide*, 58 SOC. SCI. Q. 616 (1978); Brian Forst, *The Deterrent Effect of Capital Punishment: A Cross-State Analysis of the 1960s*, 61 MINN. L. REV. 743 (1977); Stephen J. Knorr, *Deterrence and the Death Penalty: A Temporal Cross-Sectional Approach*, 70 J. CRIM. L. & CRIMINOLOGY 235 (1979); Richard O. Lempert, *Desert and Deterrence: An Assessment of the Moral Bases of the Case for Capital Punishment*, 79 MICH. L. REV. 1177, 1206-21 (1981); Peter Passell & John Taylor, *The Deterrent Effect of Capital Punishment: Another View*, 67 AM. ECON. REV. 445 (1977); Jon K. Peck, *The Deterrent Effect of Capital Punishment: Ehrlich and His Critics*, 85 YALE L.J. 359 (1976); Hans Zeisel, *The Deterrent Effect of the Death Penalty: Facts v. Faiths*, 1976 SUP. CT. REV. 317. For Ehrlich's replies, see Ehrlich & Gibbons, *supra* note 162; Isaac Ehrlich & Randall Mark, *Fear of Deterrence*, 6 J. LEGAL STUD. 293 (1977); Isaac Ehrlich, *The Deterrent Effect of Capital Punishment: Reply*, 67 AM. ECON. REV. 452 (1977); Isaac Ehrlich, *Deterrence: Evidence and Inference*, 85 YALE L.J. 209 (1975).

165.   Ruth D. Peterson & William C. Bailey, *Murder and Capital Punishment in the Evolving Context of the Post-Furman Era*, 66 SOC. FORCES 774 (1988).

166.   The average annual homicide rate was "8.46 per 100,000 population in death penalty states, 5.35 in abolitionist states, and 7.61 for the United States as a whole." Peterson & Bailey, *supra* note 165, at 785.

167.   *Id.* at 786-88. *See also* PATERNOSTER, *supra* note 116, at 223.

168.   William C. Bailey & Ruth D. Peterson, *Police Killings and Capital Punishment: The Post-Furman Period*," 25 CRIMINOLOGY 1 (1987).

169.   *See* William J. Bowers, *The Effect of Executions is Brutalization, Not Deterrence, in* KENNETH R. HAAS & JAMES A. INCIARDI, CHALLENGING CAPITAL PUNISHMENT: LEGAL AND SOCIAL SCIENCE APPROACHES 72 (1988); William C. Bailey, *Disaggregation in Deterrence and Death Penalty Research: The Case of Murder in Chicago*, 74 J. CRIM. L. & CRIMINOLOGY 827 (1983); William J. Bowers & Glenn Pierce, *Deterrence or Brutalization: What Is The Effect Of Executions?*, 26 CRIME &

years during which a state did not have the death penalty compared with the period when capital punishment was reintroduced.[170]

These studies suggest that the death penalty is not a statistically significant deterrent to the commission of homicide. If a purpose of punishment is to induce potential offenders to refrain from a course of conduct by making clear that its commission will result in a severe penalty, and evidence seems to indicate that this objective is not being achieved, perhaps some other type of sanction should be adopted. Abolitionists have in part sought to discredit the death penalty on this ground; however, notwithstanding empirical studies, deterrence, as one opponent of the death penalty conceded, can never be precisely ascertained because "no adequately controlled experiment or observation is possible or . . . ever will be possible" where, "inescapabl[y], . . . social conditions in any state are not constant through time, and . . . not the same in any two states."[171] Instead of seeking to measure deterrence from a national, interstate or intrastate perspective, retentionists have argued that, even if only a few randomly convicted felons concede that they refrained from committing murder to avoid the death penalty, the deterrent effect of capital punishment has been fulfilled.

In part because murders are often not premeditated, and, undoubtedly, since serial killers believe that they will be sufficiently clever and methodical to evade apprehension, it is difficult to assess whether murderers, before committing homicide, calculated whether the prospect of the death penalty was more undesirable than life imprisonment. One supporter of capital punishment, based on information obtained from state district attorneys, a police department study, and testimony given in the early 1970s by an assistant attorney general in the criminal division of the Justice Department to the House of Representatives, furnished accounts of individuals arrested for murder in the late 1950s and early 1960s who stated that they used a fake gun, pretended to be carrying a weapon, or refrained from killing a robbery victim to avoid the death penalty.[172] Additionally, during the ten-year moratorium on executions (voluntarily adopted by

---

DELINQ. 453 (1980); David R. King, *The Brutalization Effect: Execution Publicity and the Incidence of Homicide in South Carolina*, 57 SOC. FORCES 683 (1978).

    170.   *See* Richard O. Lempert, *The Effect of Executions on Homicides: A New Look in an Old Light*, 29 CRIME & DELINQ. 88 (1983); Peterson & Bailey, *supra* note 165.

    171.   CHARLES L. BLACK, JR., CAPITAL PUNISHMENT: THE INEVITABILITY OF CAPRICE AND MISTAKE 33 (1981).

    172.   FRANK G. CARRINGTON, NEITHER CRUEL NOR UNUSUAL 92-99 (1978).

states pending resolution of the constitutionality of the death penalty by the United States Supreme Court), from June 2, 1967, until January 17, 1977, when the carrying out of a death sentence was resumed,[173] the national homicide rate nearly doubled,[174] which may be attributable to a wide range of dynamic political, social, and economic factors, or, no less than figures suggesting that there is no appreciable difference in the homicide rates of capital and noncapital states, an indication that removing the prospect of death eliminates the fear potential killers might have felt in contemplating murder.

It appears that neither the position of the abolitionists nor the retentionists is more compelling. If deterrence could be objectively and comprehensively measured, how significant a numerical disparity between the commission of homicide in capital and noncapital states would there have to be to show that the death penalty discourages individuals from attempting murder? How long would this trend have to persist to illustrate that the death penalty is an ongoing and demonstrable deterrent? The arguments put forward by retentionists are no less statistically supportable in that a handful of statements from arrested murderers indicating fear of the death penalty does not conclusively prove that capital punishment is an effective deterrent. Ultimately, both positions appeal to the emotions: If executing just one convicted murderer will prevent that individual from ever killing again, is the death penalty not worthwhile? On the other hand, is it morally justifiable to inflict a punishment qualitatively different from any other when evidence does not indicate that the death penalty is discouraging commission of homicide? To gain a better understanding of the abolitionist and retentionist positions, it is helpful to explore both perspectives on the issue of retribution.

4.   The Relevance of Retribution in Penal Codes

Unlike deterrence, which, despite its divergent observations, can be discussed in a quantified context, retribution elicits emotions which are not empirically directed. Essentially, it may be argued that a murderer has committed such a heinous injustice to both the victim and the notion of civilized communal coexistence that society is obligated to inflict a degree of pain and suffering on the accused as a way of imparting that such conduct will not be tolerated. If this position is acceptable, it becomes necessary to define punishment, when and how it should be

---

173.   PATERNOSTER, *supra* note 116, at 18.
174.   CARRINGTON, *supra* note 172, at 86.

inflicted, and what purpose it seeks to accomplish. Because of the enormity and irreversibility of the death penalty, both its supporters and opponents have argued, respectively, that it is the only punishment commensurate with the cruelty of murder, and that government must seek to preserve the dignity of humankind by communicating that execution is morally repugnant.

The two concepts most frequently connected to the death penalty are utilitarianism and retributivism — or, as one scholar wrote, "[d]esert and [d]eterrence."[175] The doctrine of *lex talionis* — an eye for an eye — was first recognized in the Old Testament of the Bible:[176] "If a man injures his neighbor, what he has done must be done to him: broken limb for broken limb, eye for eye, tooth for tooth. As the injury inflicted, so must be the injury suffered."[177] This notion, in the modern period, refers to the need for society to be compensated for an injustice. In other words, if individuals agree to submit to the rule of civil authority, they have consented to partake in both its privileges — the protection of one's physical safety and possessions from the possible greed of others — and its responsibilities — to obey a body of laws ostensibly enacted for the well-being of all. Those who violate the laws have broken a trust with the citizenry, which, by exacting a penalty, seeks compensation for an act considered an affront to the purpose for which submission to civil authority was commenced.[178] Conceptually, *lex talionis* maintains that the punishment imposed should be commensurate with the injury inflicted. With regard to capital punishment, retentionists might argue that, since murder is unique in terms of its gravity and finality, only the death penalty is proportionate punishment.[179]

Abolitionists, on the other hand, accentuate the utilitarian component of punishment. Unlike retributivists, who view punishment as a means to impose, for the purpose of vengeance, a degree of pain and suffering on an offender proportionate to that inflicted on the victim, utilitarians maintain that the purpose of sanctions is "deterrence of potential criminals, rehabilitation of convicted criminals, and incapacitation of convicted

---

175.   Lempert, *supra* note 164.

176.   *Exodus* 21:25.

177.   *Leviticus* 24:19-20, *quoted in* Granucci, *supra* note 112, at 844.

178.   For an elaboration of this position, see IMMANUEL KANT, THE METAPHYSICAL ELEMENTS OF JUSTICE (1797).

179.   WALTER BERNS, FOR CAPITAL PUNISHMENT (1979); ERNEST VAN DEN HAAG & JOHN P. CONRAD, THE DEATH PENALTY: A DEBATE (1983). *See also* Mary E. Gale, *Retribution, Punishment, and Death*, 18 U.C. DAVIS L. REV. 973 (1985).

criminals."[180] The utilitarian conception of punishment is that, to compensate society for the violation of law incurred, a sanction is appropriate only if it is perceived by the offender to impose burdens greater than any benefit which might be gained by committing the infraction. This, presumably, would both discourage unlawful conduct and confer a benefit on society by educating the offender to refrain from recidivism.[181] Where retribution is concerned with exacting an equivalent degree of punishment on an offender as an expression of outrage toward that individual act, utilitarianism aims not so much at proportionality but rather at the perceived benefit to be gained by society from a particular type of sanction.[182]

With regard to capital punishment, there is no greater degree of morality in the position of the retributivist or utilitarian. The retributivist, likely to be a supporter of the death penalty, would generally argue that the uniqueness of murder compels a penalty qualitatively more severe than any other; that a respect for the sanctity of extinguished human life obligates society to communicate a message that it will not tolerate homicide; that some peace of mind might be communicated to a victim's family by taking the life of a convicted murderer; and that, irrespective of any possible deterrent effect, it is appropriate for lawmakers to take into account vengeance as a motive for legislation. Not all retributivists, however, believe that death is the only acceptable punishment for those convicted of murder. Two recent scholars have advocated retributivism which emphasizes punishment comparable in severity to the unlawful activity rather than seeking to mechanically inflict the same type of bodily harm on both the victim and the offender. These positions, labeled "equality"[183] and "proportional"[184] retributivism, do not disre-

---

180. Malcolm E. Wheeler, *Toward a Theory of Limited Punishment: An Examination of the Eighth Amendment,* 24 STAN. L. REV. 838, 847 (1972).

181. For an analysis of how the goals of utilitarianism may be achieved, see CESARE BECCARIA, ON CRIMES AND PUNISHMENTS (1764); JEREMY BENTHAM, AN INTRODUCTION TO THE PRINCIPLES OF MORALS AND LEGISLATION (1789); H.L.A. HART, PUNISHMENT AND RESPONSIBILITY (1968); HERBERT PACKER, THE LIMITS OF CRIMINAL SANCTION (1968); JOHN RAWLS, A THEORY OF JUSTICE (1971); John Rawls, *Two Concepts of Rules,* 64 PHIL. REV. 3 (1955).

182. For example, a retributivist would likely wish to punish one who stole money with a commensurate fine, while a utilitarian would assess the burden to be imposed on the offender by reducing, in the form of a fine, this individual's net worth, as opposed to the benefit which may accrue to the citizenry by compelling a certain number of hours of community service.

183. STEVEN NATHANSON, AN EYE FOR AN EYE? THE MORALITY OF PUNISHING BY DEATH (1987).

184. Jeffrey R. Reiman, *Justice, Civilization, and the Death Penalty: Answering van den Haag,* 14 PHIL. & PUB. AFF. 115 (1985).

gard execution as a possible penalty, but rather point out that a commensurate punishment for murder need not necessarily be death.

Opponents of capital punishment, who tend to support utilitarianism, have maintained, no less fervently than their counterparts, that retribution is an improper justification for legislation because it assumes that the convicted murderer is totally responsible for the unlawful activity. Abolitionists have argued that murderers, who have often come from broken homes and may have endured parental abuse, are "victims" who need compassion rather than retaliation from society, which perhaps by neglect of family breakdown is partly responsible for the offender's deviant behavior. A utilitarian would also likely insist that the death penalty degrades the sanctity of life by sanctioning a form of punishment which produces the same result as the conduct being condemned. As to whether the death penalty is a more cruel form of punishment than many years of incarceration, a utilitarian would probably respond affirmatively on the ground that a prisoner might perform useful work even while confined, and wages earned, however meager, can be turned over as compensation to the victim's family, or for some penological endeavor. While the life of the victim can never be restored, this, a utilitarian would probably declare, would direct punishment not toward vengeance, which would arouse base human passions, but rather to a far more desirable objective of somewhat making restitution to the community for the injustice it has suffered.

The issue of retribution is the most emotional component of discussion on capital punishment. Fundamentally, it raises questions concerning the level of dignity which government seeks to preserve with the citizenry, and the degree of civility which humankind is morally expected to follow. It is unclear whether contemporary society is retributivist or utilitarian. Since the early 1970s, public approval for the death penalty has steadily increased;[185] in 1988, it was estimated in a Gallup poll that nearly 80% of the adult population supported it for murder.[186] However, when asked whether the death penalty was preferred to life imprisonment without parole, fewer than one-third expressed support for execution,[187] suggesting perhaps that protection from possible repeat offenders, rather than retribution, was the primary motivation which has induced individuals to support

---

185. PATERNOSTER, *supra* note 116, at 26.
186. *Id.* at 25.
187. *Id.* at 275.

capital punishment.[188]   Beyond deterrence and retribution, other considerations must be weighed in assessing the position of abolitionists and retentionists.

5. Is Execution More Cost Effective Than Life Imprisonment Without Parole?

Both abolitionists and retentionists have sought to bolster their position on capital punishment by examining the financial aspects of executing a convicted murderer compared to the cost of lifetime incarceration. These arguments are not primarily intended to induce a state to more effectively practice fiscal integrity with budgetary priorities; rather, they fundamentally question the extent to which a community, compelled to emotionally deal with an extreme transgression of voluntary coexistence under the direction of civil authority, must divert attention from ongoing policy priorities and focus on an individual who, arguably, has relinquished any claim to the facilities and institutions of society. In short, retentionists have argued that execution would not enable convicted murderers to make ongoing demands on the psychological and financial resources of the community in that the death penalty is less costly and burdensome than lifetime incarceration. Abolitionists, on the other hand, have insisted that the cost of litigation in capital cases, greatly exceeding keeping an individual in prison for life, militated against sanctioning capital punishment.

In recent years there have been inquiries into the estimated cost of life imprisonment. A 1990 study reported that it costs approximately $63,000 to build a maximum security cell and about $5,000 a year on the annual principal and interest to finance construction of a prison facility.[189] It has also been estimated to cost around $20,000 a year to maintain a maximum security cell with an inmate.[190] Thus, assuming an annual cost of $25,000, a convicted murderer incarcerated for forty to forty-five years could cost the taxpayers, subject to inflation and adjustments for cost of operations, between 1-1.25 million dollars.

Comparing the cost of life imprisonment with the expense of trial proceedings prior to execution is invariably imprecise given extreme statewide fluctuations in the financial outlays for litigation. Aside from salaries paid to court personnel, empanel-

---

188. *Id.* at 276-77.
189. D.P. Cavanagh & M.A.R. Kleiman, *A Cost-Benefit Analysis of Prison Cell Construction and Alternative Sanctions*, BOTEC ANALYSIS CORP. 12-14 (1990), *quoted in* PATERNOSTER, *supra* note 116, at 209.
190. *Id.*

ing and sequestering a jury, as well as monetary outlays to operate a state adversarial system, the cost of capital proceedings is subject to the extent of due process protection to be accorded to one facing possible execution or life imprisonment. Abolitionists may argue that life imprisonment is less expensive than litigation which may statutorily result in execution, while retentionists, depending on the fervor of their support of the death penalty, may insist that court costs are variable and capable of being contained by limiting the types of evidence admissible, the extent of due process to be accorded to capital defendants, and the opportunities to appeal a verdict, among other factors.

Though the Constitution does not require more elaborate trial proceedings for those charged with capital , as opposed to noncapital, offenses,[191] a sense that the death penalty, given its finality and irreversibility, is a more severe punishment than life imprisonment, has induced states to statutorily prescribe more elaborate trial and appellate procedures for those facing possible execution. During the pretrial stage, where the prosecutor will, among other activities, seek to obtain information from psychologists and psychiatrists, as well as family members, neighbors, and fellow workers, about the character and background of the accused, and to investigate possible tangible evidence connected to the commission of the alleged offense, examine the competency of the accused to stand trial, and devise legal strategy in view of the perceived weight of evidence bearing on the defendant, it has been estimated that the state can incur costs of over $2,000 per day,[192] and that this period may last up to two years.[193]

The costs of a capital trial are affected by the elaborate procedural safeguards statutorily mandated, as well as the greater

---

191. See U.S. CONST. AMENDS. V & XIV; see supra text accompanying notes 132-33.

192. Margot Garey, The Cost of Taking a Life: Dollars and Sense of the Death Penalty, 18 U.C. DAVIS L. REV. 1221, 1253-54 (1985), cited in PATERNOSTER, supra note 116, at 194.

193. Garey, supra note 192, at 1252. In addition to the time required to locate and interview witnesses, as well as examine evidence and testimony of medical experts, there is a tendency by both the prosecutor and defense attorney to file a number of pretrial motions challenging, among other things, the constitutionality of a state's death penalty statute, admissibility of evidence, accuracy of information on the competency and lifestyle of the accused, and ability of the defendant, in view of media publicity, to obtain a fair trial. It has been estimated that "the number of pretrial defense motions in capital cases is from twice to five or six times the number in a noncapital case, and the number filed by the prosecution is twice the number filed in noncapital cases." PATERNOSTER, supra note 116, at 193 (citing Garey, supra note 192, at 1248).

time and effort expended, in view of the possible penalty to be inflicted, to meticulously verify evidence. Unlike noncapital trials, where guilt or innocence as well as sentence are determined in a single proceeding, capital defendants are tried in a bifurcated process, where a verdict and sentence are separately issued. This may require prolonged involvement by jurors, making the need for careful empaneling compelling, and inducing both the prosecution and defense to rigorously question, over a period of weeks or months, a large number of potential jurors. Assembling a jury is "[o]ne of the most expensive components of a capital trial,"[194] and, by one estimate, may take "five times longer to complete than in a noncapital case,"[195] and cost about $87,000 more in courtroom time than the expense incurred in trials where the death penalty is prohibited.[196] In addition, anticipating a possible dual stage proceeding will require extensive preparation by the prosecution and defense, both of which may in effect have to expend time for two trials, and, considering the magnitude of the possible punishment in the penalty phase, long hours seeking to uncover new information and corroborate evidence are expected. While enormous variation in the cost of capital trials from state to state makes compilation of national figures difficult, a 1982 study estimated that the cost of conducting a bifurcated trial in New York State would be around $1.5 million;[197] three years later an examination of expenses likely to be incurred in other states pointed out that California "budgets over $4 million annually just to reimburse county costs for the defense side of a capital trial."[198]

The most expensive portion of capital litigation is the appellate process. Capital defendants may pursue "a complex and multileveled system of both state and federal appellate review,"[199] where a number of years may elapse while a conviction and sentence are challenged in the state and federal courts.[200] Two stud-

---

194. PATERNOSTER, *supra* note 116, at 194.

195. Garey, *supra* note 192, at 1257.

196. PATERNOSTER, *supra* note 116, at 197.

197. NEW YORK STATE DEFENDER'S ASSOCIATION, CAPITAL LOSSES: THE PRICE OF THE DEATH PENALTY FOR NEW YORK STATE 19 (1982), *cited in* PATERNOSTER, *supra* note 116, at 201.

198. PATERNOSTER, *supra* note 116, at 201 (citing Garey, *supra* note 192, at 1260).

199. PATERNOSTER, *supra* note 116, at 201.

200. Both the conviction and sentence may be appealed up to the state supreme court, which may affirm both, affirm the conviction and remand the case for resentencing, or, after vacating the conviction, remand the case for retrial. The conviction and sentence issued following a retrial may be appealed back to the state supreme court and, subsequently, a petition for a writ of

ies published in the late 1980s indicated that, in Florida, 1700 hours of attorney time would be required to appeal a death sentence up to the federal courts.[201] Additionally, if a capital case "were to go through all avenues of appeal, it would consume approximately 1470 hours of preparation by the defense,"[202] and, as documented by some capital attorneys, as high as 2000 hours.[203] While the hourly rate charged by attorneys, as well as the time spent and expenses incurred, varies with each case and within different states, one scholar concluded that "a capital punishment system probably costs more than one that excludes the possibility of the death penalty."[204]

The exorbitant cost of litigating capital trial proceedings has been raised by abolitionists to buttress their contention that the death penalty ought to be abolished. Costs of capital litigation and lifetime incarceration, however, may fluctuate, and different aspects of these processes may be statistically accentuated by both abolitionists and retentionists to suggest that their position has greater validity. Retention or abolition of the death penalty raises profound moral and ethical questions pertaining to the capacity of humankind for virtue and justice which, arguably, cannot be reduced to fiscal considerations. Instead of tabulating the number of hours spent on litigation, and tangible expenses incurred, it might be more helpful to assess whether capital punishment comports with notions of community by examining how it is perceived in the hearts and minds of those who play a role in its administration.

---

certiorari may be filed with the U.S. Supreme Court. The Court may affirm or reverse both the conviction and sentence, with or without a remand, which, consistent with the Court's guidelines, would send the case back to state court for retrial or resentencing. A dissatisfied litigant may subsequently file a petition for writ of habeas corpus in federal district court, followed by an appeal of this action to a federal court of appeals, and, subsequently, to the U.S. Supreme Court.

201. THE SPANGENBERG GROUP CASELOAD AND COST PROJECTIONS FOR FEDERAL HABEAS CORPUS DEATH PENALTY CASES IN FY 1988 AND FY 1989, at 49 (prepared for the Administrative Office of State Courts) 49 (1989), *cited in* Robert L. Spangenberg & Elizabeth R. Walsh, *Capital Punishment or Life Imprisonment? Some Cost Considerations,* 23 LOY. L.A. L. REV. 45, 55 (1989).

202. PATERNOSTER, *supra* note 116, at 205.

203. Michael Mello, *Facing Death Alone: The Post-Conviction Attorney Crisis on Death Row,* 37 AM. U. L. REV. 513, 557 (1988).

204. PATERNOSTER, *supra* note 116, at 211. *See also* Julian H. Wright, Jr., *Life-Without-Parole: An Alternative to Death or Not Much of a Life At All?,* 43 VAND. L. REV. 529 (1990).

6. Is The Death Penalty Arbitrarily or Discriminatorily Imposed?

The enormity of possibly sentencing a defendant to death has underscored concern that weighing of evidence, application of statutory provisions, and pronunciation of verdict and sentence, be performed objectively. Avoidance of arbitrariness, racial bias, and discriminatory assessment in capital proceedings may be elusive in part because these alleged practices are difficult to define. The frequency with which a death sentence is imposed does not, by itself, indicate whether statutory provisions are being evenhandedly applied; indeed, a relatively high or low issuance of death sentences may, alternatively, indicate that a large number of convicted murderers are being punished pursuant to the maximum parameters of the law, or that, objectively applying legal guidelines, few are found to merit capital punishment. In both instances prosecutors, defense attorneys, judges, and jurors use discretion, a range of interpretation incorporated into statutory provisions, to assess whether the evidence, testimony, and character and background of an accused, merit a sentence of death or a term of imprisonment.

Discretion, an indispensable component of capital trial proceedings, has enabled courtroom participants to assess whether the totality of evidence justifies a particular punishment for one defendant, but not another. Given human frailty and conflicting perceptions of facts and circumstances, discretion, while unavoidable, has also given rise to speculation as to whether infliction of the death penalty has been to some extent motivated by racial or ethnic bias toward the accused or victim. Additionally, the exercise of discretion may result in a random or arbitrary application of statutory provisions whereby, in part due to inability to decipher complex penal codes or failure of a judge to clearly explain points of law, a jury may appear to selectively pronounce a verdict of guilty and a recommendation of death on some defendants but not others who present comparable circumstances and have been charged with similar offenses. These concerns have been extensively debated by abolitionists and retentionists. Opponents of capital punishment have in part argued that the possibility of an innocent person being executed justified statutory prohibition of the death penalty, while retentionists have maintained that the elaborate procedural safeguards accompanying capital proceedings make erroneous conviction remote, and, notwithstanding this possibility, do not negate society's legitimate desire to deem the death penalty an appropriate punishment for murder.

Statistically, the number of individuals executed is far lower than that for capital convictions. From 1976 to 1990, approximately 20,000 homicides have been committed nationally,[205] resulting in 3447 capital convictions,[206] and 140 executions,[207] all but seventeen of which were conducted in the South.[208] Moreover, nearly 70% of these executions took place in four southern states.[209] While these numbers may simply reflect more vigorous enforcement of the death penalty in the South, closer examination reveals a statistical pattern concerning the color of the defendant and victim and the likelihood of being charged and convicted of a capital crime. A series of studies seems to indicate that racial bias, dating back in the South to the harsher statutory penalties mandated for slaves and free blacks,[210] persisted into the present time in the area of capital proceedings. Evidence of a greater frequency to convict blacks who have been charged with murdering a white individual was first compiled in the early 1930s,[211] and a series of studies of conviction and sentencing patterns in capital trials conducted from the 1940s up through the 1970s has corroborated this pattern.[212] In 1983, Professor David

---

205. WELSH S. WHITE, THE DEATH PENALTY IN THE NINETIES: AN EXAMINATION OF THE MODERN SYSTEM OF CAPITAL PUNISHMENT 46 n.4 (1991).

206. *Id.* at 46 n.5.

207. PATERNOSTER, *supra* note 116, at 21.

208. *Id.*

209. From July 2, 1976 to June 3, 1990, there were 35 executions in Texas, 22 in Florida, 19 in Louisiana, and 14 in Georgia. WHITE, *supra* note 205, at 33. For a breakdown of the number of executions and individuals on death row for the period 1977-1990, see PATERNOSTER, *supra* note 116, at 22.

210. For the history of legislation enacted during the colonial period and continued in the antebellum South which mandated as capital offenses committed by blacks but not by whites, see EUGENE GENOVESE, ROLL JORDAN ROLL: THE WORLD THE SLAVES MADE (1974); KENNETH STAMPP, THE PECULIAR INSTITUTION (1956).

211. For the years 1920 to 1926, white defendants charged with murder in South Carolina were convicted 32% of the time, compared with 64% for blacks. *See* HARRINGTON C. BREARLEY, HOMICIDE IN THE UNITED STATES 110 (1932), *cited in* PATERNOSTER, *supra* note 116, at 120.

212. *See generally* CHARLES MANGUM, JR., THE LEGAL STATUS OF THE NEGRO (1940) (indicating that, in eight Southern states, the rate of executions was higher for blacks than whites); Guy Johnson, *The Negro and Crime*, 217 ANNALS AM. ACAD. POL. & SOC. SCI. 93 (1941) (examining sentencing patterns for parts of Virginia and North Carolina in the 1930s); Elmer Johnson, *Selective Factors in Capital Punishment*, 36 SOC. FORCES 165 (1957) (furnishing evidence of more frequent execution of blacks than whites for rape in North Carolina in the first half of the twentieth century); Donald H. Partington, *The Incidence of the Death Penalty for Rape in Virginia*, 22 WASH. & LEE L. REV. 43, 52-53 (1965) (stating that every rapist executed in Virginia, Louisiana, Mississippi, Oklahoma, District of Columbia, and West Virginia from 1930-1962 was black); Robert C. Koeninger, *Capital Punishment in Texas, 1924-1968*, 15 CRIME & DELINQ. 132 (1969)

Baldus and two colleagues published "the most exhaustive study of racial discrimination in capital sentencing that has ever been conducted."[213]

The Baldus study analyzed death sentences for each of 594 defendants convicted of murder in Georgia from March, 1973, to July, 1978, and 1066 prosecutions for homicide for the period 1973 to 1980.[214] Employing slightly over 200 variables — such as the race and gender and socioeconomic status of the offender and victim, existence and extent of discussion during trial of aggravating and mitigating factors, racial balance of the neighborhood where the homicide was committed, population density of the crime area, commission of felony in addition to murder, and gruesomeness of the killing, among many other factors — Baldus and his colleagues discovered a dramatic pattern of racial disparity: a black accused of killing a white person is 4.3 times more likely to receive a death sentence than instances in which the victim is black; black defendants were 1.1 times more likely to be sentenced to death; a white victim was involved in 108 of the 128 cases where the death penalty was imposed; and the prosecutors recommended the death penalty in 70% of cases involving black defendants and white victims, but in only 32% of cases

---

(reporting a higher rate of execution for blacks); Marvin Wolfgang, et. al, *Comparison of the Executed and the Commuted Among Admissions to Death Row*, 53 J. CRIM. L. CRIMINOLOGY & POLICE SCI. 301 (1962) (reporting that, in Pennsylvania during the period 1914-1958, white felony murderers were almost three times as likely as black defendants to have their sentences commuted); Marvin Wolfgang & Marc Reidel, *Race, Judicial Discretion, and the Death Penalty*, 407 ANNALS AM. ACAD. POL. & SOC. SCI. 119 (1973); Marvin Wolfgang & Marc Reidel, *Rape, Race, and the Death Penalty in Georgia*, 45 AM. J. OF ORTHOPSYCHIATRY 658 (1975); *Rape, Racial Discrimination, and the Death Penalty*, *in* CAPITAL PUNISHMENT IN THE UNITED STATES (Hugo Bedau & Chester Pierce eds., 1976) (revised earlier essays; finding in eleven Southern states during the period 1945-1965, that blacks who raped white women were eighteen to twenty times more likely to be sentenced to death than when both the offender and victim were white or black, or when a white raped a black woman), *cited in* PATERNOSTER, *supra* note 116, at 125-27. For a discussion of these and other studies on the statistical disparities concerning treatment of blacks and whites in capital proceedings, see PATERNOSTER, *supra* note 116, at 119-38.

213. WHITE, *supra* note 205, at 150, *referring to* David C. Baldus et al., *Comparative Review of Death Sentences: An Empirical Study of the Georgia Experience*, 74 J. CRIM. L. & CRIMINOLOGY 661 (1983). See also their follow up studies: EQUAL JUSTICE AND THE DEATH PENALTY (1990); David C. Baldus et al., *Arbitrariness and Discrimination in the Administration of the Death Penalty: A Challenge to State Supreme Courts*, 15 STETSON L. REV. 133 (1986); David C. Baldus, et al., *Monitoring and Evaluating Contemporary Death Sentencing Systems: Lessons from Georgia*, 18 U.C. DAVIS L. REV. 1375 (1985).

214. *See* David C. Baldus et al., *Monitoring and Evaluating Contemporary Death Sentencing Systems: Lessons from Georgia*, 18 U.C. DAVIS L. REV. 1375 (1985).

where both individuals were white.[215] It appeared from these findings, as well as earlier studies,[216] that blacks who are accused of killing a white victim are far more likely to be convicted and sentenced to death than among any other racial combination. With regard to the death penalty for rape, a statistical disparity was also evident. One scholar noted that, for the period 1930-1967, "50 percent of those executed for murder and 89 percent of those executed for rape were black, even though black males have comprised less than 20 percent of the U.S. population," and, since 1977, "about 40 percent of all those executed . . . have been black, and over 80 percent killed white victims."[217]

Abolitionists have cited statistical trends to support their contention that the death penalty has been discriminatorily imposed, while retentionists have maintained that such studies are inevitably incomplete and, irrespective of their purported accuracy and thoroughness, do not preclude infliction of death as a valid policy choice which a community may desire. Tabulation of statistics concerning the race of individuals convicted of murder and the color of victims neither confirms nor negates the position of those who support or oppose the death penalty; retentionists cannot dismiss studies illustrating possible racial bias in sentencing as insignificant and irrelevant, and abolitionists cannot definitively declare that bigotry is an inherent component of capital proceedings which can only be eradicated by prohibition of the death penalty.

Infrequent conviction and execution of those tried for a capital offense has also been addressed to bolster the position of abolitionists and retentionists, but it is unclear what constitutes arbitrariness. Convicting, for example, only 5% of those tried for homicide may mean either that a few individuals were capriciously chosen to be punished by death, or that juries, after careful deliberation, are preserving the integrity of the death penalty by pronouncing it only for the most heinous offenders. One fervent opponent of capital punishment has objected that a prosecutor's decision to recommend the death penalty for some defendants but not others may subject an accused to arbitrary action in that a defendant, wishing to avoid death, will feel coerced into pleading guilty to a serious offense raised by the prosecutor; thus, a criminal conviction would be based not on the culpability of the accused but rather on the negotiated plea

---

215. *Id.*
216. *See supra* note 213.
217. PATERNOSTER, *supra* note 116, at 156.

option dictated by the district attorney.[218] However, an accused facing a possible death sentence may feel that there is nothing to lose by rejecting a prosecutor's aggressive plea bargaining tactics and requesting a trial. Moreover, assertions by abolitionists that varying degrees of harshness displayed by prosecutors, as well as evidence that, within a state, likelihood of convicting of a capital crime varied in urban and rural settings,[219] made possible an arbitrary death sentence based on factors unrelated to the circumstances of the accused, may be countered by noting that jurors may not necessarily succumb to prosecutorial overzealousness or perceived community sentiment.

Clearly, the positions raised by abolitionists and retentionists may be reciprocally refuted, and, ultimately, their inconclusive contentions are subject to the vicissitudes of political discourse. For Justices Brennan and Marshall, however, the abolitionist's arguments were more compelling, and their opinions on the death penalty sought to convince the citizenry that capital punishment has no place in contemporary American society.

III.   THE UNITED STATES SUPREME COURT'S INTERPRETATION OF THE DEATH PENALTY

A.   *Initial Examination of Capital Punishment (1878-1947)*

Only two cases examining the Eighth Amendment's ban of "cruel and unusual punishments" in connection with the death penalty were adjudicated in the nineteenth century. In the 1878 case of *Wilkerson v. Utah*,[220] the Court held that execution by firing squad did not violate the Eighth Amendment. Acknowledging the elusiveness of defining with precision the words "cruel and unusual," the Court pointed out that "punishments of torture . . . and all others in the same line of unnecessary cruelty[221]

---

218.   BLACK, *supra* note 171, at 46-53. For a discussion of the challenges facing attorneys in capital cases, see Esther F. Lardent & Douglas M. Cohen, *The Last Best Hope: Representing Death Row Inmates*, 23 LOY. L.A. L. REV. 213 (1989); Michael E. Tigar, *Judges, Lawyers and the Penalty of Death*, 23 LOY. L.A. L. REV. 147 (1989).

219.   *See, e.g.*, BALDUS ET AL., EQUAL JUSTICE AND THE DEATH PENALTY (1990); SAMUEL GROSS & ROBERT MAURO, DEATH AND DISCRIMINATION: RACIAL DISPARITIES IN CAPITAL SENTENCING (1989); William Bowers & Glenn Pierce, *Arbitrariness and Discrimination Under Post-Furman Capital Statutes*, 26 CRIME AND DELINQ. 563 (1980); Raymond Paternoster, *Race of Victim and Location of Crime: The Decision to Seek the Death Penalty in South Carolina*, 74 J. CRIM. L. & CRIMINOLOGY 754 (1983).

220.   99 U.S. 130 (1878), *overruled by* Gregg v. Georgia, 428 U.S. 153 (1976).

221.   *Id.* at 135.

are forbidden." The Court's perception of degree of cruelty was somewhat clarified twelve years later in the case of *In re Kemmler*,[222] which, upholding electrocution as a constitutional method of execution, stated that "[p]unishments are cruel when they involve torture or a lingering death."[223] These rulings suggested that punishments inflicted without prolonged pain did not violate the Eighth Amendment.

These two rulings did not address whether the phrase "cruel and unusual" referred to punishments practiced in the founding generation or an evolving concept. In *Kemmler*, the Court referred to "burning at the stake, crucifixion, . . . [and] breaking on the wheel"[224] as "inhuman and barbarous"[225] punishments, and contrasted them with electrocution, which, though technologically novel, appeared to inflict instant death. The Court suggested that it would not confine the meaning of "cruel and unusual" to a specific method of punishment provided that the one adopted inflicted minimal physical suffering.

The Court next examined the phrase "cruel and unusual" in the 1910 case of *Weems v. United States*,[226] which presented not imposition of the death penalty but rather a protracted punishment appearing excessive in relation to the offense committed. A provision of the Philippine Penal Code punished falsifying an official document with imprisonment "for twelve years and one day, [and] a chain at ankle and wrist . . . [at] hard and painful labor."[227] Weems, a U.S. government official, received a fifteen-year term of imprisonment, during which time he was required to carry a chain hanging from his ankle and wrist, a substantial fine, a loss of voting rights, and lifetime surveillance.[228] He argued that the punishment was excessive and thus "cruel and unusual."

In *Weems*, the Court for the first time declared that punishments disproportionate to the offense committed violated the Eighth Amendment.[229] Refusing to confine interpretation of the Eighth Amendment to its understanding in the founding genera-

---

222. 136 U.S. 436 (1890), *overruled by* Gregg v. Georgia, 428 U.S. 153 (1976).
223. *Id.* at 447.
224. *Id.* at 446.
225. *Id.* at 447.
226. 217 U.S. 349 (1910).
227. *Id.* at 366.
228. *Id.* at 363-64.
229. This concept was first addressed in 1892 by Justice Stephen Field, who, in dissent, wrote that "[t]he inhibition [of the Eighth Amendment] is directed, not only against [barbaric] punishments . . . but against all punishments which by their excessive length or severity are greatly

tion, the Court noted that "[t]ime works changes, brings into existence new conditions and purposes,"[230] and compelled "progressive" application of provisions which may "acquire meaning as public opinion becomes enlightened by a humane justice."[231] Thus, the meaning of "cruel and unusual" must evolve as conceptions of justice change.[232]

By the early twentieth century the Court had ruled that lingering death and penalties excessive in relation to the offense violate the Eighth Amendment. In its sole opportunity to examine the death penalty, the Vinson Court (1946-1953), in *Louisiana ex rel. Francis v. Resweber*,[233] considered whether an individual facing the electric chair a second time following an electrical malfunction which prevented execution on the first attempt was being subjected to "cruel and unusual" punishment. Conceding that an "unforeseeable accident"[234] had occurred, the Court nevertheless held that the Eighth Amendment was not violated. Regarding the psychological stress the accused claimed to have suffered anticipating the date of the next attempted execution, the Court declared that the "cruelty against which the Constitution protects . . . is cruelty inherent in the method of punishment, not the necessary suffering involved in any method employed to extinguish life humanely."[235]

These rulings did not articulate a legal theory concerning "cruel and unusual" punishment. To be sure, the Court permitted infliction of the death penalty, but, other than ambiguous reference to the need for a punishment to be commensurate with an offense, and to the performance of an execution with minimal pain to the accused, clear standards were not furnished. It appeared that the meaning of "cruel and unusual" was to be

---

disproportioned to the offenses charged." O'Neil v. Vermont, 144 U.S. 323, 339 (1892) (Field, J., dissenting).

230. *Weems*, 217 U.S. at 373.

231. *Id.* at 378.

232. This perception may have influenced the Court in the 1932 case of Powell v. Alabama, 287 U.S. 45 (1932), which involved availability of counsel for several youths charged with the capital offense of rape. Though not directly addressing the Eighth Amendment, the Court, ruling that right to counsel is required given the illiteracy of the defendants and their inability to present a meaningful defense unaided, arguably implied that, where execution may result, fairness of treatment to the defendant (in this instance the evolving importance of counsel when seeking to apply increasingly complex penal statutes) judged by contemporary expectations is an appropriate element of constitutional adjudication.

233. 329 U.S. 459 (1947), *reh'g denied*, 330 U.S. 853 (1947).

234. *Id.* at 464.

235. *Id.*

based on the justices' perceptions of the humaneness of the form of punishment.

B. *The Warren Court (1953-1969) Addresses "Cruel and Unusual Punishments"*

Perhaps the most fundamental components of modern adjudication on the Eighth Amendment were put forward by the Warren Court in two cases which did not involve the death penalty. In the landmark 1958 case of *Trop v. Dulles*,[236] which dealt with loss of citizenship as punishment for wartime desertion, the Court declared that the Eighth Amendment "must draw its meaning from the evolving standards of decency that mark the progress of a maturing society."[237] This signaled a new perspective to examinations of "cruel and unusual" punishment. Prior to 1958, the Court had suggested that forms of execution proportionate to a crime and inflicted humanely would be upheld;[238] The *Trop* opinion, however, indicated that sanctions would be assessed in view of society's perceived changing attitudes, which may call into question, by implication, psychological effects of capital punishment, public opinion, the morality of the death penalty, its alleged deterrent effect, and the modes of proceeding by which capital trials are conducted, whenever these issues might arise.[239] Four years later, in *Robinson v. California*,[240] the Court, striking down as overbroad a statute which imposed criminal penalties for a person to be addicted to narcotics,[241] held that the Eighth Amendment's prohibition of "cruel and unusual punishments" was applicable, by the due process clause of the Fourteenth Amendment, to the states.[242]

These rulings did not signify opposition to the death penalty but rather suggested that the Court envisioned a vigorous role in overseeing both the method and appropriateness of criminal sanctions. Brennan first indicated a strong desire to have the Court examine the death penalty in a 1963 case which denied

---

236. 356 U.S. 86 (1958).
237. *Id.* at 101.
238. *See* Louisiana *ex rel.* Francis v. Resweber, 329 U.S. 459 (1947); Weems v. United States, 217 U.S. 349 (1910); *In re* Kemmler, 136 U.S. 436 (1890); Wilkerson v. Utah, 99 U.S. 130 (1878).
239. *Trop*, 356 U.S. at 86.
240. 370 U.S. 660 (1962), *reh'g denied*, 371 U.S. 905 (1962).
241. § 11721 of the California Health and Safety Code provided for a term of imprisonment of not less than ninety days or more than one year for any person convicted of ". . .use, or be[ing] under the influence of, or be[ing] addicted to the use of narcotics," except as prescribed by a physician. *Robinson*, 370 U.S. at 660 n.1.
242. *Robinson*, 370 U.S. at 667. *See supra* text accompanying notes 56-59.

certiorari to an individual convicted of rape and subject to execution.[243] Joining a brief dissent written by Justice Goldberg, Brennan, along with Justice Douglas, wished to consider: Does the death penalty for rape violate evolving conceptions of justice both in American society and in view of "standards of decency more or less universally accepted?"[244] Is "the taking of human life to protect a value other than human life" a disproportionate punishment?[245] Can some of the goals of punishment — "deterrence, isolation, rehabilitation" — be achieved with a sanction less severe than execution for rape?[246]

Brennan did not, at this point in his tenure, urge categorical rejection of capital punishment, and, in the handful of cases decided in the 1960s dealing with procedures followed in state capital trials, it appeared that the Warren Court accepted the constitutionality of the death penalty and was unwilling to consider whether it violated the Eighth Amendment per se.

The Warren Court did not articulate a comprehensive position on capital punishment; instead, it addressed admissibility of evidence in proceedings statutorily punishable by death. In *Davis v. North Carolina,*[247] the Court objected that testimony furnished to police by an individual arrested for rape and murder, and subsequently interrogated over a sixteen-day period of incarceration, was coercively obtained.[248] The Court also invalidated confessions to a capital crime on the ground that the nature and implications of the guilty plea were insufficiently explained and thus involuntary.[249] At no time did the Court discuss applicability of "cruel and unusual punishments" or give any indication that the death penalty was unacceptable.

The Warren Court's unwillingness to declare the death penalty in violation of the Eighth Amendment was most apparent in cases dealing with waiving trial by jury and empaneling of jurors in capital proceedings. In *United States v. Jackson,*[250] the Court examined a provision of the Federal Kidnaping Act of 1932[251] which punished interstate kidnaping by death or life imprison-

---

243. Rudolph v. Alabama, 375 U.S. 889, *reh'g denied,* 375 U.S. 917 (1963).

244. Rudolph v. Alabama, 375 U.S. at 889 (1963) (Goldberg, J., dissenting) (*quoting* Francis v. Resweber, 329 U.S. 459, 469 (1947)).

245. *Id.* at 891.

246. *Id.*

247. 384 U.S. 737 (1966).

248. *Id.* at 752.

249. *See* Boykin v. Alabama, 395 U.S. 238 (1969); Jackson v. Denno, 378 U.S. 368 (1964).

250. 390 U.S. 570 (1968).

251. Federal Kidnapping Act of 1932, ch. 271, 47 Stat. 236 (1932) (codified as amended at 18 U.S.C. § 1201(a) (1988)).

ment, as "the verdict of the jury shall so recommend."[252] This suggested that a defendant who relinquished jury trial by pleading guilty, or who was sentenced by a judge, may evade the death penalty, since its infliction was possible only by a jury. This prospect, the Court believed, would compromise the Sixth Amendment's protection of trial by jury.[253] Moreover, the Court insisted that the statute refrained from specifying procedures for an accused who pleaded guilty or waived jury trial, and did not clarify the relationship between the jury and judge concerning determination of sentence.[254]

The Court's concern with jury deliberations was also evident in the cases of *Whitus v. Georgia*[255] and *Witherspoon v. Illinois*,[256] both of which addressed procedures for empaneling jurors in capital trials. The *Whitus* case involved a provision of Georgia law which authorized jury commissioners to select grand and petit jurors from lists of county tax digests which, prior to 1965, used separate tax return sheets for white and black taxpayers.[257] Though state authorities claimed to have employed a revised jury list on which no one had been included or excluded on the basis of race or color, the Court held that the petitioners, convicted of murder, confronted a "prima facie case of purposeful discrimination"[258] by which an extreme disparity between the "percentage of Negroes listed on the tax digest (27.1%) and that of the grand jury venire (9.1%) and the petit jury venire (7.8%)"[259] suggested an ongoing pattern of selective empaneling.

In *Witherspoon*, the Court also objected to a practice which it believed compromised the objectivity of a jury. A provision of Illinois law which permitted a judge to disqualify potential jurors who expressed "conscientious scruples against capital punishment, or that he is opposed to the same,"[260] was construed by the petitioner to produce a biased jury which, unopposed to the death penalty, would "too readily . . . accept the prosecution's

---

252.   390 U.S. at 570-71.

253.   The Sixth Amendment in pertinent part states that: "In all criminal prosecutions, the accused shall enjoy the right to a speedy and public trial, by an impartial jury. . . ." U.S. CONST. amend. VI. For identical reasons, the Court, per curiam, vacated and remanded a sentence of death under the Federal Bank Robbery Act, 18 U.S.C. § 2113(e) (1988). *See* Pope v. United States, 392 U.S. 651 (1968).

254.   *Jackson*, 390 U.S. at 580-84.

255.   385 U.S. 545 (1967).

256.   391 U.S. 510 (1968), *reh'g denied*, 393 U.S. 898 (1968).

257.   *Whitus*, 385 U.S. at 548-49.

258.   *Id.* at 551.

259.   *Id.* at 552.

260.   *Witherspoon*, 391 U.S. at 512.

version of the facts, and return a verdict of guilt."[261]   Though
stating that this position was "tentative and fragmentary,"[262] the
Court reversed the death sentence and suggested that only those
potential jurors who indicated that they would vote against the
death penalty regardless of the evidence brought out in trial be
excluded.[263]

The Warren Court was concerned with procedural fairness
in capital deliberations and refrained from examining whether
capital punishment violated the Eighth Amendment per se.
Interestingly, Brennan at no time during Warren's tenure wrote
a concurring or dissenting opinion expressing his views on capital punishment.   In view of the strong opposition to capital punishment which Brennan articulated following Warren's
retirement,[264] it is surprising that, in *Witherspoon*, he did not write
a concurring opinion expressing concern over possible arbitrariness of the death penalty arising from the subjectivity accompanying jury empaneling.   In other words, Brennan might have
emphasized that jury bias, which no procedural safeguards can
completely eliminate, compelled a form of punishment (other
than execution) capable of suspension if courtroom improprie-
ties are subsequently proved.   Marshall, who joined the Court in
1967, did not participate in any cases on this subject.

---

261.   *Id.* at 516-17.

262.   *Id.* at 517.

263.   *Id.* at 522 n.21. *See also* Bumper v. State of North Carolina, 391 U.S.
543 (1968) (considerig a similar objection from a defendant sentenced to life
imprisonment).   For an analysis of jury empaneling in capital cases, see HARRY
KALVEN, JR., & HANS ZEISEL, THE AMERICAN JURY 437-49 (1966); Marshall Dayan
et al., *Searching For an Impartial Sentencer Through Jury Selection in Capital Trials*, 23
LOY. L.A. L. REV. 151 (1989); Robert E. Knowlton, *Problems of Jury Discretion in
Capital Cases*, 101 U. PA. L. REV. 1099 (1953); Walter E. Oberer, *Does
Disqualification of Jurors for Scruples Against Capital Punishment Constitute Denial of
Fair Trial on Issue of Guilt?*, 39 TEX. L. REV. 545 (1961).   For an analysis of the
Witherspoon opinion, see WHITE, *supra* note 205, at 186-207; Edward Bronson,
*On the Conviction Proneness and Representativeness of the Death-Qualified Jury: An
Empirical Study of Colorado Veniremen*, 42 U. COLO. L. REV. 1 (1970); Faye
Goldberg, *Toward Expansion of Witherspoon: Capital Scruples, Jury Bias and Use of
Psychological Data to Raise Presumptions in the Law*, 5 HARV. C.R.-C.L. L. REV. 53
(1970); Craig Haney, *Examining Death Qualification: Further Analysis of the Process
Effect*, 8 J.L. & HUM. BEHAV. 133 (1984); George L. Jurow, *New Data on the Effect
of a 'Death Qualified' Jury on the Guilt Determination Process*, 84 HARV. L. REV. 567
(1971); David Rotman, *Jury Selection and the Death Penalty: Witherspoon in the Lower
Courts*, 37 U. CHI. L. REV. 759 (1970); Welsh S. White, *The Constitutional
Invalidity of Convictions Imposed by Death-Qualified Juries*, 58 CORNELL L. REV. 1176
(1973).

264.   *See infra* text accompanying notes 404-85.

C.   *The Burger Court (1969-1986) Upholds the Death Penalty and Discusses Procedural Guidelines to be Followed in its Imposition*

At the time Warren Burger commenced his tenure as Chief Justice in October, 1969, a voluntary moratorium on execution had been in effect for two years. Pending clarification of procedural guidelines in capital trials, states, as of June, 1967, adopted a de facto moratorium on execution.[265] In 1969, forty-six petitions concerning the death penalty were filed with the Court, followed by thirty-eight others the next year.[266] In 1970, the Court refrained from addressing the constitutionality of capital punishment, and confined itself to issues dealing with fairness of procedural standards comparable to those adjudicated in the last two years of Warren's tenure.[267] In the pivotal cases of *McGautha v. California*[268] and *Crampton v. Ohio*,[269] decided on the same day in 1971, the Court discussed discretion to be accorded to states in administering the death penalty.

The *McGautha* and *Crampton* cases examined the range of discretion available to juries which may impose the death penalty, and whether both the verdict and sentence may be pronounced in a single stage.[270] California was one of six states which provided for a bifurcated trial in capital cases whereby guilt would be determined in the first stage, and, in a subsequent proceeding, sentence would be pronounced based on an examination of aggravating and mitigating factors.[271] Ohio statutes, similar to those in twenty-six other states, provided that both guilt and punishment are to be determined in a single trial.[272]

---

265.   BOWERS, *supra* note 117, at 419.

266.   MICHAEL MELTSNER, CRUEL AND UNUSUAL: THE SUPREME COURT AND CAPITAL PUNISHMENT 214 (1973).

267.   The position put forward in *Witherspoon*, 391 U.S. at 512, was applied in Maxwell v. Bishop, 398 U.S. 262 (1970), first set aside for review in 1968, 393 U.S. at 997, argued before the Court on March 4, 1969, and, following the resignation on May 14 of Justice Abe Fortas, reargued on May 4, 1970. Allegations of coerced confession in a capital offense, examined in Davis v. State of North Carolina, 384 U.S. 737 (1966), were considered in three 1970 cases: Brady v. United States, 397 U.S. 742 (1970); Parker v. North Carolina, 397 U.S. 790 (1970); and North Carolina v. Alford, 400 U.S. 25 (1970). The opportunity of a defendant to question the testimony of twenty witnesses called by the prosecution was considered in Dutton v. Evans, 400 U.S. 74 (1970).

268.   402 U.S. 183 (1971), *reh'g denied*, 406 U.S. 978 (1972).

269.   *Id.*

270.   *Id.*

271.   *Id.* at 185.

272.   *Id.*

Speaking on behalf of six members, Justice Harlan declared that state statutes which left absolute discretion to juries to impose the death penalty, without any standards to guide them, did not violate the due process clause of the Fourteenth Amendment.[273] While the contention that conferring on juries unconfined discretion may result in arbitrary infliction of the death penalty had an "undeniable surface appeal,"[274] Harlan emphasized that it was impossible to identify the myriad factors which jurors in capital trials may consider. Thus, he concluded that, "[i]n light of history, experience, and the present limitations of human knowledge, we find it quite impossible to say that committing to the untrammeled discretion of the jury the power to pronounce life or death in capital cases is offensive to anything in the Constitution."[275] The Court did not explicitly state whether the death penalty per se violated the Eighth Amendment; it merely indicated that states may choose to punish offenses as capital and to devise trial proceedings free from judicial interference.

Only fourteen months after *McGautha* and *Crampton* were decided, the Court retracted its position by expressing concern for the alleged arbitrary enforcement of capital statutes and commanding states to reexamine their modes of proceeding in trials where the death penalty may be inflicted. In the landmark case of *Furman v. Georgia*,[276] decided on June 29, 1972, the Court, believing that statutes in Georgia and Texas enabled arbitrary imposition of capital punishment, ruled per curiam that "the imposition and carrying out of the death penalty *in these cases* constitutes cruel and unusual punishment in violation of the Eighth and Fourteenth amendments."[277]

This brief statement was followed by nine separate opinions totaling 217 pages.[278] In varying degrees and levels of intensity, the justices elaborated on the constitutionality of capital punishment, the infrequency with which it is imposed, the alleged arbitrariness and racial bias accompanying its infliction, its alleged deterrent effect, its acceptability in contemporary society, and

---

273. *Id.* at 221; *see also supra* note 57.

274. 402 U.S. at 206-07.

275. *Id.* at 207.

276. 408 U.S. 238 (1972), *reh'g denied*, 409 U.S. 902 (1972). (This case was decided together with *Jackson v. Georgia* and *Branch v. Texas.* In *Furman*, the jury recommended the death penalty for the petitioner, who killed the head of household in a burglary attempt. *Id.* at 239, 252. In both *Jackson* and *Branch*, an individual arrested for rape was sentenced by the jury to death.

277. 408 U.S. at 239-40 (emphasis added).

278. 408 U.S. at 240-470.

the role of the judiciary regarding supervision of criminal justice in the states.[279] The *Furman* ruling, categorized by one scholar as a "jurisprudential debacle,"[280] left unanswered whether capital punishment violated the Eighth Amendment, and, absent procedural guidelines, failed to instruct thirty-five states and the District of Columbia which had death penalty statutes how to revise their laws and deal with six hundred forty-two persons then on death row who at least temporarily had been granted a stay of execution.[281]

By confining itself to the jury's pronouncements "in these cases," the *Furman* decision avoided ruling that capital punishment per se was unconstitutional, that the death penalty is impermissible for certain types of crimes, or that mandatory death sentences are "cruel and unusual." Failing to furnish standards[282] for determining what penalties or procedures constituted "cruel and unusual" punishment, the *Furman* ruling presented a difficult obstacle for state statutes which established discretionary rather than mandatory capital punishment. The opinions of the concurring justices (Brennan, Marshall, Douglas, Stewart, and White) in *Furman*, taken together, suggested that the death penalty constituted cruel and unusual punishment because of its arbitrary and infrequent imposition.[283] This presented states with a paradox in that unlimited discretion enabled jurors to arbitrarily inflict the death penalty, while mandatory capital punishment laws eliminated discretion but prevented jurors from weighing aggravating and mitigating circumstances. In addition, the *McGautha* and *Furman* rulings contradictorily told states, respectively, that unlimited jury discretion in sentencing was not unconstitutional, and that too much discretion may result in discriminatory infliction of the death penalty.

After *Furman* was decided, all thirty-five states that had death penalty statutes revised their laws, narrowing the range of discretion available to jurors.[284] Twenty-five of these statutes established a bifurcated process whereby judges and juries were required to take into account specific aggravating and mitigating circumstances in determining guilt or innocence, and, in a sec-

---

279. *See* PATERNOSTER, *supra* note 116, at 54-59; Daniel D. Polsby, *The Death of Capital Punishment? Furman v. Georgia,* 1972 SUP. CT. REV. 1.

280. Margaret J. Radin, *The Jurisprudence of Death: Evolving Standards for the Cruel and Unusual Punishments Clause,* 126 U. PA. L. REV. 989, 998 (1978).

281. GORECKI, *supra* note 124, at 93.

282. *Furman,* 408 U.S. at 240.

283. *Id.*

284. GORECKI, *supra* note 124, at 17.

ond trial, the decision whether to impose the death penalty would be rendered.[285] Ten other statutes sought to eliminate any possibility that capital punishment might be arbitrarily imposed by enacting mandatory death sentences for those convicted of specific offenses.[286] Four years after the *Furman* ruling, the Court examined five of these revised death penalty statutes, all decided on July 2, 1976: *Gregg v. Georgia*,[287] *Jurek v. Texas*,[288] *Proffitt v. Florida*,[289] *Woodson v. North Carolina*,[290] and *Roberts v. Louisiana*.[291] In 1978, Ohio's revised statute was considered in *Bell v. Ohio*[292] and *Lockett v. Ohio*.[293]

The Court upheld statutes which allowed the sentencing body to refrain from imposing the death penalty even after finding the accused guilty (Georgia, Texas, and Florida),[294] and struck down those imposing mandatory death sentences (North Carolina, Louisiana, Ohio).[295] States which provided a discretionary death sentence established a bifurcated trial in which a finding, beyond a reasonable doubt, of guilt or innocence would be determined in the first stage, and sentence imposed in the second.[296] At least one aggravating factor among a list of statutorily enumerated aggravating and mitigating circumstances had to be linked to the accused in order to impose the sentence of death.[297] Though jurors retained considerable discretion,[298] the

---

285. See generally id.

286. Id.

287. 428 U.S. 153, reh'g denied, 429 U.S. 875 (1976).

288. 428 U.S. 262, reh'g denied sub nom. Gregg v. Georgia, 429 U.S. 875 (1976).

289. 428 U.S. 242, reh'g denied sub nom. Gregg v. Georgia, 429 U.S. 875 (1976).

290. 428 U.S. 280 (1976).

291. 428 U.S. 325, reh'g denied, 429 U.S. 890 (1976).

292. 438 U.S. 637 (1978).

293. 438 U.S. 586 (1978).

294. Gregg v. Georgia, 428 U.S. 153, reh'g denied, 429 U.S. 875 (1976); Jurek v. Texas, 428 U.S. 262, reh'g denied sub nom. Gregg v. Georgia, 429 U.S. 875 (1976); Proffitt v. Florida, 428 U.S. 242, reh'g denied sub nom. Gregg v. Georgia, 429 U.S. 875 (1976).

295. Woodson v. North Carolina, 428 U.S. 280 (1976); Roberts v. Louisiana, 428 U.S. at 325; Bell v. Ohio, 438 U.S. at 637; Lockett v. Ohio, 438 U.S. at 586.

296. Gregg, 428 U.S. at 158; Jurek, 428 U.S. at 267; Proffitt, 428 U.S. at 245-46.

297. Gregg, 428 U.S. at 165 n.9; Jurek, 428 U.S. at 269; Proffitt, 428 U.S. at 250 n.6.

298. Jurek, 428 U.S. at 262. Jurors, according to Texas law, had to find two aggravating circumstances in order for the death penalty to be imposed: First, the conduct that caused the victim's death had to be "committed deliberately and with the reasonable expectation that the death of the deceased

Court believed that limiting the category of offenses for which the death penalty might be imposed, and requiring jurors to weigh aggravating and mitigating circumstances, confined their discretion and, presumably, reduced the likelihood of arbitrary infliction of capital punishment.[299] By contrast, the Court held that statutes which required imposition of the death penalty once guilt of a capital offense was established[300] were "unduly harsh and unworkably rigid"[301] alternatives. This arrangement, the Court believed, could result in capricious sentencing if jurors, aware that the death penalty must be imposed for certain crimes, purposely found guilt for a lesser offense if they believed that a particular defendant did not warrant execution.[302] In addition, the Court pointed out that, by taking away all discretion, mandatory capital statutes precluded jurors from fully taking into consideration the particular circumstances of the accused.

These cases made permissible imposition of the death penalty for some crimes; indeed, in *Gregg* the Court for the first time explicitly acknowledged that capital punishment "does not invariably violate the Constitution."[303] However, the Court refrained from specifying which crimes are capital, and acknowledged the power of states to refuse to "select the least severe penalty possible so long as the penalty selected is not cruelly inhumane or disproportionate to the crime involved."[304] In sum, the Court concluded that unconfined discretion made possible arbitrariness in reaching a verdict, while removing all discretion (by mandatory capital statutes) might inhibit jury flexibility by precluding consideration of individual circumstances.[305] The Court

---

or another would result." Second, the jury had to find "a probability that the defendant would commit criminal acts of violence that would constitute a continuing threat to society." *Id.* If jurors could not definitively find both aggravating circumstances, the defendant was sentenced to life imprisonment. *Id.* The *Woodson* case involved a North Carolina statute which provided for a mandatory death penalty for all persons convicted of first-degree murder, defined as "willful, deliberate and premeditated killing" or murder in the course of committing particular crimes. *Woodson*, 428 U.S. at 286.

299.   Gregg v. Georgia, 428 U.S. 153, 196-98, *reh'g denied*, 429 U.S. 875 (1976); Jurek v. Texas, 428 U.S. at 262, 276, *reh'g denied sub nom.* Gregg v. Georgia, 429 U.S. 875 (1976); Proffitt v. Florida, 428 U.S. 242, 251-52, *reh'g denied sub nom.* Gregg v. Georgia, 429 U.S. 875 (1976).

300.   Woodson v. North Carolina, 428 U.S. 280-86 (1976); Roberts v. Louisiana, 428 U.S. 325, 329 n.3.

301.   *Woodson*, 428 U.S. at 293.

302.   *Id.* at 303.

303.   *Gregg*, 428 U.S. at 169.

304.   *Id.* at 175.

305.   *Id.* at 206. For an analysis of *Gregg* and its companion cases, see Charles L. Black, Jr., *Due Process For Death:* Jurek v. Texas *and Companion Cases,*

wished to give juries the option of recommending death or a term of imprisonment after fully examining an array of aggravating and mitigating evidence, and preclude their ability to base a verdict on extraneous factors. Its position in *Bell*[306] and *Lockett*,[307] however, indicated that, once jury discretion is accorded, arbitrariness cannot be fully prevented.

The *Bell* and *Lockett* cases, decided on the same day in 1978, dealt with an Ohio statute which mandated death for seven classes of murder if the defendant failed to establish one of the following mitigating factors: the victim of the offense induced it; the offender was under duress or provoked; or the offender suffered from a mental deficiency.[308] Unable to meet this statutory requirement, the defendants were convicted and sentenced to death.[309]

The Court struck down this law, holding that it did not adequately permit individual consideration of mitigating circumstances.[310] Conceding that standards to be followed in capital trials are difficult to enumerate and that the kinds of mitigating factors to be considered had never been specified in earlier rulings, the Court held that sentencing authorities must consider, "*as a mitigating factor,* any aspect of a defendant's character or record and any of the circumstances of the offense that the defendant proffers as a basis for a sentence less than death."[311] By allowing consideration of only three mitigating factors, the Court believed that adequate examination of the range of events which may have accompanied the defendant's circumstances had not transpired.

The *Bell* and *Lockett* decisions, seeking to prevent arbitrariness in sentencing, made it inevitable. The Court, hoping to confine jury discretion to consideration of factors relating to the particular circumstances of an accused, instead enabled raising of issues — such as the race of the victim and accused compared with statistical patterns in the state as a whole — which may merit investigation but are not relevant to the determination of guilt.

---

26 CATH. U. L. REV. 1 (1976); Kenneth M. Murchison, *Toward A Perspective on the Death Penalty Cases,* 27 EMORY L.J. 469, 491-508 (1978); L.S. Tao, *The Constitutional Status of Capital Punishment: An Analysis of* Gregg, Jurek, Roberts, *and* Woodson, 54 U. DET. J. URB. L. 345 (1977); Franklin E. Zimring & Gordon Hawkins, *Capital Punishment and the Eighth Amendment:* Furman *and* Gregg *in Retrospect,* 18 U.C. DAVIS L. REV. 927 (1985); Radin, *supra* note 280, at 1002-13.

306.   Bell v. Ohio, 438 U.S. 637 (1978).
307.   Lockett v. Ohio, 438 U.S. 586 (1978).
308.   *Id.* at 593.
309.   *Id.* at 594.
310.   *Id.* at 608-09.
311.   *Id.* at 604 (emphasis in original).

Moreover, these decisions, along with the positions taken in McGautha,[312] Furman,[313] Gregg[314] and its companion cases,[315] communicated ambiguous and contradictory guidelines to states. After telling states, in 1971,[316] that the Court would not attempt to prepare a list of factors to be considered by jurors, thus leading the states to believe that they were free to devise capital trial proceedings according to their own notions of justice, the states were subsequently directed, one year later,[317] to eliminate alleged arbitrariness in deliberations, but were not furnished guidance on how this might be accomplished. In 1976, the Court indicated that it would approve statutes which displayed a sincere effort to confine jurors' discretion but simultaneously warned states not to attempt this too severely;[318] two years later, a state, seeking to comply with this directive by confining discretion, was told to expand it subject only to the parameters of the range of issues a litigant seeks to introduce.[319] The Lockett opinion, which reminded states that they must not allow jurors unconfined discretion but simultaneously insisted that they were free to take into account any mitigating circumstances,[320] unleashed, noted one scholar, "the floodgates of discretion that the Court's demand for 'standards' was meant to limit."[321]

After its Furman ruling in 1972, the Burger Court, not counting petitions for certiorari and stays of execution decided without an opinion, examined the death penalty in thirty-seven cases.[322] The issues presented included: the weighing by jurors

---

312. McGautha v. California, 402 U.S. 183 (1971), reh'g denied, 406 U.S. 978 (1972).
313. Furman v. Georgia, 408 U.S. 238, reh'g denied, 409 U.S. 902 (1972).
314. Gregg v. Georgia, 428 U.S. 153, reh'g denied, 429 U.S. 875 (1976).
315. See supra text accompanying notes 288-91.
316. McGautha, 402 U.S. at 207-08.
317. Furman, 408 U.S. at 239-40.
318. See supra text accompanying notes 287-91.
319. See supra text accompanying notes 292-93.
320. Lockett v. Ohio, 438 U.S. 586, 602-05 (1978).
321. BERGER, supra note 113, at 151.
322. See Ford v. Wainwright, 477 U.S. 399 (1986); Turner v. Murray, 476 U.S. 28 (1986); Skipper v. South Carolina, 476 U.S. 1 (1986); Cabana v. Bullock, 474 U.S. 376 (1986); Baldwin v. Alabama, 472 U.S. 372 (1985); Caldwell v. Mississippi, 472 U.S. 320 (1985); Francis v. Franklin, 471 U.S. 307 (1985); Ake v. Oklahoma, 470 U.S. 68 (1985); Wainwright v. Witt, 469 U.S. 412 (1985); Spaziano v. Florida, 468 U.S. 447 (1984); Arizona v. Rumsey, 467 U.S. 203 (1984); Strickland v. Washington, 466 U.S. 668, reh'g denied, 467 U.S. 1267 (1984); Pulley v. Harris, 465 U.S. 37 (1984); Maggio v. Williams, 464 U.S. 46 (1983); California v. Ramos, 463 U.S. 992 (1983); Barclay v. Florida, 463 U.S. 939, reh'g denied, 464 U.S. 874 (1983); Zant v. Stephens, 462 U.S. 862 (1983); Enmund v. Florida, 458 U.S. 782 (1982); Eddings v. Oklahoma, 455 U.S. 104 (1982); Estelle v. Smith, 451 U.S. 454 (1981); Bullington v. Missouri, 451 U.S.

of aggravating and mitigating circumstances;[323] sentencing discretion at the appellate stage;[324] method of empaneling jurors[325] and conveying information on their responsibilities in assessing guilt or innocence;[326] presentence introduction of testimony or a written report;[327] the death penalty for accomplices;[328] the death penalty for commission of rape,[329] and for the mentally insane;[330] comments made by a prosecutor or judge prior to sentencing;[331] competency of counsel for the accused;[332] and revision by a state of its capital statute.[333] Its pronouncements, taken in the aggregate, indicated that states may enact capital statutes provided that application is limited to clearly defined classes of murder, and that due process requirements have been fol-

---

430 (1981); Adams v. Texas, 448 U.S. 38 (1980); Beck v. Alabama, 447 U.S. 625 (1980); Godfrey v. Georgia, 446 U.S. 420 (1980); Sandstrom v. Montana, 442 U.S. 510 (1979); Green v. Georgia, 442 U.S. 95 (1979); Bell v. Ohio, 438 U.S. 637 (1978); Lockett v. Ohio, 438 U.S. 586 (1978); Coker v. Georgia, 433 U.S. 584 (1977); Dobbert v. Florida, 432 U.S. 282, *reh'g denied*, 434 U.S. 882 (1977); Gardner v. Florida, 430 U.S. 349 (1977); Davis v. Georgia, 429 U.S. 122 (1976); Roberts v. Louisiana, 428 U.S. 325, *reh'g denied*, 429 U.S. 890 (1976); Woodson v. North Carolina, 428 U.S. 280 (1976); Jurek v. Texas, 428 U.S. 262, *reh'g denied sub nom.* Gregg v. Georgia, 429 U.S. 875 (1976); Proffitt v. Florida, 428 U.S. 242, *reh'g denied sub nom.* Gregg v. Georgia, 429 U.S. 875 (1976); Gregg v. Georgia, 428 U.S. 153, *reh'g denied*, 429 U.S. 875 (1976); Donnelly v. DeChristoforo, 416 U.S. 637 (1974).

323. *Skipper*, 476 U.S. at 1; *Ramos*, 463 U.S. at 992; *Barclay*, 463 U.S. at 939; *Zant*, 462 U.S. at 862; *Eddings*, 455 U.S. at 104; *Beck*, 447 U.S. at 625; *Godfrey*, 446 U.S. at 420; *Bell*, 438 U.S. at 637; *Lockett*, 438 U.S. at 586; *Roberts*, 428 U.S. at 325; *Woodson*, 428 U.S. at 280; *Jurek*, 428 U.S. at 262; *Proffitt*, 428 U.S. at 242; *Gregg*, 428 U.S. at 153.

324. *Baldwin*, 472 U.S. at 372; *Spaziano*, 468 U.S. at 447; *Arizona*, 467 U.S. at 203; *Pulley*, 465 U.S. at 37; *Bullington*, 451 U.S. at 430.

325. *Turner*, 476 U.S. at 28; *Wainwright*, 469 U.S. at 412; *Adams*, 448 U.S. at 38; *Davis*, 428 U.S. at 122.

326. *Francis*, 471 U.S. at 307; *Sandstrom*, 442 U.S. at 510.

327. Ake v. Oklahoma, 470 U.S. 68 (1985); Green v. Georgia, 442 U.S. 95 (1979); Gardner v. Florida, 430 U.S. 349 (1977).

328. *Cabana*, 474 U.S. at 376 (1986); *Enmund*, 458 U.S. 782 (1982).

329. Coker v. Georgia, 433 U.S. 584 (1977).

330. *Ford*, 447 U.S. at 399. For a discussion of execution of the mentally insane prior to the *Ford* decision, see James S. Liebman & Michael J. Shepard, *Guiding Capital Sentencing Discretion Beyond the 'Boiler Plate': Mental Disorder as a Mitigating Factor*, 66 GEORGETOWN L.J. 757 (1978). For an analysis of the *Ford* ruling, see John Blume & David Bruck, *Sentencing the Mentally Retarded to Death: An Eighth Amendment Analysis*, 41 ARK. L. REV. 725, 756-757 (1988).

331. *Caldwell*, 472 U.S. at 320; *Donnelly*, 416 U.S. at 637.

332. *Strickland*, 466 U.S. at 668. For a discussion of circumstances confronted by attorneys in capital trials, see, generally, WHITE, *supra* note 205; Gary Goodpaster, *The Trial For Life: Effective Assistance of Counsel in Death Penalty Cases*, 58 N.Y.U. L. REV. 299 (1983).

333. *Dobbert*, 432 U.S. at 282.

lowed.[334] Though the Burger Court, after 1972, overturned convictions in twenty-two cases,[335] it never articulated clear standards to be followed by states, prompting one scholar to conclude that its opinions "engendered confusion" and "created a minefield through which the perplexed legislators tread at their peril."[336]

D. *The Rehnquist Court (1986-   ) and Capital Punishment Up to the Retirements of Brennan and Marshall*

Up to the time of Marshall's retirement on June 28, 1991 (Brennan announced his decision to step down on July 20, 1990), the Rehnquist Court had handed down thirty-nine rulings on the death penalty — seven in 1987,[337] six in 1988,[338] seven in 1989,[339] twelve in 1990,[340] and seven in 1991.[341] With the excep-

---

334. BERGER, *supra* note 113, at 131.
335. *Ford*, 477 U.S. at 399; *Turner*, 476 U.S. at 28; *Skipper*, 476 U.S. at 1; *Caldwell*, 472 U.S. at 320; *Francis*, 471 U.S. at 307; *Ake*, 470 U.S. at 68; *Arizona*, 467 U.S. at 203; *Enmund*, 458 U.S. at 782; *Eddings*, 455 U.S. at 104; *Bullington*, 451 U.S. at 430; *Adams*, 448 U.S. at 38; *Beck*, 447 U.S. at 625; *Godfrey*, 446 U.S. at 420; *Sandstrom*, 442 U.S. at 510; *Green*, 442 U.S. at 95; *Bell*, 438 U.S. at 637; *Lockett*, 438 U.S. at 586; *Coker*, 433 U.S. at 584; *Gardner*, 430 U.S. at 349; *Davis*, 429 U.S. at 122; *Roberts*, 428 U.S. at 325; *Woodson*, 428 U.S. at 280.
336. BERGER, *supra* note 113, at 152.
337. Burger v. Kemp, 438 U.S. 776, *reh'g denied*, 483 U.S. 1056 (1987); Sumner v. Shuman, 483 U.S. 66 (1987); Booth v. Maryland, 482 U.S. 496, *reh'g denied*, 483 U.S. 1056 (1987), *and overruled by* Payne v. Tennessee, 111 S. Ct. 2597 (1991); Hitchcock v. Dugger, 481 U.S. 393 (1987); McCleskey v. Kemp, 481 U.S. 279, *reh'g denied*, 482 U.S. 920 (1987); Tison v. Arizona, 481 U.S. 137, *reh'g denied*, 482 U.S. 921 (1987); California v. Brown, 479 U.S. 538 (1987).
338. Thompson v. Oklahoma, 487 U.S. 815 (1988); Johnson v. Mississippi, 486 U.S. 578 (1988); Mills v. Maryland, 486 U.S. 367 (1988); Maynard v. Cartwright, 486 U.S. 356 (1988); Satterwhite v. Texas, 486 U.S. 249 (1988); Lowenfield v. Phelps, 484 U.S. 231, *reh'g denied*, 485 U.S. 944 (1988).
339. Powell v. Texas, 492 U.S. 680 (1989); Stanford v. Kentucky, 492 U.S. 361, *reh'g denied*, 492 U.S. 937 (1989); Penry v. Lynaugh, 492 U.S. 302 (1989); Murray v. Giarratano, 492 U.S. 1 (1989); South Carolina v. Gathers, 490 U.S. 805, *reh'g denied*, 492 U.S. 938 (1989), *and overruled by* Payne v. Tennessee, 111 S. Ct. 2597 (1991); Hildwin v. Florida, 490 U.S. 638, *reh'g denied*, 492 U.S. 927 (1989); Dugger v. Adams, 489 U.S. 401, *reh'g denied*, 490 U.S. 1301 (1989).
340. Cage v. Louisiana, 498 U.S. 39 (1990); Shell v. Mississippi, 498 U.S. 1 (1990); Lewis v. Jeffers, 497 U.S. 764, *reh'g denied*, 497 U.S. 1050 (1990); Walton v. Arizona, 497 U.S. 639, *reh'g denied*, 497 U.S. 1050 (1990); Sawyer v. Smith, 497 U.S. 227, *reh'g denied*, 497 U.S. 1050 (1990); Demosthenes v. Baal, 495 U.S. 731 (1990); Whitmore v. Arkansas, 495 U.S. 149 (1990); Clemons v. Mississippi, 494 U.S. 738 (1990); Saffle v. Parks, 494 U.S. 484 (1990); McKoy v. North Carolina, 494 U.S. 433 (1990); Boyde v. California, 494 U.S. 370, *reh'g denied*, 495 U.S. 924 (1990); Blystone v. Pennsylvania, 494 U.S. 299 (1990).
341. Payne v. Tennessee, 111 S. Ct. 2597, *reh'g denied*, 112 S. Ct. 28 (1991); Schad v. Arizona, 111 S. Ct. 2491, *reh'g denied*, 112 S. Ct. 28 (1991); Mu'Min v. Virginia, 111 S. Ct. 1899, *reh'g denied*, 112 S. Ct. 13 (1991); Yates v. Evatt, 111 S. Ct. 1884 (1991); Lankford v. Idaho, 111 S. Ct. 1723 (1991); McCleskey v. Zant,

tion of four issues — the admissibility of testimony on the emotional impact of a victim's death on family members,[342] right to counsel in appellate capital proceedings,[343] abuse of the writ of habeas corpus,[344] and the death penalty for minors[345] — none of these cases presented questions which had not been considered by the Burger Court. Early in its tenure, the Rehnquist Court signaled that it would be guided in its consideration of capital proceedings by precedents established in earlier cases. In the 1987 case of *McCleskey v. Kemp*,[346] one of its first rulings on the death penalty,[347] the Rehnquist Court elaborated on its intended examination of state capital statutes:

> In sum, our decisions since *Furman* have identified a constitutionally permissible range of discretion in imposing the death penalty. First, there is a required threshold below which the death penalty cannot be imposed. In this context, the State must establish rational criteria that narrow the decision maker's judgment as to whether the circumstances of a particular defendant's case meet the threshold. Moreover, a societal consensus that the death penalty is disproportionate to a particular offense prevents a State from imposing the death penalty for that offense. Second, States cannot limit the sentencer's consideration of any relevant circumstances that could cause it to decline to impose the penalty. In this respect, the State cannot channel the sentencer's discretion, but must allow it to consider any relevant information offered by the defendant.[348]

---

111 S. Ct. 1454, *reh'g denied*, 111 S. Ct. 2841 (1991); Parker v. Dugger, 111 S. Ct. 731, *reh'g denied*, 111 S. Ct. 1340 (1991).

342.   Booth v. Maryland, 482 U.S. 496, *reh'g denied*, 483 U.S. 1056 (1987), *and overruled by* Payne v. Tennessee, 111 S. Ct. 2597 (1991).

343.   Murray v. Giarratano, 492 U.S. 1 (1989).

344.   McCleskey v. Zant, 111 S. Ct. 1454, *reh'g denied*, 111 S. Ct. 2841 (1991).

345.   Stanford v. Kentucky, 492 U.S. 361, *reh'g denied*, 492 U.S. 937 (1989), *decided together with* Wilkins v. Missouri, 492 U.S. 361, *reh'g denied*, 492 U.S. 937 (1989); Thompson v. Oklahoma, 487 U.S. 815 (1988). In Eddings v. Oklahoma, 455 U.S. 104 (1982), the majority refrained from deciding whether the execution of minors is constitutional.

346.   481 U.S. 279 (1987).

347.   *See* Hitchcock v. Dugger, 481 U.S. 393 (1987) (decided the same day as *McCleskey*, Apr. 22, 1987); Tison v. Arizona, 481 U.S. 137 (decided Apr. 21, 1987).

348.   *McCleskey*, 481 U.S. at 306-07. The Court reiterated its adherence to this standard in *Payne*, 111 S. Ct. at 2597, and *Blystone*, 494 U.S. at 299.

Up to the time of Brennan and Marshall's departure, the Rehnquist Court continued to adhere to this standard. However, this did not produce a coherent approach in capital adjudication; of 39 cases,[349] the Court reversed 19 convictions perceived to have violated the defendant's right to due process of law.[350] A consistent position has appeared neither in the frequency with which state convictions have been overturned[351] nor in the application of precedents. This has been most evident in the Court's examination of statutory enumeration of aggravating and mitigating circumstances, the most frequently adjudicated issue in the Rehnquist Court's first five Terms. Of eighteen cases,[352] ten convictions, examined in light of precedents established in *Gregg* and its companion cases,[353] and *Lockett v. Ohio*,[354] were reversed.[355] While this may suggest that the Court has been more sympathetic to protection of due process of law than states, other decisions — such as those disallowing alleged patterns of racial discrimination in capital sentencing to be considered in an instance where a black defendant is convicted of killing a white

---

349.   *See supra* notes 337-41.

350.   *Parker*, 498 U.S. at 308; *Yates*, 111 S. Ct. at 1884; *Lankford*, 111 S. Ct. at 1723; *Cage*, 498 U.S. at 39; *Shell*, 498 U.S. at 1; *McKoy*, 494 U.S. at 433; *Powell*, 492 U.S. at 680; *Murray*, 492 U.S. at 1; *Gathers*, 490 U.S. at 805; *Dugger*, 489 U.S. at 401; *Thompson*, 487 U.S. at 815; *Johnson*, 486 U.S. at 578; *Maynard*, 486 U.S. at 356; *Satterwhite*, 486 U.S. at 249; *Mills*, 486 U.S. at 367; *McCleskey*, 481 U.S. at 279; *Sumner*, 483 U.S. at 66; *Hitchcock*, 481 U.S. at 393; *Booth*, 482 U.S. at 496.

351.   The breakdown of reversed convictions for each Term is as follows:

Term	Number of Cases Decided	Reversed State Convictions
October, 1990	7	3
October, 1989	12	3
October, 1988	7	4
October, 1987	6	5
October, 1986	7	4

352.   *Parker*, 498 U.S. at 308; *Shell*, 498 U.S. at 1; *Lewis*, 497 U.S. at 764; *Walton*, 497 U.S. at 639; *Clemons*, 494 U.S. at 738; *Saffle*, 494 U.S. at 484; *McKoy*, 494 U.S. at 433; *Boyde*, 494 U.S. at 370; *Blystone*, 494 U.S. at 299; *Penry*, 492 U.S. at 302; *Hildwin*, 490 U.S. at 638; *Johnson*, 486 U.S. at 578; *Mills*, 486 U.S. at 367; *Maynard*, 486 U.S. at 356; *Lowenfield*, 484 U.S. at 231; *Sumner*, 483 U.S. at 66; *Hitchcock*, 481 U.S. at 393; *McCleskey*, 481 U.S. at 279.

353.   *Gregg v. Georgia*, 428 U.S. 153, *reh'g denied*, 429 U.S. 875 (1976); *Jurek v. Texas*, 428 U.S. 262, *reh'g denied sub nom.* Gregg v. Georgia, 429 U.S. 875 (1976); *Proffitt v. Florida*, 428 U.S. 242, *reh'g denied sub nom.* Gregg v. Georgia, 429 U.S. 875 (1976); *Woodson v. North Carolina*, 428 U.S. 280 (1976); *Roberts v. Louisiana*, 428 U.S. 325, *reh'g denied*, 429 U.S. 890 (1976).

354.   438 U.S. 586 (1978). *See also* Bell v. Ohio, 438 U.S. 637 (1978).

355.   *Parker*, 498 U.S. at 308; *Shell*, 498 U.S. at 1; *McKoy*, 494 U.S. at 433; *Penry*, 492 U.S. at 302; *Johnson*, 486 U.S. at 578; *Maynard*, 486 U.S. at 356; *Mills*, 486 U.S. at 367; *McCleskey*, 481 U.S. at 279; *Hitchcock*, 481 U.S. at 393; *Sumner*, 483 U.S. at 66.

victim,[356] upholding the death penalty for minors[357] and the mentally retarded,[358] and filing a petition for habeas corpus[359] — indicate insensitiveness to the position of the accused. The Court's adherence to precedent — as evidenced in its overturning, after just four years, of its initial decision to disallow, as irrelevant to the culpability of the accused, use of testimony on the psychological trauma suffered by the victim's family members;[360] its contention that the death penalty is permissible, in light of evolving societal standards of decency, for sixteen and seventeen-year-olds,[361] but not for those who are fifteen years of age;[362] and its reinterpretation of the death penalty for accomplices[363] — was also uneven.

In short, the Rehnquist Court, like its immediate predecessor, has not articulated and implemented a coherent position on capital punishment. Its rulings appear to have been based on subjective perceptions of fairness to the accused as determined by a fluctuating majority.[364] This trend, as well as a belief that the range of issues surrounding the death penalty have not been satisfactorily addressed, impelled both Brennan and Marshall to forcefully elaborate on their views of capital punishment.

IV.   JUSTICE BRENNAN'S OPINIONS ON CAPITAL PUNISHMENT

A.   Early Voting Pattern and First Elaboration of Position in McGautha v. California (1971)

The Burger Court, it will be recalled, did not examine whether the death penalty constituted "cruel and unusual" pun-

---

356.   McCleskey v. Kemp, 481 U.S. 279, *reh'g denied*, 482 U.S. 920 (1987). *See infra* text accompanying notes 506-25.

357.   Stanford v. Kentucky, 492 U.S. 361, *reh'g denied*, 492 U.S. 937 (1989), and its companion, Wilkins v. Missouri, 492 U.S. 361, *reh'g denied*, 492 U.S. 937 (1989). *But see* Thompson v. Oklahoma, 487 U.S. 815 (1988).

358.   Penry v. Lynaugh, 492 U.S. 302 (1989).

359.   Sawyer v. Smith, 497 U.S. 227 (1990).

360.   Booth v. Maryland, 482 U.S. 496, *reh'g denied*, 483 U.S. 1056 (1987), and South Carolina v. Gathers, 490 U.S. 805, *reh'g denied*, 492 U.S. 938 (1989) *and both overruled by* Payne v. Tennessee, 111 S. Ct. 2597 (1991).

361.   *Stanford*, 492 U.S. at 361 (upheld death penalty for seventeen-year-old); *Wilkins*, 492 U.S. at 361 (upheld death penalty for sixteen-year-old).

362.   *Thompson*, 487 U.S. at 815.

363.   *Cf.* Tison v. Arizona, 481 U.S. 137, *reh'g denied*, 482 U.S. 921 (1987); Cabana v. Bullock, 474 U.S. 376 (1986); Enmund v. Florida, 458 U.S. 782 (1982).

364.   For a detailed examination of the Rehnquist Court's approach to capital punishment in its first five Terms (1986-1991), see Alan I. Bigel, *The Rehnquist Court on Right to Life: Forecast for the 1990s*, 18 OHIO N.U. L. REV. 515, 531-56 (1992).

ishment in several 1970 cases which largely focused on admissibility of testimony in trial proceedings for offenses statutorily punishable by death.[365] Brennan also refrained from addressing this question, focusing instead on assessing voluntariness of a confession. In the companion 1970 cases of *Parker v. North Carolina*[366] and *Brady v. United States*,[367] Brennan, writing a single opinion expressing both dissent from and concurrence with the majority's position, respectively,[368] discussed application of precedent. In *United States v. Jackson*,[369] decided in 1968, the Warren Court indicated that statutory provisions which made possible a less severe penalty for capital defendants who choose to forego trial by jury were invalid.[370] Brennan maintained that the majority failed to adhere to this position in *Parker*.[371]

The *Parker* case involved a North Carolina law which authorized a jury to recommend a penalty of death or life imprisonment for first-degree burglary.[372] After consulting with counsel, the accused, aware that entering a plea of guilty would result in a sentence of life imprisonment,[373] signed a confession,[374] which the Court upheld as an informed and voluntary act.[375]

Acknowledging the difficulty which the Court has encountered in seeking to assess the myriad factors potentially affecting the voluntariness of a confession,[376] Brennan nevertheless emphasized that, based on the precedent in *Jackson*,[377] Parker's guilty plea was unconstitutional. Unlike plea bargaining, where a defendant may elect to plead guilty to an offense based on an assessment of the weight of evidence and its possible affect on a jury, an accused who exercised a statutory provision mandating life imprisonment for a crime punishable by death by entering a plea of guilty was coerced to relinquish the constitutional protec-

---

365. *See supra* note 267. *Witherspoon*, 391 U.S. at 512; Maxwell v. Bishop, 398 U.S. 262 (1970); *Davis*, 384 U.S. at 737; *Brady*, 397 U.S. at 742; *Parker*, 397 U.S. at 790; *Alford*, 400 U.S. at 25; Dutton v. Evans, 400 U.S. 74 (1970).

366. 397 U.S. 790 (1970).

367. 397 U.S. 742 (1970).

368. *Parker*, 397 U.S. at 799 (Brennan, J., dissenting in part, concurring in part); *Brady*, 397 U.S. at 775 (Brennan, J., dissenting).

369. 390 U.S. 570 (1968).

370. *See supra* text accompanying notes 250-54.

371. 397 U.S. at 799.

372. N.C. Gen. Stat. §§ 14-51, and 52 (1969). (Current version at N.C. Gen. Stat. § 14-52). *Parker*, 397 U.S. at 792 n.1.

373. N.C. Gen. Stat. § 15-162.1 (1965), *repealed by* 1971 N.C. Sess. Laws c.1225. *Parker*, 397 U.S. at 792, n.2.

374. *Parker*, 397 U.S. at 792.

375. *Id.* at 795-96.

376. *Id.* at 799-804.

377. 390 U.S. 570 (1968).

tion of trial by jury.[378] Moreover, Brennan maintained, potential exercise of constitutional rights is more compelling when death, "the most severe and awesome penalty known to our law,"[379] may be imposed. Noting that the Court "has recognized that capital cases are treated differently in some respects from noncapital cases,"[380] and that "the threat of a death penalty [has been raised] as a factor to be given considerable weight in determining whether a defendant has deliberately waived his constitutional rights,"[381] Brennan suggested that heightened judicial scrutiny of statutory provisions is imperative where the death penalty may result. In 1971, however, the Court, in *McGautha v. California*[382] and its companion, *Crampton v. Ohio*,[383] expressed unwillingness to undertake detailed examination of state capital guidelines.[384]

The Court's contention in *McGautha* that it is both impossible and inappropriate to devise a list of factors to be considered by a jury in a capital trial,[385] and that jurors, "confronted with the truly awesome responsibility of decreeing death for a fellow human,"[386] will undoubtedly consider a wide range of circumstances in careful deliberation, brought forth a lengthy dissent[387] by Brennan (which Marshall and Douglas joined) which, primarily, addressed the importance of, and prior rulings on, preserving due process of law under the Fourteenth Amendment,[388] as well as historical delegation of power by a legislature.[389] While acknowledging a state's considerable discretion to devise policy and select methods of implementation, Brennan emphasized that this power is not unlimited. The purpose of the due process clause,[390] Brennan pointed out, is "to protect individuals against the arbitrary exercise of state power."[391] This is constitutionally fulfilled by explicitly articulating the objectives of legislation and channeling the range of discretion to be exercised by those authorized to implement statutory policy. By proceeding in this

---

378.   U.S. Const. amend. VI. *See supra* note 253.
379.   *Parker*, 397 U.S. at 809.
380.   *Id.* at 809-10 (citing Williams v. Georgia, 349 U.S. 375, 391 (1955)).
381.   *Id.* at 810 (citing Green v. United States, 355 U.S. 184 (1957) and Fay v. Noia, 372 U.S. 391 (1963)).
382.   402 U.S. 183 (1971).
383.   *Id.*
384.   *See supra* text accompanying notes 268-75.
385.   *Id.* 402 U.S. at 207.
386.   402 U.S. at 208.
387.   402 U.S. at 248-312.
388.   U.S. Const. amend. XIV, § 1.
389.   402 U.S. at 271-87.
390.   *See supra* note 57.
391.   *McGautha*, 402 U.S. at 270.

manner, allegations of abuse of power may be more readily detected. Capital statutes enacted in California and Ohio, Brennan argued, did not meet this standard; they merely directed the jury to reach a verdict and recommend death or life imprisonment after examining evidence deemed pertinent. This standardless discretion, Brennan maintained, violated both due process and delegation of power requirements formulated by the Court since the late nineteenth century.[392]

Brennan did not believe that *McGautha* directly addressed the meaning of "cruel and unusual punishments;" indeed, he pointed out that the issue presented did not "in the slightest way draw into question the power of States to determine whether or not to impose the death penalty itself,"[393] or whether the penalty of death "'is appropriate punishment' for the petitioners before us."[394] The obligation of a state to comply with due process of law in formulating and providing for the application of penal codes was, as perceived by Brennan, the key issue presented, and he objected to the majority's failure to address this concern by merely asserting, as if it were necessary to devise "predetermined standards so precise as to be capable of purely mechanical application,"[395] that this subject is inappropriate for judicial consideration.

It is impossible to definitively determine Brennan's position on the death penalty in *McGautha*, though it may appear that he would not object to a capital statute which explicitly confined the range of discretion to be exercised in trial proceedings. Brennan could have declared that the death penalty violated the Eighth Amendment irrespective of the meticulous procedural protections which a state may have devised. Instead, however, he seemed to encourage state innovation on assessing appropriate punishment for criminal offenses, and did not foreclose the possibility that capital punishment may be enacted. He declared:

> . . . I do not believe that the legislatures of the 50 States are so devoid of wisdom and the power of rational thought that they are unable to face the problem of capital punishment directly, and to determine for themselves the criteria under which convicted capital felons should be chosen to live or die.[396]

---

392. *Id.* at 252-57.
393. *Id.* at 310.
394. *Id.*
395. *Id.* at 249.
396. *Id.*

In other words, Brennan's dissent focused not on the majority's willingness to sanction the death penalty but rather on its assumption that this issue was too complex to be subject to due process and delegation of power standards traditionally applied to other areas of criminal law. Rather than "stark legislative abdication"[397] by which a state, absent any direction, merely authorizes juries to weigh evidence and issue a recommendation of death or life imprisonment, a statute must address: the "ends any given State seeks to achieve by imposing the death penalty" and whether they "will or will not be served in any given case;"[398] a state's possible desire to execute "only those first-degree murderers who cannot be rehabilitated;"[399] its attitude toward retribution, deterrence, recidivism, and rehabilitation;[400] the willingness of lawmakers to authorize jurors to examine a range of aggravating and mitigating circumstances;[401] and the opportunity, by judicial review, to examine the reasons which impelled a jury to issue a particular verdict.[402]

Though he expressed dissatisfaction that these factors were not incorporated into the California and Ohio statutes, and objected to the majority's unwillingness to examine them, Brennan did not categorize execution as a constitutionally impermissible form of punishment. "[L]ife itself," Brennan concluded, "is an interest of such transcendent importance that a decision to take a life may require procedural regularity far beyond a decision simply to set a sentence at one or another term of years."[403] He urged states — and the Court — to give this careful consideration where capital punishment may be inflicted.

B. *Brennan's Most Elaborate Discussion of Capital Punishment: Furman v. Georgia (1972)*

The Court's rejection, in *Furman v. Georgia*,[404] of capital trial procedures in Georgia and Texas, and its implicit objection to the alleged arbitrariness of capital statutes as then administered in all thirty-five states (and the District of Columbia) which sanctioned the death penalty,[405] elicited a far-ranging concurring opinion by Brennan which addressed the original understanding

---

397. *Id.* at 252.
398. *Id.* at 283.
399. *Id.*
400. *Id.* at 284.
401. *Id.* at 285-86.
402. *Id.* at 286.
403. *Id.* at 311.
404. 408 U.S. 238, *reh'g denied,* 409 U.S. 902 (1972).
405. *See supra* text accompanying notes 276-83.

of capital punishment, judicial precedents, and the perceived meaning of "cruel and unusual punishment" in contemporary society. For the first time, Brennan explicitly concluded that the death penalty is categorically unconstitutional.[406]

Brennan began with an inquiry into the Framers' perception of punishment. He pointed out that few statements were made on the "cruel and unusual punishments" clause; the brief comments in the First Congress,[407] as well as concerns put forward in the Massachusetts and Virginia ratifying conventions,[408] furnished inconclusive evidence on the original understanding of this phrase. While Brennan believed that the Framers "intended to ban torturous punishments,"[409] he envisioned an original purpose wider in scope. Though he conceded that the original meaning of "cruel and unusual" was unclear, Brennan interestingly asserted that "the reach of the Clause," as the framers intended, "was not limited to the proscription of unspeakable atrocities," and was not perceived "simply to forbid punishments considered 'cruel and unusual' at the time."[410]

Brennan might have declared that widespread existence of the death penalty at the time the Eighth Amendment was drafted and submitted to the states for ratification,[411] as well as failure by anyone to explicitly express opposition to this form of punishment, rendered it constitutionally acceptable for states wishing to enact capital offenses. After all, it may have been a "cruel" sanction, but it was not "unusual." Does use of the word "unusual" in the Eighth Amendment refer to the infrequency with which a punishment is inflicted or the number of legislatures willing to adopt it? Seeking to obtain a more clear understanding of "cruel

---

406. *Furman*, 408 U.S. at 305.

407. *See supra* text accompanying notes 121-22.

408. Abraham Holmes and Patrick Henry, delegates to the Massachusetts and Virginia ratifying conventions, respectively, expressed concern that the original Constitution contained no provision expressly limiting Congress' power to punish. Holmes pointed out that Congress would not be "restrained from inventing the most cruel and unheard-of punishments, and annexing them to crimes," J. ELLIOT'S DEBATES 2:111 (1876), while Henry, noting that the Virginia bill of rights prohibited infliction of "cruel and unusual punishments," and restrained legislators from mandating "tortures, or cruel and barbarous punishment," objected to the absence of a comparable clause for Congress. This omission, Henry feared, would place no limits on the kinds of punishments Congress might impose; members would be "let . . . loose" to prescribe sanctions which "depart from the genius of . . . [the] country." J. ELLIOT'S DEBATES 3:447 (1876) (quoted in *Furman*, 408 U.S. at 258-60 (Brennan, J., concurring).

409. *Furman*, 408 U.S. at 263.

410. *Id.*

411. *See supra* text accompanying note 123.

and unusual," Brennan examined statements made by the Court in precedents on capital punishment.[412]

The Court, Brennan pointed out, put forward an evolving interpretation of the death penalty which gradually went beyond the original understanding of "cruel and unusual." At first, the Court restricted its position on capital punishment to practices in effect during the founding generation;[413] however, beginning in the early twentieth century, a perception of "cruel and unusual" which emphasized flexible construction of provisions in light of changing expectations was adopted.[414] Precedents, Brennan noted, emphasized that a provision of the Constitution is not to be interpreted with a fixed and unalterable meaning.

Brennan envisioned an active role by the judiciary in developing changing applications of cruel and unusual punishments. The Framers, he believed, inserted ambiguous words into the Constitution to enable future generations to revise the original understanding. While this conferred considerable policymaking discretion to the legislative branch, it was limited by the Bill of Rights, which, Brennan maintained, placed "'certain subjects . . . beyond the reach of majorities and officials. . . .'"[415] Enforcement of this objective, Brennan emphasized, "lies with the courts"[416] by preventing exercises of legislative power which may jeopardize "maintenance of individual freedom."[417]

Brennan insisted that the Court's role was not to assess legislation based on its perceived reasonableness or necessity; indeed, he quoted approvingly a statement in *Weems v. United States*[418] which pointed out that, in examining the constitutionality of punishments challenged as "cruel and unusual," the justices "must avoid the insertion of 'judicial conception[s] of . . . wisdom or propriety.'"[419] However, it appeared that Brennan was willing to make value judgments on the death penalty. After noting that the Court must assess sanctions "'from the evolving standards of decency that mark the progress of a maturing society,'"[420] Bren-

---

412. *See supra* text accompanying notes 220-39.
413. *In re* Kemmler, 136 U.S. 436 (1890); Wilkerson v. Utah, 99 U.S. 130 (1878). *See supra* text accompanying notes 220-25.
414. Trop v. Dulles, 356 U.S. 86 (1958); Weems v. United States, 217 U.S. 349 (1910). *See supra* text accompanying notes 226-32, 236-39.
415. *Furman*, 408 U.S. at 268-69 (quoting West Virginia State Bd. of Education v. Barnette, 319 U.S. 624, 638 (1943)).
416. *Furman*, 408 U.S. at 267.
417. *Id.* (quoting Weems v. United States, 217 U.S. at 377).
418. 217 U.S. 349 (1910).
419. *Id.* at 379 (*quoted in Furman*, 408 U.S. at 269).
420. Trop v. Dulles, 356 U.S. 86, 101 (1958). *See supra* text accompanying notes 236-39 (*quoted in Furman*, 408 U.S. at 269-70).

nan declared that the constitutionality of punishment is to be examined by the following four criteria: A punishment "must not be so severe as to be degrading to the dignity of human beings;"[421] it "must not [be] arbitrarily inflict[ed];"[422] it "must not be unacceptable to contemporary society;"[423] and it "must not be excessive."[424] Brennan concluded that capital punishment could not be reconciled with any of these conditions.

Judicial precedents, Brennan pointed out, have indicated that punishments which, by their severity, offend human dignity, are impermissible.[425] Primitive forms of punishment, such as the pillory, gallows, and stretching of limbs, among other measures inflicted earlier in history,[426] have in time been rejected not only for the degree of physical pain inflicted but, primarily, because "they treat members of the human race as nonhumans, as objects to be toyed with and discarded."[427] While the Court had initially recognized forms of punishment which appeared to involve a minimum degree of pain and suffering due to the relative swiftness in execution,[428] in time the requirement of proportionality between an offense and punishment had been adopted[429] on the premise that "even the vilest criminal remains a human being possessed of common human dignity."[430] The death penalty, Brennan believed, violated this principle.

Brennan also maintained that the arbitrary infliction of capital punishment rendered it cruel and unusual. Again he cited precedents[431] to indicate that punishments which have been carried out with relative frequency following conviction left "little likelihood that the State . . . [has been] inflicting it arbitrarily."[432] The frequency with which a punishment is imposed, Brennan added, is related to its degree of acceptance by contemporary society in that a penalty rarely inflicted is perceived disproportionate to the offense committed. The infrequent execution of

---

421. *Furman*, 408 U.S. at 271.
422. *Id.* at 274.
423. *Id.* at 277.
424. *Id.* at 279.
425. *Id.* at 305.
426. *See supra* notes 129-30.
427. *Furman*, 408 U.S. at 272-3.
428. *See* Louisiana *ex rel.* Francis v. Resweber, 329 U.S. 459 (1947); *In re* Kemmler, 136 U.S. 436 (1890); Wilkerson v. Utah, 99 U.S. 130 (1878); *see also supra* text accompanying notes 220-25, 233-35.
429. *See* Weems v. United States, 217 U.S. 349 (1910); *see also supra* text accompanying notes 226-32.
430. *Furman*, 408 U.S. at 273.
431. *See Wilkerson*, 99 U.S. at 130.
432. *Furman*, 408 U.S. at 276.

individuals convicted of a capital offense has underscored its increasing rejection as a humane form of punishment, and lack of predictability as to which defendants will be executed makes the death penalty arbitrary and thus irreconcilable with the prohibition against "cruel and unusual" punishments.

Brennan also believed that the "pointless infliction of suffering"[433] rendered the death penalty unconstitutional. The Court's early recognition of the need for punishment to be proportionate to the offense committed[434] has underscored that the legislature, in adopting particular penalties, must demonstrate an objective to discourage recidivism by seeking to rehabilitate the offender, and to compensate society for the injustice committed. Brennan believed that the death penalty, intended to exact retribution,[435] failed to achieve the educational purpose of punishment, and thus violated the Eighth Amendment.

Having put forward four principles by which the constitutionality of the death penalty is to be assessed,[436] Brennan proceeded to examine provisions of the Constitution which made reference to capital punishment, legislative trends, frequency of executions, and perceived social attitudes. Brennan acknowledged that capital offenses were recognized in the Fifth Amendment,[437] but insisted that this was not permissible in light of the Eighth Amendment's prohibition of "cruel and unusual" punishments. He also maintained that the Framers' insertion of the word "capital," which recognized "the existence of what was then a common punishment,"[438] was no longer applicable in view of evolving conceptions of treatment of defendants.

Brennan did not attempt to ignore the views of the founders. He believed that the Framers put forward not practices which were to be unwaveringly followed but rather principles of justice which each generation will be compelled to apply in light of perceived contemporary needs. One may argue that the death penalty itself is explicitly recognized in the Fifth and Fourteenth

---

433. *Id.* at 279.

434. *See Weems*, 217 U.S. at 349; *see also supra* text accompanying notes 230-32. This principle, Brennan argued, was recognized in the nineteenth century. *See* Trop v. Dulles, 356 U.S. 86, 99 (1958); Weems v. United States, 217 U.S. 349, 381 (1910); O'Neil v. Vermont, 144 U.S. 323, 339 (1892) (Field, J., dissenting), *supra* note 229; Pervear v. Commonwealth of Massachusetts, 5 Wall. 475, 480 (1867) (cited *Furman*, 408 U.S. at 279-81 n. 23-25).

435. For a discussion of this concept, see *supra* text accompanying notes 175-88.

436. See text accompanying *supra* notes 421-24.

437. See text accompanying *supra* note 132.

438. *Furman*, 408 U.S. at 283.

Amendments[439] and that power to regulate its mode of infliction, based on compliance with due process of law,[440] does not authorize proscription of capital punishment; hence, the scope of "cruel and unusual" is limited either to noncapital offenses or methods employed by a state in the trial and execution of individuals. Brennan, however, argued that the "cruel and unusual punishments" clause confined the scope of the Fifth Amendment on the ground that open-ended provisions of the Bill of Rights, reflecting the Framers' aspirational goals of constitutional protections, are controlling over specific words such as "capital" which merely depicted a practice in effect in their time. Notwithstanding the Framers' possible belief that the meaning of the Constitution is to evolve, one may argue that explicit recognition of the death penalty in the Fifth and Fourteenth Amendments as an option of punishment did not compel states to adopt it but also precluded the Court from prohibiting its infliction. The four criteria[441] set forth by Brennan to assess punishment, however, furnished discretion to the Court to establish parameters which legislative policy choices may not exceed.

Brennan argued that the death penalty, "an unusually severe punishment, unusual in its pain, in its finality, and in its enormity,"[442] is unacceptable in "a society that so strongly affirms the sanctity of life."[443] Brennan noted that there has been "no national debate about punishment, in general or by imprisonment, comparable to the debate about punishment by death,"[444] but this did not prove that the death penalty was abhorrent to contemporary society. The moratorium on further execution, in effect for five years prior to the *Furman* decision,[445] was instituted not because of increasing opposition to capital punishment but rather because states were unclear as to the process by which it was to be carried out; indeed, thirty-five states and the District of Columbia authorized the death penalty at the time of the *Furman* decision,[446] and public opinion polls conducted from 1969 and up to the time of *Furman* indicated that a majority of Americans surveyed favored the death penalty.[447] To be sure, Brennan's citing of statistics indicating a decline in the number of executions

---

439. *See supra* text accompanying note 133.
440. *See supra* text accompanying notes 132-33.
441. *See supra* text accompanying notes 421-24.
442. *Furman*, 408 U.S. at 287.
443. *Id.* at 286.
444. *Id.*
445. *See supra* text accompanying note 173.
446. HUGO BEDAU, THE DEATH PENALTY IN AMERICA 248-49 (1982).
447. *Id.* at 85-92. *See supra* text accompanying notes 185-86.

for each succeeding decade beginning with the 1930s[448] may indicate increasing attention and concern over the utility of capital punishment;[449] however, this trend does not establish the unconstitutionality of the death penalty.

Brennan compared the death penalty to other forms of severe punishment, such as lengthy imprisonment[450] and expatriation,[451] and contended that "the deliberate extinguishment of human life by the State is uniquely degrading to human dignity."[452] Unlike all other penalties, where an individual may suffer constriction of mobility, diminished reputation, embarrassment, and monetary burdens from exorbitant fines and orders for restitution, among other consequences, death "involves, by its very nature, a denial of the executed person's humanity."[453] Arguably, however, subjecting an individual to confinement for many years, absent the comforts of modern life and an opportunity to interact with a wide circle of individuals both in the workplace and in one's neighborhood, and confronting the constant fear of harm from inmates, prolongs suffering which may be more psychologically devastating than execution. Brennan did not distinguish the punishment of death from its method of infliction. Does "cruel and unusual" refer to the penalty itself or the manner in which it is administered? Perhaps the Eighth Amendment proscribed barbaric treatment of criminals[454] while leaving open the type of penalty to be imposed. Death may be perceived as the only appropriate commensurate punishment for extremely heinous acts,[455] and, it may be argued, refraining from imposing it would deny not "the executed person's humanity"[456] but rather the humanity comprising communal existence by which citizens engage in lawful behavior and, to validate this arrangement, expect severe transgressors to be strongly penalized.[457] Brennan did not address this subject.

---

448.   *Furman,* 408 U.S. at 291-93 nn. 40-44. Brennan pointed out that "[i]n the 1930's, executions averaged 167 per year; in the 1940's, the average was 128; in the 1950's, it was 72; and in the years 1960-1962, it was 48. There have been a total of 46 executions since then, 36 of them in 1963-1964." *Furman,* 408 U.S. at 291.

449.   *See supra* text accompanying notes 175-88.

450.   *Furman,* 408 U.S. at 290.

451.   *Id.* at 289-90.

452.   *Id.* at 291.

453.   *Id.* at 290.

454.   *See supra* notes 129-130.

455.   *See supra* text accompanying notes 175-88.

456.   *Furman,* 408 U.S. at 290.

457.   *See supra* text accompanying notes 175-88.

The possibility that an innocent person may be executed, and the allegedly arbitrary infliction of the death penalty, were also cited by Brennan to bolster his contention that capital punishment is unconstitutional. To the extent that human beings are not infallible, one may realistically surmise that "the punishment of death must inevitably be inflicted upon innocent men,"[458] and, should this occur, "the finality of death precludes relief."[459] Brennan did not explore this contention. Though one who has been executed obviously cannot receive some form of compensation available to an innocent individual who has been imprisoned, has the incidence of wrongful infliction of death been sufficient to warrant abolition of capital punishment? A study completed in 1987 indicated that at least twenty-three innocent persons were executed between 1900 and 1982;[460] however, an article published in 1962 which advocated abolition of capital punishment cited only one instance — in 1898 — of a wrongfully executed individual.[461] The precise number — or, indeed, whether any verifiable instances of wrongful execution have taken place — can never be determined because methods of ascertaining the reliability or admissibility of evidence, both at the time of an arrest and trial many years after a sentence is pronounced, are imprecise. Brennan's position is speculative, and the severity, awesomeness, and uniqueness of a punishment does not establish or negate its constitutionality.

In view of the potentially numerous opportunities to appeal a verdict in capital proceedings,[462] and the range of civil liberties challenges likely to be raised,[463] Brennan expressed concern about possible arbitrariness in sentencing. After citing the steady statistical decline in the number of executions since the 1930s,[464] Brennan declared that, "[w]hen a country of over 200 million people inflicts an unusually severe punishment no more than 50 times a year, the inference is strong that the punishment is not being regularly and fairly applied."[465] He did not believe that statutes and trial procedures could be sufficiently meticulous to properly determine which defendants should be sentenced to

---

458. *Furman*, 408 U.S. at 290.
459. *Id.*
460. Hugo A. Bedau & Michael L. Radelet, *Miscarriages of Justice in Potentially Capital Cases*, 40 Stan. L. Rev. 21, 72-73 (1987).
461. Sarah R. Ehrmann, *For Whom The Chair Waits*, Fed. Prob. Q. March 1962, 14-25 (*quoted in* Carrington, *supra* note 172, at 122-23).
462. *See supra* note 200.
463. Paternoster, *supra* note 193, at 192.
464. *Furman*, 408 U.S. at 291-93 nn.40-44.
465. *Furman*, 408 U.S. at 293.

death or a term of imprisonment, and maintained that this obstacle is reflected in the small number of sentences for execution. While studies on the alleged racially discriminatory patterns of capital sentencing[466] lend credence to Brennan's concern, it is interesting, in view of his confidence expressed one year earlier in *McGautha* that state legislatures may be presumed competent to devise trial proceedings with sufficient procedural safeguards,[467] that he no longer believed states could conduct capital trials in an unbiased manner. Infrequent execution of individuals may signify either arbitrariness in sentencing or evidence that, after careful deliberation, only those defendants found to have committed the most heinous crimes are executed. In other words, a relatively high rate of execution may indicate mechanical infliction of the death penalty, while its seldom imposition may reflect meticulous attention to the circumstances of the crime and defendant. Brennan did not explore these possibilities; he could have made reference to the handful of studies undertaken prior to *Furman* on alleged patterns of racial discrimination in capital sentencing[468] to assess whether trial proceedings are irremediably unconstitutional. Instead, he merely asserted that infrequent executions furnish a "compelling [presumption] that there is a deep-seated reluctance to inflict it."[469]

The final area of inquiry examined by Brennan addressed a state's perceived interest in the death penalty. At the time *Furman* was decided, only a handful of studies had been done on the alleged deterrent effect of capital punishment,[470] and none had furnished conclusive evidence that states which had the death penalty experienced a statistically significant reduction in homicide rates than those which punished murder by life imprisonment.[471] Brennan made reference to this empirical evidence,[472] and observed that it is virtually impossible to assess the frequency with which an accused murderer had contemplated the prospect of death or long imprisonment.[473] Of paramount concern for Brennan was the current administration of capital statutes. Unwilling to explore abstract theories of deterrence,[474]

---

466. *See supra* text accompanying notes 205-19.

467. *See supra* text accompanying note 396.

468. *See supra* text accompanying note 212.

469. *Furman,* 408 U.S. at 300.

470. *See supra* text accompanying notes 155-63. For studies of deterrence prior to the *Furman* ruling, see *supra* text accompanying notes 155-57.

471. *See supra* text accompanying notes 155-61.

472. *Furman,* 408 U.S. at 301.

473. *But see supra* text accompanying note 172.

474. *See supra* text accompanying notes 155-74.

Brennan maintained that the small number of individuals convicted of murder who are executed, as well as the likelihood that many years will elapse before a death sentence is carried out, undermined the potency of state assertions that capital punishment is the only suitable measure to reduce homicide rates. Brennan also did not agree with the contention that the death penalty is needed to protect society from possible repeat offenders; he believed that "effective administration of the State's pardon and parole laws," as well as strict "techniques of isolation,"[475] may effectively achieve this objective.

Brennan was unsympathetic to arguments that the death penalty was an appropriate means for society to express its outrage toward a heinous act. In view of the small number of convicted murderers who are executed, Brennan believed that retribution, a sense that "criminals are put to death because they deserve it,"[476] is not a justifiable objective. Brennan refrained from exploring philosophical arguments on retribution;[477] infrequent execution of individuals undermined a state's contention that there is a public desire for revenge which needs to be fulfilled, and precluded the need to elaborate on this concept.

Brennan's perception of judicial power is evident in his *Furman* opinion. His belief that the meaning of constitutional provisions evolves was reflected in construing the death penalty as incompatible with enlightened notions of "cruel and unusual" punishment. As "concepts of justice change,"[478] the Court must reassess principles bequeathed by the founders. This may entail vigorous exercise of judicial power in which perceptions of morality affect adjudication. Notwithstanding that a majority of states (and the District of Columbia) had the death penalty,[479] and that public opinion polls indicated support for its infliction,[480] Brennan insisted that death "stands condemned as fatally offensive to human dignity,"[481] and that the states, consistent with the Eighth Amendment, "may no longer inflict it as a punishment for crimes."[482] His position suggests that it is permissible for the Court to devise a moral code of conduct for the states independent of the perceived position of the populace. Brennan might have confined his reservations about the death penalty to

---

475. *Furman*, 408 U.S. at 300-01.
476. *Id.* at 304.
477. *See supra* text accompanying notes 175-88.
478. *Furman*, 408 U.S. at 304.
479. *See supra* text accompanying note 446.
480. *See supra* text accompanying note 447.
481. *Furman*, 408 U.S. at 305.
482. *Id.*

its alleged arbitrary application at the time *Furman* was decided, and put forward guidelines to be addressed by states during revision of statutes. This would have established an ongoing dialogue between the Court and the states and perhaps resulted in elaborate due process safeguards designed to accommodate Brennan's procedural concerns.[483]

Brennan's categorical rejection of the death penalty as irreconcilable with the Eighth Amendment was based on a belief that it inherently violated his four criteria[484] by which punishment was to be assessed. He significantly restricted policymaking discretion to punish heinous offenders based on legislative perceptions of justice by imposing a moral judgment on states which limited prospects of the majority to statutorily achieve capital punishment in those states where the death penalty is believed to be representative of the peoples' views. The per curiam opinion, however, expressed disapproval with capital statutes as then administered,[485] and, without precluding retention of the death penalty, directed states to reexamine their laws. A few years after the *Furman* decision, several revised statutes were considered by the Court.

C.   *1976: Brennan Responds to the Court's Explicit Acknowledgment of the Death Penalty's Constitutionality*

The Court's first opportunity to reexamine the death penalty was presented in 1976, when, in five cases,[486] mandatory and discretionary capital statutory proceedings were considered.[487] The position of the Court, expressing support for statutes which gave jurors and judges, after considering aggravating and mitigating circumstances, the option of recommending a sentence of death or imprisonment,[488] while rejecting as too inflexible those which required a death sentence for defendants linked with one or more aggravating factors,[489] was criticized as ambiguous and

---

483.   *Id.*

484.   *Id.*

485.   *Id.* at 239-40.

486.   Gregg v. Georgia, 428 U.S. 153, *reh'g denied,* 429 U.S. 875 (1976); Jurek v. Texas, 428 U.S. 262, *reh'g denied sub nom.* Gregg v. Georgia, 429 U.S. 875 (1976); Proffitt v. Florida, 428 U.S. 242, *reh'g denied sub nom.* Gregg v. Georgia, 429 U.S. 875 (1976); Woodson v. North Carolina, 428 U.S. 280 (1976); Roberts v. Louisiana, 428 U.S. 325, *reh'g denied,* 429 U.S. 890 (1976).

487.   *See supra* text accompanying notes 284-305.

488.   *Gregg,* 428 U.S. at 153; *Jurek,* 428 U.S. at 262; *Proffitt,* 428 U.S. at 242. *See supra* text accompanying notes 294-99.

489.   *Woodson,* 428 U.S. at 280; *Roberts,* 428 U.S. at 325. *See supra* text accompanying notes 300-02.

failing to furnish clear standards to states.[490]   In *Gregg*,[491] Brennan wrote a brief dissenting opinion[492] expressing disapproval of both mandatory and discretionary capital statutes.[493]

Reaffirming his position in *Furman*, Brennan maintained that "'evolving standards of decency'"[494] render the death penalty "degrading to human dignity"[495] and unconstitutional regardless of procedural safeguards contained in a statute. Brennan did not examine whether revised statutes minimized arbitrariness in sentencing or consider public support of the death penalty reflected in legislative retention of capital punishment following the *Furman* ruling. The prohibition of "cruel and unusual punishments," Brennan emphasized, embodied "in unique degree moral principles restraining the punishments that our civilized society may impose on those persons who transgress its laws."[496]

Brennan believed that constitutional provisions erect a moral code of behavior which the Court was bound to apply to the citizenry. He did not perceive this as discretion to impose a value judgment on the nation; rather, Brennan maintained that the Court "inescapably has the duty, as the ultimate arbiter of the meaning of our Constitution, to say whether . . . 'moral concepts' require us to hold that . . . [particular] punishments . . . [are] no longer morally tolerable in our civilized society."[497] These standards of morality, Brennan argued, are not derived from the justices' personal perception of civility but rather are contained in the principles of the Bill of Rights.

Brennan's position indicated that morality is an integral component of constitutional adjudication, and that its application may be counter to the sentiments of the majority. The Court's role, Brennan believed, is not to merely endorse public opinion but rather to embark the nation on a moral plane embodied in the aspirational tone of the Eighth Amendment.

---

490.   *See* Charles L. Black, Jr., *Due Process for Death:* Jurek v. Texas *and Companion Cases*, 26 CATH. U. L. REV. 1 (1976); L.S. Tao, *The Constitutional Status of Capital Punishment: An Analysis of* Gregg, Jurek, Roberts, *and* Woodson, 54 U. DET. J. URB. L. 345 (1977); Murchison, *supra* note 305, at 491-508.

491.   428 U.S. at 153.

492.   *Id.* at 227-31 (Brennan, J., dissenting).

493.   *Id. See also Roberts*, 428 U.S. at 325, 336 (Brennan, J., concurring).

494.   *Gregg*, 428 U.S. at 153, 227 (quoting Trop v. Dulles, 356 U.S. 86, 101 (1958)).

495.   428 U.S. at 229.

496.   *Id.*

497.   *Id.*

D. *Brennan Unwaveringly Continues to Oppose Capital Punishment (1977-1990)*

The Court's recognition, in *Gregg*, of the constitutionality of capital punishment,[498] and its indication that statutes which make a careful effort to confine the discretion of jurors would be upheld,[499] appeared to give states considerable flexibility in revising procedural provisions. The lack of clarity displayed in *Gregg* and its companion cases,[500] however, left uncertainty as to what types of capital trial proceedings would be deemed constitutional, and, between 1977 and 1990, Brennan's last thirteen years on the bench, the Court decided 63 cases on the death penalty — 31 from 1977 up to the retirement of Chief Justice Warren Burger in 1986,[501] and 32 during the first four Terms of the Rehnquist Court in which Brennan served.[502] The most frequent issue examined by the Court was the weighing by jurors of aggravating and mitigating circumstances. Of 18 cases[503] dealing with this subject, Brennan wrote an opinion on five occasions,[504] and, in a brief concurring statement, reiterated his categorical opposition to capital punishment in five others.[505] His first lengthy opinion on consideration of aggravating and mitigating factors,

---

498.   *See supra* text accompanying note 303.

499.   *See supra* text accompanying notes 284-305.

500.   *Id.*

501.   *See supra* note 322.

502.   *See supra* notes 337-40 (*Cage*, 498 U.S. at 39, and *Shell*, 498 U.S. at 1, were decided after Brennan's retirement).

503.   *See supra* note 352 (*Parker*, 498 U.S. at 308, and *Shell*, 498 U.S. at 1, were decided after Brennan left the bench).

504.   Walton v. Arizona, 497 U.S. 639, *reh'g denied*, 490 U.S. 1050 (1990) (Brennan, J., dissenting); Saffle v. Parks, 494 U.S. 484 (1990) (Brennan, J., dissenting); Blystone v. Pennsylvania, 494 U.S. 299 (1990) (Brennan, J., dissenting); Penry v. Lynaugh, 492 U.S. 302 (1989) (Brennan, J., concurring in part and dissenting in part); McCleskey v. Kemp, 481 U.S. 279, *reh'g denied*, 482 U.S. 920 (1987) (Brennan, J., dissenting).

505.   Clemons v. Mississippi, 494 U.S. 738, 755 (1990) (Brennan, J., concurring); Hildwin v. Florida, 490 U.S. 638, 640, *reh'g denied*, 492 U.S. 927 (1989) (Brennan, J., concurring); Maynard v. Cartwright, 486 U.S. 356, 366 (1988) (Brennan, J., concurring); Mills v. Maryland, 486 U.S. 367, 389 (1988) (Brennan, J., concurring); Johnson v. Mississippi, 486 U.S. 578, 591 (1988) (Brennan, J., concurring); Eddings v. Oklahoma, 455 U.S. 104, 117 (1982) (Brennan, J., concurring). In these cases Brennan wrote a two or three sentence concurring statement expressing, at the outset, support of the majority's judgment, and typically ending with the following declaration: "Adhering to my view that the death penalty is in all circumstances cruel and unusual punishment prohibited by the Eighth and Fourteenth Amendments [citation omitted], I would direct that the resentencing proceedings be circumscribed such that the State may not reimpose the death sentence." *Mills*, 486 U.S. 367, 389.

and the possibility of racial bias in pronouncing a verdict, did not appear until the 1987 case of *McCleskey v. Kemp*.[506]

The *McCleskey* petitioner was a black man convicted for the murder of a white police officer.[507] Though statutorily eligible to receive the death penalty for failing to furnish any mitigating evidence, McCleskey, based on a study by University of Iowa law professor David Baldus and associates,[508] argued that there was a disparity in Georgia between the percentage of black and white murderers sentenced to death and the frequency with which the death penalty is inflicted for the murder of black and white individuals.[509] McCleskey also contended that sentencing of capital defendants is racially discriminatory in violation of the equal protection clause of the Fourteenth Amendment.[510] Without questioning the legitimacy of the Baldus study, the Court, by a 5-4 vote, concluded that an individual must prove discrimination in

---

Brennan on several occasions expressed this sentiment in cases which did not focus on the weighing by jurors of aggravating and mitigating circumstances. *See, e.g.*, Cabana v. Bullock, 474 U.S. 376 (1986) (Brennan, J., dissenting), and Enmund v. Florida, 458 U.S. 782 (1982) (Brennan, J., concurring) (addressing death penalty for accomplices); Green v. Georgia, 442 U.S. 95 (1979) (Brennan, J., concurring) (involving introduction of testimony furnished at one trial in separate proceedings of an accomplice); Gardner v. Florida, 430 U.S. 349 (1977) (Brennan, J., concurring) (furnishing an accused a parole commission's presentence report); Dobbert v. Florida, 432 U.S. 282, *reh'g denied*, 434 U.S. 882 (1977) (Brennan, J., dissenting) (involving conviction of a capital defendant following judicial invalidation of applicable statutory provisions); Coker v. Georgia, 433 U.S. 584 (1977) (Brennan, J., concurring) (considering death penalty for rape).

506.   481 U.S. 279, *reh'g denied*, 482 U.S. 920 (1987).

507.   *Id.* at 283.

508.   *See supra* note 213. Examining over 2000 murder cases in Georgia during the 1970s, Baldus et al. discovered a pattern in capital sentencing based on the race of the victim and the defendant. They concluded that "defendants charged with killing white persons received the death penalty in 11% of the cases, but defendants charged with killing blacks received the death penalty in only 1% of the cases;" that "the death penalty was assessed in 22% of the cases involving black defendants and white victims; 8% of the cases involving white defendants and white victims; 1% of the cases involving black defendants and black victims; and 3% of the cases involving white defendants and black victims;" that "prosecutors sought the death penalty in 70% of the cases involving black defendants and white victims; 32% of the cases involving white defendants and white victims; 15% of the cases involving black defendants and black victims; and 1% of the cases involving white defendants and black victims;" and that "defendants charged with killing white victims were 4.3 times as likely to receive a death sentence as defendants charged with killing blacks," while "black defendants were 1.1 times as likely to receive a death sentence as other defendants." *McCleskey*, 481 U.S. at 286.

509.   *McCleskey*, 481 U.S. at 286.

510.   *Id.*

his own case, rather than citing statewide statistical trends, to demonstrate an equal protection violation and discriminatory application of a state statute.[511]

At the outset of his dissenting opinion, Brennan reiterated his categorical opposition to capital punishment.[512] The Baldus study underscored the validity of objections to capital punishment which Brennan put forward in *Furman*.[513] Brennan disagreed with the majority's contention that it was necessary for the defendant to prove that he was personally subjected to discriminatory treatment; in its examination of capital proceedings, the Court, he emphasized, "has been concerned with the *risk* of the imposition of an arbitrary sentence, rather than the proven fact of one."[514] He believed that this had been amply demonstrated by the Baldus study, which "relentlessly documents" that "there is a better than even chance in Georgia that race will influence the decision to impose the death penalty. . . ."[515]

More fundamentally, Brennan believed that the Baldus study confirmed the inherent arbitrariness of capital trial proceedings, based in large part on historically entrenched discrimination in state penal codes which has persisted to the present time. After briefly reviewing statutory provisions, dating back to the colonial period, which punished as capital offenses commit-

---

511.   *Id.* at 306-07. For an analysis of the *McCleskey* case while it was under review in the lower federal courts, see Fredric J. Bendremer et al., McCleskey v. Kemp: *Constitutional Tolerance for Racially Disparate Capital Sentencing*, 41 U. MIAMI L. REV. 295 (1986). For an examination of the Court's ruling, see Randall L. Kennedy, McCleskey v. Kemp: *Race, Capital Punishment, and the Supreme Court*, 101 HARV. L. REV. 1388 (1988).

512.   *McCleskey*, 481 U.S. at 320.

513.   *Furman*, 408 U.S. at 305. *See also supra* text accompanying notes 421-24.

514.   *McCleskey*, 481 U.S. at 322 (emphasis in original).

515.   *Id.* at 328. After examining the statistical evidence put forward in the Baldus study, Brennan concluded that "blacks who kill whites are sentenced to death at nearly *22 times* the rate of blacks who kill blacks, and more than 7 *times* the rate of whites who kill blacks." *McCleskey*, 481 U.S. at 327 (emphasis in original). By the time *McCleskey* was decided, several studies indicating a lingering pattern of racial disparities in capital sentencing had been published. *See, e.g.* Steven D. Arkin, *Discrimination and Arbitrariness in Capital Punishment: An Analysis of Post-*Furman *Murder Cases in Dade County, Florida, 1973-1976,"* 33 STAN. L. REV. 75 (1980); Arnold Barnett, *Some Distribution Patterns for the Georgia Death Sentence*, 18 U.C. DAVIS L. REV. 1327 (1985); Ursula Bentele, *The Death Penalty in Georgia: Still Arbitrary*, 62 WASH. U. L.Q. 573 (1985); Samuel R. Gross, *Race and Death: The Judicial Evaluation of Evidence of Discrimination in Capital Sentencing*, 18 U.C. DAVIS L. REV. 1275 (1985); Michael L. Radelet & Glenn L. Pierce, *Race and Prosecutorial Discretion in Homicide Cases*, 19 LAW & SOC'Y REV. 587 (1985).

ted by blacks but not by whites,[516] Brennan observed that Georgia has operated under the "legacy of a race-conscious criminal justice system."[517] The Court, he pointed out, has always been cognizant of the magnitude of capital as opposed to noncapital proceedings, and has accordingly placed the burden on the state, rather than the accused, to demonstrate that sentencing has not been arbitrarily conducted. While "every nuance of decision cannot be statistically captured,"[518] the totality of circumstances, measured in large part by the political and social environment which has shaped a state's criminal justice system, compelled rejection of a sentence in capital cases where there existed any indication that arbitrariness has infected — much less permeated — deliberations.

Brennan did not believe that arbitrariness could be removed from capital proceedings. The number of subjective considerations which characterized the trial of capital defendants "provides considerable opportunity for racial considerations, however subtle and unconscious, to influence charging and sentencing decisions."[519] Brennan seemed to indicate that trial participants are incapable of overcoming racial bias, both individual and societal, regardless of the elaborateness of statutory procedural protections, and that, in view of the enormity of capital punishment, the only realistic alternative is prohibition of this penalty.

Brennan's position in McCleskey was that a defendant's culpability is to be assessed in light of the perceived social environment which has affected comparably situated litigants. The death penalty, an expression of society's moral degradation, can never be acceptable regardless of how extensive a range of procedural protections may have been available to a defendant, and, Brennan believed, the mere existence of this punishment constituted abridgment of a constitutional commitment to respect the humanity of each individual. Brennan was not primarily concerned with the treatment McCleskey received; indeed, other than citing the Baldus study to allege an ongoing pattern of racial discrimination in capital sentencing,[520] the petitioner did not challenge his opportunity to offer mitigating evidence. Arguably, then, Georgia's treatment of McCleskey fulfilled the Court's earlier pronouncements that each defendant in a capital case should be treated "with that degree of respect due the uni-

---

516.   McCleskey, 481 U.S. at 329-30.
517.   Id. at 328.
518.   Id. at 335.
519.   Id. at 334.
520.   Id. at 291-92, 299.

queness of the individual,"[521] and that there must be "particular-ized consideration of relevant aspects of the character and record of each convicted defendant."[522] Brennan, however, believed that any indication of racial disparity in sentencing patterns compromised the objectivity of individual trial deliberations, and rendered a guilty verdict suspect, and thus unconstitutional. He objected that Georgia "provides juries with no list of aggravating and mitigating factors, nor any standard for balancing them against one another;"[523] however, no enumeration, or degree of explicitness, would have been sufficient for Brennan to render McCleskey's sentence valid.

Aside from the majority's willingness to sustain the constitutionality of capital punishment, the most fervent objection expressed by Brennan in *McCleskey* was that the Court failed to adhere to precedents. Specifically, Brennan believed that the underpinning of *Lockett v. Ohio*[524] — where the Court maintained that any mitigating factor raised by the defendant had to be examined by jurors[525] — was ignored in *McCleskey* by refusing to consider the allegedly racially biased environment in which capital trials proceeded. His perception that the Rehnquist Court was too willing to recognize considerable state discretion in administering the death penalty without carefully assessing adherence by jurors to due process requirements established in precedents was evident in three dissenting opinions written in the 1990 cases of *Walton v. Arizona,*[526] *Saffle v. Parks,*[527] and *Blystone v. Pennsylvania.*[528]

All three of these cases examined whether statutory provisions precluded giving full consideration to mitigating evidence. In *Walton,* the Court held that an aggravating circumstance requiring the trial judge to determine whether an alleged offense was "especially heinous, cruel, or depraved,"[529] sufficiently channeled the sentencing authority's discretion and facilitated concentration on aspects of the defendant's background and alleged

---

521.   Lockett v. Ohio, 438 U.S. 586, 605 (1978).

522.   Woodson v. North Carolina, 428 U.S. 280, 303 (1976).

523.   *McCleskey,* 481 U.S. at 333.

524.   438 U.S. 586 (1978).

525.   *See supra* text accompanying note 311.

526.   497 U.S. 639, 674 (1990), *reh'g denied,* 497 U.S. 1050 (1990) (Brennan, J., dissenting). Brennan indicated that his objections also applied to Lewis v. Jeffers, 497 U.S. 764, 784, *reh'g denied,* 497 U.S. 1050 (1990) (Brennan, J., joining the dissenting opinion of Blackmun, J.).

527.   494 U.S. 484, 495 (1990) (Brennan, J., dissenting).

528.   494 U.S. 299, 309 (1990) (Brennan, J., dissenting).

529.   *Walton,* 497 U.S. at 643 (citing ARIZ. REV. STAT. ANN. § 13-703(F)(6) (1989)).

actions which most directly related to culpability. The extent to which a jury's ability to examine mitigating evidence may have been undermined was also at issue in *Saffle*, where the majority ruled that a judge's instructions that the jurors "avoid any influence of sympathy, sentiment, passion, prejudice, or other arbitrary factor when imposing sentence,"[530] did not undermine consideration of mitigating factors. The judge, pointed out the Court, merely cautioned members to refrain from basing a sentencing decision "on the vagaries of particular jurors' emotional sensitivities"[531] without impairing the jurors' ability to consider mitigating evidence. Broad discretion to administer capital statutory provisions was also recognized in *Blystone*, where a Pennsylvania statute which stipulated that the "verdict must be a sentence of death if the jury unanimously finds at least one aggravating circumstance . . . and no mitigating circumstance or if the jury unanimously finds one or more aggravating circumstances which outweigh any mitigating circumstances,"[532] was held as sufficiently confining the range of factors to be considered by sentencing authorities. In all three cases the Court emphasized that the impossibility of devising precise rules to be followed in capital trials compelled examination of proceedings in totality to assess whether fairness has been accorded to the accused.

Brennan objected in all three cases that the Court allowed sentencing authorities to issue verdicts without fully examining the individual circumstances of the accused. His brief dissent in *Walton* expressed concern that the Court, by upholding ambiguously worded aggravating circumstances, enabled states "to execute prisoners with as little interference as possible from our established Eighth Amendment doctrine"[533] which compelled consideration of the particular situation of an accused.[534] While the majority believed that the absence of proof that jurors were improperly instructed established the validity of trial proceedings, Brennan argued that the existence of imprecise phrasing in statutory provisions rendered a verdict unconstitutional on its face by making possible introduction and consideration of extraneous matters.

---

530. *Saffle*, 494 U.S. at 487.
531. *Id.* at 493.
532. *Blystone*, 494 U.S. at 302 (quoting 42 Pa. Cons. Stat. § 9711(C)(1)(iv) (1988)).
533. *Walton*, 497 U.S. at 676-77.
534. Brennan cited precedents in *Furman*, 408 U.S. 238; *Gregg*, 428 U.S. 153; *Woodson*, 428 U.S. 280; *Eddings*, 455 U.S. 104. He also cited *Walton*, 497 U.S. at 675-76 (Brennan, J., dissenting).

Brennan's concern that the Court was departing from guide-lines put forward in precedents was more extensively addressed in *Saffle*. Comparable to his position in *McCleskey*, which expressed apprehension that the Court was abandoning its tradi-tional concern for the prospect of discriminatory action in light of the general environment of trial proceedings,[535] Brennan argued in *Saffle* that, irrespective of evidence indicating arbitrary proceeding against an accused, the mere possibility that this may occur with ambiguous wording of aggravating and mitigating cir-cumstances was sufficient to invalidate a conviction. Agreeing with the respondent's contention that the judge's instructions to jurors to reach a verdict without being influenced by personal biases[536] "could have [been] *interpreted* . . . as barring considera-tion of mitigating evidence,"[537] Brennan maintained that full examination of the character and circumstances of the accused was precluded. This violated the express command of *Lockett v. Ohio*[538] and *Eddings v. Oklahoma*,[539] both of which mandated that "a jury may not be prohibited from considering and giving effect to all relevant mitigating evidence when deciding whether to impose the death penalty."[540] Brennan also disagreed with the majority's contention that these precedents merely required an opportunity to introduce mitigating evidence without addressing how it is to be examined. This distinction, Brennan insisted, is "meaningless" in that "a rule that limits the *manner* in which the jury considers mitigating evidence is unconstitutional if it limits the jury's ability to consider and give effect to that evidence."[541] Brennan concluded that, in all likelihood, the jury "interpreted the antisympathy instruction as a command to ignore the mitigat-ing evidence."[542]

A fundamental concern of Brennan's was that the Court might shift the burden of proof to the accused. He sensed that the majority's "growing displeasure with the litigation of capital cases on collateral review"[543] encouraged deference to proceed-ings which may not have explicitly based a verdict and sentence on an arbitrary factor but which operated in an atmosphere which did not foreclose this possibility. This, Brennan con-

---

535. *See supra* text accompanying notes 514-18.
536. *See supra* text accompanying note 530.
537. *Saffle*, 494 U.S. at 498-99 (emphasis in original).
538. 438 U.S. 586 (1978).
539. 455 U.S. 104 (1982).
540. *Saffle*, 494 U.S. at 499-500.
541. *Id.* at 504 (emphasis in original).
542. *Id.* at 508.
543. *Id.* at 507.

tended, "denied an individualized sentencing determination as required by the Eighth Amendment."[544]

In addition to the method by which a judge communicated instructions to the jury, Brennan believed that preserving the individualized element of sentencing proceedings required examination of aggravating and mitigating factors and giving greater weight to those deemed compelling. This may be circumvented by an arrangement, presented in *Blystone*,[545] which enabled jurors to reach a verdict without having to consider mitigating evidence.[546] A jury which, at the outset of deliberations, has unanimously found an aggravating circumstance, may "end the decisionmaking process"[547] by claiming that the need to examine possible mitigating factors has been precluded. Unlike the majority in *Blystone*, which believed that constitutional requirements are met by furnishing a forum to examine, in varying degrees, aggravating and mitigating circumstances, Brennan maintained that prevention of arbitrariness required the Court to ascertain whether both types of evidence have been introduced and considered.

Brennan insisted that prevention of arbitrariness in capital sentencing required careful examination of all phases of trial proceedings. This was especially important with regard to jury deliberations; jurors who are improperly empaneled or instructed, or compelled to listen to prejudicial comments of a judge or prosecutor, are unlikely to apply even the most comprehensive statutory provisions in an unbiased manner. On behalf of the majority, Brennan addressed the manner in which instructions are communicated to the jury in the 1979 case of *Sandstrom v. Montana*.[548]

The *Sandstrom* case examined instructions to the jury to presume that "a person intends the ordinary consequences of his voluntary acts."[549] Speculating that the likelihood of conviction would increase, Brennan declared that this command in effect shifted to the defendant the burden of proving that he was mentally incapable of comprehending the magnitude of his alleged crime, and unconstitutionally relieved the state of having to establish guilt beyond a reasonable doubt.[550] Whether the jury actually formed biases on the culpability of the accused was

---

544. *Id.* at 508.
545. 494 U.S. 299.
546. *See supra* text accompanying note 532.
547. *Blystone*, 494 U.S. at 322.
548. 442 U.S. 510 (1979).
549. *Id.* at 512.
550. *Id.* at 513.

immaterial for Brennan, who maintained that its mere possibility rendered proceedings invalid.

Six years after the *Sandstrom* ruling, the Court, in *Francis v. Franklin* (1985),[551] once again considered whether jury instructions conceivably enabled members to make unsubstantiated inferences regarding the motives of an accused. The *Francis* case dealt with jury instructions stating in part that "[t]he acts of a person of sound mind and discretion are presumed to be the product of the person's will, but the presumption may be rebutted."[552] Relying on the position in *Sandstrom*, Brennan, on behalf of the majority, again held that this instruction unconstitutionally relieved the state of its burden of proving the charges against the accused.

Brennan examined whether the tone of the instructions imparted a "mandatory presumption" that the jury "must infer the presumed fact if the State proves certain predicate facts,"[553] or a "permissive inference" that jurors may draw "a possible conclusion . . . if the State proves predicate facts,"[554] but are not compelled to do so. While the state argued that communication to the jurors that a presumption of voluntariness "may be rebutted"[555] compelled trial participants, if the accused presented an appropriate challenge, to establish guilt beyond a reasonable doubt, Brennan emphasized that instructions to the jury must be construed not by taking words "in isolation" but by examining "the potentially offending words . . . in the context of the charge as a whole."[556] He believed that the instructions were "cast in the language of command"[557] in that the trial judge did not explain that jurors were not obligated to construe failure by the accused to satisfactorily prove that the alleged offense was unintended as a presumption of guilt. This, Brennan believed, diminished the jury's perception of its responsibility to independently establish guilt or innocence. Brennan also rejected arguments that other aspects of the instructions to the jury — that the state was required to prove "the defendant's guilt as charged . . . beyond a reasonable doubt;"[558] that a person "will not be presumed to act with criminal intention;"[559] and that a jury "may find criminal

---

551. 471 U.S. 307 (1985).
552. *Id.* at 311.
553. *Id.* at 314.
554. *Id.*
555. *See supra* text accompanying note 552.
556. *Francis*, 471 U.S. at 315.
557. *Id.* at 316.
558. *Id.* at 319 n.6.
559. *Id.* at 319.

intention upon a consideration of the words, conduct, demeanor, motive and all other circumstances connected with the act for which the accused is prosecuted;"[560] — compelled it to establish guilt beyond a reasonable doubt. Jurors, he concluded, were compelled to deliberate with ambiguous and contradictory instructions which may diminish their sense of responsibility.

In both *Sandstrom* and *Francis*, Brennan was concerned not primarily with specific actions of sentencing authorities but rather with the environment in which trial proceedings were conducted. In the 1987 case of *California v. Brown*,[561] Brennan once again elaborated on the affect jury instructions may have on consideration of a range of possible mitigating factors.

The *Brown* case focused on instructions during the penalty stage that the jury must not "be swayed by 'mere sentiment, conjecture, sympathy, passion, prejudice, public opinion or public feeling'"[562] in its deliberations. Believing that this directive confined jury discretion "by cautioning it against reliance on extraneous emotional factors"[563] which have no bearing on the culpability of the accused, the majority concluded that appropriate guidance had been furnished. Brennan, in dissent, argued that this wording, and the tone of its communication, discouraged jurors from examining a wide range of mitigating circumstances. Citing precedent in *Lockett v. Ohio*,[564] where the majority directed that any mitigating factors introduced by the defendant must be considered,[565] Brennan declared that instructions which leave a jury "unclear as to whether it may consider such evidence"[566] are invalid. This, he believed, was evident by the wording of the instruction. For example, what kind of "sympathy" is the jury to disregard? How does one distinguish adverse circumstances which a defendant may have endured from subjective emotions which have no relationship to the offense or alleged offender? Citing *Eddings v. Oklahoma*,[567] where the Court overturned a conviction on the ground that all pertinent mitigating evidence had not been considered,[568] Brennan maintained that

---

560. *Id.* at 320.
561. 479 U.S. 538 (1987) (Brennan, J., dissenting).
562. *Id.* at 542.
563. *Id.* at 543.
564. 438 U.S. 586 (1978).
565. *See supra* text accompanying note 311.
566. California v. Brown, 479 U.S. 538, 547 (1987) (Brennan, J., dissenting).
567. 455 U.S. 104 (1982).
568. Eddings, a sixteen-year-old defendant convicted of murder, introduced evidence concerning physical abuse by his father and neglect by his

instructions must be clearly worded and explained to make clear the kinds of testimony which is relevant to a defendant's circumstances. After examining state precedents dating back to 1970,[569] Brennan observed a pattern in which jurors had not been clearly instructed as to what kinds of mitigating evidence are impertinent, and concluded that this trend has persisted in *Brown.*

Unlike the majority, which could find no evidence that the instructions had been misconstrued and thus no justification to rule that an unlawful conviction had occurred, Brennan, as he had maintained in *Sandstrom* and *Francis,* declared that its mere possibility warranted invalidation of trial proceedings. The potential for diminution of due process safeguards, apart from its actual occurrence, was his underlying focus. This concern was also apparent in cases dealing with empaneling of jurors, which was first addressed in the 1968 case of *Witherspoon v. Illinois,*[570] and examined by the Burger Court twelve years later in *Adams v. Texas.*[571]

The *Adams* case addressed a statutory provision which provided that a prospective juror would be excluded unless the individual could state under oath "that the mandatory penalty of death[572] or imprisonment for life would not affect his deliberations on any issue of fact."[573] The Court struck down the oath requirement[574] on the belief that a jury likely to be composed of individuals firmly against or in favor of capital punishment would bias the verdict and result in a jury unrepresentative of a cross

---

alcoholic mother. Stating that statutory provisions precluded consideration of this evidence, the trial judge ruled that the aggravating circumstances outweighed mitigating factors. The Court declared that full consideration of mitigating evidence had not taken place, and struck down the death sentence. *Id.* at 114-15. Brennan wrote a concurring statement. *Id.* at 117. *See also,* Beck v. Alabama, 447 U.S. 625 (1980) (Brennan, J., concurring). Brennan wrote a brief statement joining the majority opinion but reiterating his categorical opposition to capital punishment. *Id.* at 646.

569. Brown, 479 U.S. at 552-55. Brennan cited People v. Walker, 711 P.2d 465 (1985); People v. Robertson, 655 P.2d 279 (1982); and People v. Bandhauser, 463 P.2d 408 (1970).

570. 391 U.S. 510 (1968).

571. 448 U.S. 38 (1980).

572. Texas statutes provided for a bifurcated capital trial. If a jury in the second stage of the trial answered "yes" to three questions — "(1) whether the defendant's conduct causing the death at issue was deliberate, (2) whether the defendant's conduct in the future would constitute a continuing threat to society, and (3) whether his conduct in killing the victim was unreasonable in response to the victim's provocation, if any" — a death sentence was mandatory. *Id.*

573. *Id.* at 42.

574. *Id.* at 49-51.

section of the community.[575] Instead of asking whether automatic imposition of the death penalty might affect their performance, jurors, the Court ruled, should have been asked whether they would follow the trial judge's instructions. While a state may continue to excuse potential jurors who declared that they would automatically vote against the death penalty regardless of evidence presented, the Court emphasized that persons opposed to capital punishment may not be excluded unless their views would impair performance of their duties as stipulated by an oath.[576]

Brennan, concurring in *Adams*,[577] wrote a brief statement reiterating his categorical opposition to capital punishment.[578] He did, however, express his views on empaneling jurors in capital trials in two cases — *Wainwright v. Witt*[579] and *Turner v. Murray*[580] — which examined the applicability of the *Witherspoon* and *Adams* pronouncements.

The *Wainwright* case examined procedures under which prospective jurors may be excluded and considered standards to be followed by federal courts in assessing challenges of a trial judge's disqualification order. Respondent Johnny Paul Witt argued that three of eleven prospective jurors, after alluding to religious reservations against the death penalty, and responding affirmatively to the prosecutor's question that this would "interfere with judging the guilt or innocence"[581] of the accused, were improperly excluded.

Citing precedents in *Witherspoon v. Illinois*[582] and *Adams v. Texas*,[583] the majority pointed out that, unlike a potential juror who expressed personal reservations about capital punishment, one who claimed that opposition to the death penalty would inhibit reaching a verdict of guilty irrespective of the validity of

---

575.   *Id.* at 43-45. For an examination, prior to the *Adams* decision, of the perceived effect of questions concerning attitudes toward capital punishment on the objectivity of juries, see *supra* note 263. For an analysis of issues raised by the Adams v. Texas ruling, see Claudia L. Cowan et al., *The Effects of Death Qualification on Jurors' Predisposition to Convict and On the Quality of Deliberations*, 8 L. & HUM. BEHAV. 53 (1984); Michael Finch & Mark Ferraro, *The Empirical Challenge to Death- Qualified Juries: On Further Examination*, 65 NEB. L. REV. 21 (1986); Samuel R. Gross, *Determining the Neutrality of Death- Qualified Juries: Judicial Appraisal of Empirical Data*, 8 L. & HUM. BEHAV. 7 (1984).
576.   *Adams*, 448 U.S. at 50.
577.   *Id.* at 51.
578.   *See supra* note 505.
579.   469 U.S. 412, 439 (1985) (Brennan, J., dissenting).
580.   476 U.S. 28, 38 (1986) (Brennan, J., concurring in part and dissenting in part).
581.   469 U.S. at 416.
582.   391 U.S. 510 (1968). *See supra* text accompanying notes 260-63.
583.   448 U.S. 38 (1980). *See supra* text accompanying notes 572-76.

incriminating evidence which may be presented, violated the Sixth Amendment's command for trial by an "impartial jury."[584] This, the majority declared, cannot be ascertained with "'unmistakable clarity';"[585] a trial judge, unable to absolutely conclude whether a prospective juror would permit personal biases to affect consideration of evidence and pronouncement of a verdict, must be accorded discretion to ask a range of questions in seeking to assess possible objectivity, and federal appellate judges, in examining a petition for habeas corpus, are to adopt a "'presumption of correctness'" regarding a state court determination on the "'factual issues'"[586] presented during voir dire.

Brennan, in dissent, objected that the Court conferred too wide a range of discretion on trial judges to exclude potential jurors. Disagreeing with the majority's position that *Witherspoon* did not preclude judges from asking a range of questions on the attitudes of potential jurors toward capital punishment to more fully determine whether they would likely reach a verdict based on an objective weighing of evidence, Brennan maintained that this ruling,[587] along with *Adams*,[588] prevented judges from inquiring into areas which had no bearing on the potential jurors' fitness to discharge obligations set forth in the oath. "Exclusion of those opposed to capital punishment," Brennan pointed out, "keeps an identifiable class of people off the jury in capital cases and is likely systematically to bias juries."[589] This, Brennan believed, would occur if there were exclusion of potential jurors "whose views [on capital punishment] would simply make these tasks [concerning abidance to an oath] more psychologically or emotionally difficult,"[590] whose "responses to death-qualification inquiries are ambiguous or vacillating,"[591] or who "do not know at voir dire whether their views about the death penalty will prevent them abiding by their oaths at trial."[592] In short, Brennan argued that the majority diminished the significance of *Witherspoon's* prohibition against exclusion "of the ambiguous, evasive, or uncertain juror."[593]

---

584. *See supra* note 253.

585. *Wainwright*, 469 U.S. at 424.

586. *Id.* at 426. (interpreting 28 U.S.C. § 2254(D)).

587. Witherspoon v. Illinois, 391 U.S. 510 (1968). *See supra* text accompanying notes 260-63.

588. *See supra* text accompanying notes 572-76.

589. 448 U.S. at 38; *Wainwright*, 469 U.S. at 442.

590. *Id.* at 443.

591. *Id.* at 444.

592. *Id.*

593. *Id.* at 445.

Fundamentally, Brennan believed that the Court had departed from its precedents insisting that the discretion of trial participants be confined to prevent infusion of arbitrariness. Acknowledging a broad range of discretion by the trial judge to examine and exclude potential jurors on their views toward capital punishment, and discouraging federal appellate courts from questioning assessments regarding fitness to serve,[594] Brennan maintained, diminished the Court's earlier insistence on stricter standards of due process in capital proceedings.[595] This, Brennan maintained, reduced the risk that the " 'overzealous prosecutor and . . . the compliant, biased, or eccentric judge' "[596] may, particularly when "elected, or when they harbor political ambitions,"[597] work to obtain convictions.

Brennan concluded with a denunciation of the Court's increasing insensitiveness to compelling procedural safeguards relied on by defendants in capital trials. He decried the majority's unwillingness to hold sentencing authorities to strict standards, and declared that the Court "increasingly acts as the adjunct of the State and its prosecutors in facilitating efficient and expedient conviction and execution irrespective of the Constitution's fundamental guarantees."[598]

Brennan's opinion in *Wainwright* presented a dilemma for trial judges. On the one hand, Brennan did not wish to accord a trial judge unconfined discretion to question prospective jurors, which potentially may result in disqualification of those who expressed ambivalent positions on capital punishment, or who revealed attitudes toward crime and heinous offenders incompatible with the judge's personal beliefs; at the same time, Brennan's desire for an unbiased jury may induce a judge to ask a range of questions touching on the circumstances of an accused, and thereby compelling elicitation of testimony which has no bearing on one's fitness to discharge an oath. This prospect was presented in the 1986 case of *Turner v. Murray*,[599] which dealt with an alleged murder committed by a black defendant in Virginia. The jury, consisting of eight whites and four blacks, had not been told during empaneling that the victim was white. The

---

594. See *id.* at 426-29 for the discussion of discretion on habeas review in the majority opinion.

595. *Id.* at 454 (citing Eddings v. Oklahoma, 455 U.S. 104 (1982), and Woodson v. North Carolina, 428 U.S. 280 (1976)).

596. *Wainwright*, 469 U.S. at 459 (quoting Duncan v. Louisiana, 391 U.S. 145 (1968)).

597. *Wainwright*, 469 U.S. at 459.

598. *Id.* at 463.

599. 476 U.S. 28 (1986).

majority ruled that, to ensure trial by an impartial jury, "a capital defendant accused of an interracial crime is entitled to have prospective jurors informed of the race of the victim and questioned on the issue of racial bias."[600]

Brennan, concurring and dissenting in part, declared that the "reality of race relations in this country is such that we simply may not presume impartiality,"[601] and supported questioning of potential jurors on possible racial overtones of an alleged offense. He disagreed, however, with the majority's vacating of the petitioner's death sentence without ordering a retrial on the issue of guilt.[602] The "*risk* of bias," Brennan argued, is not less compelling than the "*consequences* of bias," both of which may be displayed by a jury "at a guilt trial and . . . at a sentencing hearing. . . ."[603] Thus, Brennan declared, the conviction, as well as the sentence itself, should be vacated.[604]

Brennan emphasized that the Sixth Amendment's protection of trial by an impartial jury required judges "to strike those jurors who manifest an inability to try the case solely on the basis of the evidence."[605] This, the Court pointed out in *Witherspoon* and *Adams*, confined judges to inquire as to whether prospective jurors could discharge an oath based on the weight of evidence and irrespective of their personal views on capital punishment.[606] Arguably, requiring judges to determine whether a prospective juror embraced racial biases violated the pronouncements of *Witherspoon* and *Adams* in that this, in the abstract, did not implicate one's ability to reach a verdict with a specific accused based on evidence presented. The Court's pronouncement may result in the disqualification of potential jurors who give an ambiguous response to questions on racial bias — which Brennan opposed with regard to questioning on one's support of, or opposition to, capital punishment.[607] In *Turner*, Brennan agreed that " 'essential demands of fairness' may require a judge to ask jurors whether they entertain any racial prejudice;"[608] however, unlike the majority, which did not foreclose inquiries into whether

---

600. *Id.* at 36-37.

601. *Id.* at 39.

602. *Id.*

603. *Id.* (emphasis in original).

604. *Id.* at 39-40.

605. *Id.* at 40.

606. Witherspoon v. Illinois, 391 U.S. 510 (1968); Adams v. Texas, 448 U.S. 38 (1980). *See supra* text accompanying notes 260-63, 571-76.

607. Wainwright v. Witt, 469 U.S. 412 (1985) (Brennan, J., dissenting). *See supra* text accompanying notes 587-93.

608. *Turner*, 476 U.S. at 40 (quoting Aldridge v. United States, 283 U.S. 308 (1931)).

potential jurors had stereotypes on the perceived behavior of blacks or the absence of racial parity,[609] Brennan confined questioning to whether "the race of either the victim or the accused will bear on . . . [jurors'] ability to render a decision *based solely on the evidence.*"[610] Brennan's position was more consistent with the tone of *Witherspoon* and *Adams* than that of the majority.

Brennan's insistence that the possibility of racial bias was no less present at the time a verdict of guilt or innocence is issued than during pronouncement of sentence underscored his belief that phases in capital proceedings are not separate and distinct components but rather are a comprehensive demonstration of a state's commitment to protection of civil liberties. The presence of racial bias, he maintained, "should be of [no] less concern at the guilt phase than at the sentencing phase"[611] in that a trial "to determine guilt or innocence is, at bottom, nothing more than the sum total of a countless number of small discretionary decisions made by each individual who sits in the jury box."[612] The totality of proceedings must be examined, and suspicion of racially biased deliberations in one part of a trial equally compromised objectivity in its earlier stages. As Brennan had pointed out in *Sandstrom, Franklin,* and *Brown,*[613] and strongly emphasized in *McCleskey v. Kemp,*[614] the possibility of jury bias, apart from its actual existence, compelled invalidation of trial proceedings.

Brennan's concern with potential abridgment of due process safeguards, which may occur in jury deliberations if racial biases preclude reaching a verdict based on an objective assessment of admissibility and applicability of evidence, was also apparent in other aspects of trial proceedings. In the 1984 case of *Strickland v. Washington,*[615] the Court for the first time established standards to determine whether a defendant had been effectively represented by counsel. A two-prong test had to be satisfied by an accused who challenged a conviction based on inadequate performance by a defense attorney. It stipulated that:

> First, the defendant must show that counsel's performance was deficient. This required showing that counsel made errors so serious that counsel was not functioning as the 'counsel' guaranteed the defendant by the Sixth Amend-

---

609. *Turner,* 476 U.S. at 35.
610. *Id.* at 41 (emphasis added).
611. *Id.* at 42.
612. *Id.*
613. *See supra* text accompanying notes 548-69.
614. 481 U.S. 279, 322 (1987); *see supra* text accompanying note 514.
615. 466 U.S. 668, *reh'g denied,* 467 U.S. 1267 (1984).

ment. Second, the defendant must show that the deficient performance prejudiced the defense. This requires showing that counsel's errors were so serious as to deprive the defendant of a fair trial, a trial whose result is reliable.[616]

The Court did not articulate what type of behavior by defense counsel needed to be exhibited for the defendant to prove inadequate representation, except to state that "[a]ctual or constructive denial of the assistance of counsel altogether is legally presumed to result in prejudice."[617] In effect, an accused somehow needed to furnish evidence that the outcome of the trial would have been different if not for the alleged improper actions or omissions by the defense attorney.

Brennan, concurring and dissenting in part, supported the majority's attempt to enable a defendant to prove negligence by a defense attorney, and believed that lower courts will receive "helpful guidance . . . [in] considering claims of actual ineffectiveness of counsel" and opportunities "to achieve progressive development of this area of the law."[618] However, Brennan believed that assessing performance of counsel should not be confined to the penalty stage. Mindful of the potential for violation of due process protections at any point in deliberations, Brennan emphasized that "capital proceedings [needed to] be policed at all stages by an especially vigilant concern for procedural fairness and for the accuracy of factfinding."[619] Conceding that varying circumstances and conceivable measures which a defense attorney may employ precluded erection of a "particular set of detailed rules for counsel's conduct,"[620] Brennan nevertheless insisted on holding a lawyer accountable for quality of representation at the time mitigating evidence is presented for determination of guilt or innocence. This, he believed, would "minimize the possibility" of a death sentence being " 'imposed out of whim, passion, prejudice, or mistake' "[621] by accentuating commitment to due process requirements throughout the developmental stages of capital proceedings.

Brennan's unwavering opposition to capital punishment, in part based on a perception that sufficiently extensive due process protections could not be formulated to prevent the risk of arbitrariness entering into proceedings, impelled him to address

---

616. *Strickland,* 466 U.S. at 687.
617. *Id.* at 692.
618. *Id.* at 702.
619. *Id.* at 704.
620. This was the phrase used by the majority opinion. *Id.* at 688.
621. *Id.* at 705 (quoting Eddings v. Oklahoma, 455 U.S. 104, 118 (1982) (O'Connor, J., concurring)).

stages of deliberations which the majority had not focused on. The tone of Brennan's opinion in *Strickland* was that the potential for abridgment of Bill of Rights protections needed to be anticipated to prevent conviction arising from denial of opportunities to introduce mitigating evidence or attempts to misrepresent the circumstances of the accused. This was reiterated by Brennan in the 1989 case of *South Carolina v. Gathers.*[622] In a brief opinion on behalf of the majority, Brennan invalidated, as irrelevant to the defendant's culpability and potentially distorting the jury's perception of aggravating and mitigating evidence, comments by the prosecutor on religious messages found on the person of the accused.[623] Irrespective of whether jurors were influenced by testimony pertaining to the defendant's alleged religious beliefs, the possibility that deliberations may have been diverted from the blameworthiness of the accused tainted proceedings and compelled reversal of a death sentence.

While Brennan's opinions on capital punishment tended to focus on procedural inadequacies, he never wavered from his *Furman* pronouncement that the death penalty was offensive to human dignity.[624] This sentiment induced him, in the late 1980s, to strongly oppose capital punishment for those — such as minors,[625] the mentally retarded,[626] and the insane[627] — who he believed were incapable of comprehending their behavior, as well as those who, arguably, could not be shown to be responsible for a homicide. The Court addressed the death penalty for accomplices in the 1982 case of *Enmund v. Florida*[628] and again four years later in *Cabana v. Bullock;*[629] in 1987, Brennan, dissenting in *Tison v. Arizona,*[630] first addressed this subject at length.[631]

---

622. 409 U.S. 805 (1989), *overruled by* Payne v. Tennessee, 111 S. Ct. 2597 (1991).
623. *Id.* at 2211. *See also* Booth v. Maryland, 482 U.S. 496, *reh'g denied*, 483 U.S. 1056 (1987), *overruled by* Payne v. Tennessee, 111 S. Ct. 2597 (1991).
624. *Furman*, 408 U.S. at 305. *See supra* text accompanying notes 452-53.
625. Stanford v. Kentucky, 492 U.S. 361 (1989) (Brennan, J., dissenting); Thompson v. Oklahoma, 487 U.S. 815 (1988) (Brennan, J., joining the majority opinion of Stevens, J.).
626. Penry v. Lynaugh, 492 U.S. 302 (1989) (Brennan, J., concurring in part and dissenting in part).
627. Ford v. Wainwright, 477 U.S. 399 (1986) (Brennan, J., joining the majority opinion of Marshall, J.). *See infra* text accompanying notes 880-91.
628. 458 U.S. 782 (1982).
629. 474 U.S. 376 (1986).
630. Tison v. Arizona, 481 U.S. 137, *reh'g denied*, 482 U.S. 921 (1987).
631. In *Enmund*, 458 U.S. at 782, and *Cabana*, 474 U.S. at 376, Brennan wrote brief statements confined to expressing his categorical opposition to capital punishment. *Enmund, id.* at 801 (Brennan, J., concurring); *Cabana, id.* at 393 (Brennan, J., dissenting).

The *Tison* case involved three sons who, following a successful attempt to help their father escape from prison, killed a driver and three passengers after the motorist, led to believe that the Tisons needed assistance, stopped to examine a flat tire. Though it was uncertain whether the entire Tison family was equally responsible for the killings, all were convicted of first-degree murder.

Modifying its earlier rulings in *Enmund* and *Cabana*, where the Court held that an accomplice did not sufficiently participate in the commission of murder to qualify for the death penalty,[632] a 5-4 majority declared in *Tison* that it was permissible for abettors "whose participation is major and whose mental state is one of reckless indifference to the value of human life"[633] to be sentenced to death. Given that only eleven of the thirty-seven states which authorized capital punishment prohibited its imposition for accomplices who significantly participated in the commission of murder, the Court concluded that its ruling is consistent with prevailing societal attitudes.[634]

The dissenting opinion written by Brennan criticized infliction of the death penalty on those whose degree of involvement in commission of murder cannot be precisely ascertained. After attempting to reconstruct the factual evidence, Brennan observed that it was impossible to assess which individuals were primarily or tangentially responsible for the murders,[635] and objected to the state statute for failing to articulate degrees of complicity among several individuals who are charged with homicide.[636]

Brennan strongly opposed the death penalty for accomplices as a "living fossil"[637] from a bygone period during which sentencing authorities summarily subjected all participants in a killing, however indirect or remote involvement of some may have been, to execution. This concept, Brennan maintained, is contrary to enlightened notions of justice followed "in most American jurisdictions and in virtually all European and Commonwealth countries" which refrain from executing an individual "for a murder that he or she did not commit or specifically intend or attempt to commit."[638]

---

632.   *Edmund,* 458 U.S. at 782; *Cabana,* 474 U.S. at 376.
633.   *Tison,* 481 U.S. at 152.
634.   *Id.* at 154.
635.   *Id.* at 164-68.
636.   *Id.* at 159.
637.   *Id.*
638.   *Id.* at 160.

Brennan objected to the Court's departure from precedent and its uneven application of principles established in Eighth Amendment jurisprudence. The position in *Enmund*,[639] which refused to support the death penalty for individuals whose degree of involvement in a homicide did not indicate an intention to kill,[640] was, insisted Brennan, controlling in the present case because sentencing authorities did not establish that all petitioners convicted of murder actually committed a killing or expected to do so. An accomplice sentenced to death who has not killed is, in effect, being punished for one's "mental state with regard to an act committed by another."[641] This, Brennan argued, "cannot serve . . . as independent grounds for imposing the death penalty."[642] He also maintained that the Court's categorization of the petitioners' behavior as "reckless indifference to the value of human life"[643] did not prove intent to kill. Acting "with intent is qualitatively different from a determination that the defendant acted with reckless indifference to human life" in that the "reckless actor has not *chosen* to bring about the killing in the way the intentional actor has."[644] This statute, Brennan insisted, failed to require a finding that those who kill intended the consequences of their behavior.

Brennan also did not agree with the majority's contention that the death penalty for accomplices was in accord with prevailing national sentiment. Examining states which have abolished capital punishment, as well as those which authorize it for a narrow class of offenses, Brennan maintained that "three-fifths of American jurisdictions did not authorize the death penalty for a nontriggerman absent a finding that he intended to kill."[645] He also pointed out that, in the quarter century preceding the *Enmund* decision, as well as the 65 executions which have taken place since its adjudication, not a single individual who did not kill or intend to commit murder was put to death.[646]

The objections which Brennan raised in *Furman* concerning capital punishment were, he believed, implicated in the *Tison* opinion.[647] The death penalty for accomplices, he insisted, was offensive to contemporary society, and the Court's failure to

---

639. 458 U.S. 782.
640. *Id.* at 801.
641. *Tison*, 481 U.S. at 170.
642. *Id.*
643. *Id.* at 152.
644. *Id.* at 170 (emphasis in original).
645. *Id.* at 175.
646. *Id.* at 176-79.
647. *See supra* text accompanying notes 420-24.

articulate clear standards concerning physical and mental responsibility for murder contradicted precedent which mandated examination of the proportionality between an offense and its punishment.[648] Brennan acknowledged the Court's earlier recognition of retribution as a legitimate outlet for society to express its anger at a heinous act;[649] however, he insisted that the Court's failure in *Tison* to compel the state to impose punishment based on the individual culpability of an accused made this argument inapplicable.[650]

The *Tison* case, Brennan concluded, illustrated the futility of attempting to remove arbitrariness from capital trial proceedings. Adoption of the death penalty encouraged resorting to excessive punishment based on emotional outrage which, invariably, did not follow due process safeguards; with regard to its infliction on accomplices to a homicide, Brennan insisted, a state gave expression to its "retributive instincts" in a manner "tragically anachronistic in a society governed by our Constitution."[651] This sentiment was reiterated in the 1989 cases of *Stanford v. Kentucky*[652] and *Penry v. Lynaugh,*[653] which dealt with the death penalty for minors and the mentally retarded, respectively.

The Court in *Stanford* upheld statutory provisions which authorized capital punishment for seventeen-year-olds.[654] Pointing out that capital statutes are to be examined in light of evolving societal standards of decency,[655] the Court noted that a majority of states which sanctioned the death penalty authorized it for offenders who are sixteen or older.[656] Brennan, in dissent, disagreed with the majority's contention that the death penalty for minors is consistent with contemporary notions of justice,[657] and insisted that "'evolving standards of decency'"[658] rendered capital punishment for juveniles abhorrent.

---

648. Weems v. United States, 217 U.S. 349 (1910). *See supra* text accompanying notes 226-32.

649. Lockett v. Ohio, 438 U.S. 586, 605 (1978); Furman v. Georgia, 408 U.S. 238, 308 (1972). *Tison,* 481 U.S. at 181. For a discussion of this concept, see *supra* text accompanying notes 175-88.

650. *Tison,* 481 U.S. at 181.

651. *Id.* at 184.

652. 109 S. Ct. 2969, *reh'g denied,* 110 S. Ct. 23 (1989).

653. 109 S. Ct. 2934 (1989).

654. In the companion case of *Wilkins v. Missouri,* the Court upheld a statute which mandated the death penalty for sixteen-year-olds. 109 S. Ct. at 2969. See, however, Thompson v. Oklahoma, 487 U.S. 815 (1988), which invalidated the death penalty for fifteen-year-olds.

655. 109 S. Ct. at 2974.

656. *Id.* at 2976.

657. *Id.* at 2980.

658. *Id.* at 2982 (quoting Trop v. Dulles, 356 U.S. 86, 101 (1958)).

Examining statistical trends, Brennan maintained that the death penalty for minors was unacceptable to contemporary society. Of thirty-five states which then authorized capital punishment, twelve, calculated Brennan, "specifically mandate that offenders under age 18 not be sentenced to death," while three others "explicitly refuse to authorize sentences of death for those who committed their offense when under 17."[659] When these states are added to the fifteen which prohibited capital punishment, Brennan concluded that thirty do not allow execution of minors under age 17.[660] He also cited the infrequency with which minors have been executed, as well as widespread opposition to the death penalty in industrialized European nations, to further challenge the majority's contention that this punishment was not repugnant to modern society.[661]

More fundamentally, however, Brennan believed that execution of minors violated the prohibition of "cruel and unusual punishments" on its face. This wording, he insisted, as well as a series of precedents,[662] compelled evaluation of the severity of punishment in relation to the offense and offender. Though he conceded that some individuals "mature more quickly than their peers,"[663] Brennan maintained that minors "so generally lack the degree of responsibility for their crimes that it is a predicate for the constitutional imposition of the death penalty that the Eighth Amendment forbids that they receive that punishment."[664] Employing a comparable position in *Penry*,[665] Brennan, in a brief dissent, insisted that subjecting the mentally retarded to the death penalty constituted a disproportionate punishment which did not take into account the blameworthi-

---

659.   *Id.* at 2982-83.

660.   *Id.* at 2983.

661.   Brennan pointed out that only "[e]leven minors were sentenced to die in 1982; 9 in 1983; 6 in 1984; 5 in 1985; 7 in 1986; and 2 in 1987." *Stanford*, 109 S. Ct. at 2984. He also noted the "small proportion of [juvenile offenders on] the current death row population: 30 out of a total of 2,186 inmates, or 1.37 percent." *Id.* at 2984. Moreover, Brennan emphasized that the death penalty itself has been abolished or "limited . . . to exceptional crimes such as treason" in "over 50" countries, and "not enforced in 27 others." *Id.* at 2985.

662.   Brennan cited Booth v. Maryland, 482 U.S. 496, 502, *reh'g denied*, 483 U.S. 1056 (1987), *and overruled by* Payne v. Tennessee, 111 S. Ct. 2597 (1991); California v. Brown, 479 U.S. 538, 545 (1987); Solem v. Helm, 463 U.S. 277, 286 (1983); Enmund v. Florida, 458 U.S. 782, 815 (1982) (O'Connor, J., dissenting); Coker v. Georgia, 433 U.S. 584, 598 (1977); Weems v. United States, 217 U.S. 349, 369 (1910); O'Neil v. Vermont, 144 U.S. 323, 339-40 (1892) (Field, J., dissenting).

663.   *Stanford*, 109 S. Ct. at 2989.

664.   *Id.* at 2988.

665.   109 S. Ct. 2934.

ness of the accused or the ability to comprehend the magnitude of an alleged offense.[666]

In both his *Stanford* and *Penry* opinions, Brennan addressed, as he had done in *Furman*,[667] the relevance of retribution and deterrence as factors which may induce authorization of capital punishment.[668] Without elaboration, he declared that a punishment disproportionate to the culpability of the offender "by definition is not justly deserved"[669] and thus cannot be said to further alleged objectives of retribution; similarly, Brennan maintained that execution of juveniles and the mentally retarded did not "measurably contribute to the goal of deterrence."[670] In both instances Brennan speculated on the possible gain to society by extending capital punishment to these offenders. A punishment, he declared, has deterrent value only if an individual refrained from criminal activity after having determined that the penalty outweighed any possible benefits from unlawful conduct. It is highly unlikely, Brennan reasoned, that juveniles, having "little fear of death,"[671] will take this into consideration, and the intellectual and cognitive impairment of the mentally retarded similarly made remote the possibility that they would examine aforethought the consequences of contemplated action.[672]

Brennan's contention that the alleged purposes of retribution and deterrence were inapplicable with regard to these classes of defendants was based on his moral outrage toward capital punishment as "'nothing more than the purposeless and needless imposition of pain and suffering.'"[673] It is conceivable, however, that jurors, taking into account the individualized

---

666. *Id.* at 2960-62. The majority opinion written by Justice O'Connor in *Penry, id.* at 2934, objected that jurors were not informed that they may consider an accused's mental state (the petitioner, arrested for murder, was diagnosed as mildly to moderately retarded and having "the mental age of a 6 1/2 year old. . . ."), *id.* at 2941, and concluded that full consideration of mitigating evidence was precluded. *Id.* at 2947. The Court did not, however, rule that the mentally retarded may not be subject to capital punishment; rather, it concluded that "at present, there is insufficient evidence of a national consensus against executing mentally retarded people" to warrant its categorical prohibition by the Eighth Amendment. *Id.* at 2955.

667. 408 U.S. 238, *reh'g denied*, 409 U.S. 902 (1972). *See supra* text accompanying notes 433-35, 470-72.

668. *See supra* text accompanying notes 155-88.

669. *Stanford*, 109 S. Ct. at 2993. *See also, Penry*, 109 S. Ct. at 2962 (Brennan, J., dissenting).

670. *Stanford*, 109 S. Ct. at 2993; *Penry*, 109 S. Ct. at 2962.

671. *Stanford*, 109 S. Ct. at 2993.

672. *Penry*, 109 S. Ct. at 2962-63.

673. *Stanford*, 109 S. Ct. at 2994 (quoting Coker v. Georgia, 433 U.S. 584, 592 (1977)).

circumstances of the accused and the alleged offense, may conclude that a particular defendant, though a minor or of subnormal intelligence, comprehended the magnitude of one's conduct and committed an act with knowledge of its consequences. By categorizing an entire class of offenders as free from culpability for homicide, Brennan made possible inconsistent pronouncement of verdicts in that jurors, aware that minors and the mentally retarded cannot receive the death penalty, may weigh aggravating and mitigating circumstances differently than what would transpire with defendants who were eligible for execution. This may introduce arbitrariness in sentencing — which the majority sought to prevent in *Furman.*[674]

Brennan's pronouncements on capital punishment were motivated by compassion. While his foremost objective was to proscribe the death penalty, Brennan also emphasized the importance — given the enormity and finality of execution — of preserving due process safeguards in trial proceedings through the appellate stages and extending to petitions for writ of certiorari.

The Court's role in reviewing petitions for certiorari may have a major impact on an accused's ability to challenge the legality of capital proceedings. A petition for certiorari affords an accused an opportunity to request the Court to review the proceedings of a lower court and assess whether constitutional guidelines have been followed. A stay of execution is typically requested; however, whether granted or denied, further opportunities to appeal capital sentences are not foreclosed.

A petition for a writ of certiorari raises issues concerning the degree to which the Court should examine capital proceedings. Should the Court overturn state convictions only when explicit constitutional violations have been found, or is it appropriate for the justices to examine proceedings based on subjective notions concerning the morality or perceived reasonableness of statutory provisions? Granting a petition for certiorari may result in prompt execution of the sentence if no violation is found; on the other hand, denial may give rise to protracted litigation — and affect prompt administration of criminal justice — in that a defendant who has already exhausted numerous opportunities to appeal a capital conviction may feel encouraged to challenge the Court's refusal to consider a petition for certiorari, and thereby raise legal issues which likely have been examined.

---

674.   *Furman,* 408 U.S. at 239-40. *See supra* text accompanying notes 276-77.

A related option available to capital defendants is a petition for a writ of habeas corpus. A litigant who has incurred an abridgment of personal liberty may, by filing this petition, request a judge to examine the legality of incarceration. The Constitution does not define unlawful imprisonment or specify circumstances in which the writ is to be granted.[675]

Both petitions for certiorari and habeas corpus relate to standing, which deals with one's eligibility to have a grievance heard in the federal courts. The Court noted in two 1990 cases that, "before a federal court can consider the merits of a legal claim, the person seeking to invoke the jurisdiction of the court must establish the requisite standing to sue."[676] To satisfy the requirement in Article III that gives federal courts jurisdiction over "cases" and "controversies," a litigant must demonstrate that a direct and personal impairment of constitutional or statutory rights has been sustained.[677] Establishing one's alleged deprivation of rights is difficult because this is often not apparent until all appellate challenges have been exhausted, compelling a defendant, while litigation is pending, to speculate on the eventual outcome. In *Whitmore v. Arkansas*,[678] the Court ruled that an inmate's claim that legal rulings which might emanate from appellate proceedings may someday benefit him is "nothing more than conjecture"[679] and insufficient to meet the "case" and "controversies" requirement. The possibility of applying a rule formulated in appellate review retroactively to other litigants was rejected in the 1989 case of *Teague v. Lane*,[680] where the Court declared that "new constitutional rules of criminal procedure will not be applicable to those cases which have become final before the new rules are announced."[681] A new ruling will only be applied retroactively, the majority in *Teague* pronounced, if it

---

675. The Constitution forbids suspension of the writ "unless when in Cases of Rebellion or Invasion the public Safety may require it." U.S. CONST. art. I, § 9. For an analysis of concerns presented by petition for a writ of habeas corpus in capital cases, see Robert S. Catz, *Federal Habeas Corpus and the Death Penalty: Need for a Preclusion Doctrine Exception*, 18 U.C. DAVIS L. REV. 1177 (1985); Timothy J. Foley, *The New Arbitrariness: Procedural Default of Federal Habeas Corpus Claims in Capital Cases*, 23 LOY. L.A. L. REV. 193 (1989). *See also* Demosthenes v. Baal, 110 S. Ct. 2223 (1990).

676. Whitmore v. Arkansas, 110 S. Ct. 1717, 1722 (1990). *See also,* Demosthenes v. Baal, 110 S. Ct. 2223, 2226 (1990).

677. U.S. CONST. art. III, § 2.

678. 110 S. Ct. at 1717.

679. *Id.* at 1724. *See also* Demosthenes v. Baal, 110 S. Ct. 2223 (1990) (Brennan, J., dissenting).

680. 489 U.S. 288, *reh'g denied,* 490 U.S. 1031 (1989).

681. *Id.* at 310.

"places 'certain kinds of primary, private individual conduct beyond the power of the criminal lawmaking authority to proscribe,'"[682] and if it demands new procedures without which the likelihood of obtaining a valid conviction is significantly impaired.[683]

By placing a formidable burden of proof on the defendant, the Court underscored its desire to leave state capital proceedings subject to minimal federal intervention. Moreover, its contention in *Sawyer v. Smith*,[684] decided one year after *Teague*, that the purpose of a habeas corpus petition "is to ensure that state convictions comply with the federal law in existence at the time the conviction became final, and not to provide a mechanism for the continuing reexamination of final judgments based upon later emerging legal doctrine,"[685] diminished the likelihood that the Court would agree to review capital proceedings alleged to violate evolving standards of decency, morality, and proportionality — a major component of Brennan's Eighth Amendment jurisprudence.

Unsurprisingly, Brennan objected that these guidelines would make it difficult to appeal capital convictions beyond allegations that narrowly defined due process guidelines have been violated. In the 1980s, the Burger Court, usually without divulging individual votes, denied petitions for writ of certiorari on a number of occasions;[686] in two cases — *Smith v. Kemp*[687] and *Campbell v. Washington*[688] — Brennan appended a brief statement

---

682. *Id.* at 307 (quoting Mackey v. United States, 401 U.S. 667, 692 (1971) (Harlan, J., concurring)).

683. *Id.* at 315. In Saffle v. Parks, 110 S. Ct. 1257, *reh'g denied*, 110 S. Ct. 1960 (1990), the Court applied this standard to both capital and noncapital cases.

684. 497 U.S. 227 (1990).

685. *Id.* at 234. One year later, the Court in McCleskey v. Zant, 111 S. Ct. 1454 (1991), addressed the proper exercise of a habeas corpus petition in capital proceedings. It held that one who fails to raise a legal claim in an initial petition for a writ of habeas corpus must demonstrate, in a second or subsequent application seeking to refute the government's assertion that the writ had been abused, that "a fundamental miscarriage of justice would result from failure to entertain the claim." *Id.* at 1470.

686. *See, e.g.*, Coleman v. Balkcom, 451 U.S. 949, *reh'g denied*, 452 U.S. 955 (1981); Williams v. King, 719 F.2d 730 (5th Cir.), *cert. denied*, 464 U.S. 1027 (1983); Barefoot v. Estelle, 697 F.2d 593 (5th Cir.), *aff'd*, 463 U.S. 880, *and reh'g denied*, 464 U.S. 874 (1983); Estelle v. Jurek, 623 F.2d 929 (5th Cir. 1980), *cert. denied*, 450 U.S. 1001, *and cert. denied*, 450 U.S. 1014, *and reh'g denied*, 451 U.S. 1011 (1981).

687. 849 F.2d 481 (11th Cir.), *cert. denied*, 464 U.S. 1032 (1983).

688. 691 P.2d 929, *cert. denied*, 471 U.S. 1094 (1985).

reiterating his categorical opposition to capital punishment;[689] in two others — *Maggio v. Williams* (1983)[690] and *Glass v. Louisiana* (1985)[691] — which also involved denial of certiorari and rejection of a request for stay of execution — Brennan elaborated on his concern for making appellate proceedings accessible.

Dissenting in *Maggio*, Brennan maintained that the petitioner's claim, in part, that the state supreme court had not examined the proportionality of his death sentence based on statewide rather than regional sentencing patterns, merited review by the Court of a petition for certiorari. This type of allegation, he declared, is "nonfrivolous,"[692] and the failure of the Court to have formulated clear standards on the review of proportionality challenges compelled granting the petition. Examining state sentencing patterns, Brennan believed that disparities existed in different judicial districts,[693] and urged the Court to avoid appearing to condone "arbitrary and capricious imposition of the death penalty"[694] by refusing to approve a state mode of appellate review which "results in different sentences for similarly situated defendants."[695] In the *Glass* decision, where the Court denied a petition for certiorari from a defendant sentenced to death by electrocution, Brennan, in dissent, maintained that a form of punishment which is inconsistent with contemporary perceptions of human dignity "demands measured judicial consideration."[696]

These opinions make clear that Brennan wished the Court to exercise wide discretion in deciding to consider petitions for writ of certiorari. The magnitude of capital punishment compelled furnishing the accused with unrestricted appellate opportunities to challenge a death sentence on both substantive and procedural grounds, and evolving conceptions of acceptable forms of punishment convinced Brennan that new interpretations of trial proceedings which hold sentencing authorities to increasingly meticulous standards are to be applied retroactively. This position was contrary to the Court's pronouncements in

---

689. *Smith*, 464 U.S. at 1032 (Brennan, J., dissenting); *Campbell*, 471 U.S. at 1094 (Brennan, J., dissenting). *See supra* note 505.

690. 719 F.2d 730 (5th Cir.), *cert. denied*, 464 U.S. 46 (1983) (Brennan, J., dissenting).

691. 471 U.S. 1080 (1985) (Brennan, J., dissenting).

692. *Maggio*, 464 U.S. at 57.

693. *Id.* at 60-61.

694. *Id.* at 61.

695. *Id.*

696. *Glass*, 471 U.S. at 1081.

Teague,[697] which Brennan, in dissent, addressed in two cases: *Penry v. Lynaugh*[698] and *Saffle v. Parks*.[699]

In *Penry*, Brennan insisted that standards for appellate review are not similar in capital and noncapital proceedings. The *Teague* case dealt with a noncapital proceeding, and Brennan, who dissented in that decision,[700] emphasized in *Penry* that its pronouncements were inapplicable to capital trials. The *Teague* plurality, he insisted, put forward "a novel threshold test for federal review of state criminal convictions"[701] which erected a formidable burden of proof on litigants to justify applying new judicial interpretations retroactively. Ability to benefit from revised rulings should not be limited to defendants whose conviction and sentence have not yet been pronounced.[702]

In *Saffle*, Brennan elaborated further on the diminished ability of litigants, based on *Teague*, to successfully appeal capital proceedings. *Saffle*, it will be recalled, declared that the judge's instruction to the jury to reach a verdict free from personal biases and emotions did not prevent unrestricted consideration of mitigating evidence.[703] Brennan, in dissent, objected that *Teague* would make it virtually impossible for defendants to challenge the jurors' mode of deliberation. To obtain appellate relief, it was necessary for the accused to show that failure to apply a revised judicial pronouncement to capital proceedings already completed would "'implicat[e] the fundamental fairness and accuracy of the criminal proceeding.'"[704] In *Saffle*, Brennan contended, the majority, other than stating that the "precise contours of this exception may be difficult to discern,"[705] did not articulate how an accused may demonstrate that retroactive application of a new rule was warranted.

Brennan's objections to capital punishment were underscored in his opinions concerning appellate review of trial proceedings. Brennan did not believe that the Court's pronouncements concerning the need for jurors, free from prejudicial comments of a judge or prosecutor, to take into account

---

697.   489 U.S. at 288. *See supra* text accompanying notes 680-83.

698.   492 U.S. 302 (1989) (Brennan, J., dissenting). *See supra* text accompanying notes 665-66.

699.   494 U.S. 484 (1990) (Brennan, J., dissenting).

700.   Teague v. Lane, 489 U.S. 288, *reh'g denied*, 490 U.S. 1031 (1989) (Brennan, J., dissenting).

701.   *Penry*, 492 U.S. at 341.

702.   *Id.*

703.   *See supra* text accompanying notes 530-31.

704.   *Saffle*, 494 U.S. at 505 (quoting Teague v. Lane, 489 U.S. at 311).

705.   *Id.*

the individualized circumstances of the accused based on an unbiased assessment of mitigating evidence, could be implemented. He maintained that jury bias, often based on psychological prejudices against a particular class of offender, is difficult to prove, and the mere risk of its appearance is sufficient to justify prohibition of a punishment which could furnish no recourse to an accused later found to be wrongly executed. In short, beyond generalizations on the need to confine the discretion of sentencing authorities, Brennan believed that clear standards concerning admissibility and examination of evidence, pronouncement of sentence, and appeal of trial proceedings, could not be articulated. He expressed this sentiment in the 1984 case of *Pulley v. Harris.*[706]

Dissenting from an opinion which held that it was unnecessary for a state supreme court to determine whether a sentence of death was proportionate to the manner in which other defendants were treated in comparable cases,[707] Brennan expressed doubt that capital proceedings could ever be administered in an unbiased manner. The Court, declared Brennan in *Pulley,* is "simply deluding itself, and also the American public, when it insists that those defendants who have already been executed or are today condemned to death have been selected on a basis that is neither arbitrary nor capricious, under any meaningful definition of those terms."[708] He also stated that, "[g]iven the emotions generated by capital crimes, it may well be that juries, trial judges, and appellate courts considering sentences of death are invariably affected by impermissible considerations."[709] While "we may tolerate such irrationality in other sentencing contexts,"[710] it is inexcusable in proceedings which may result in the extinguishment of life.

This perception, along with his belief that the meaning of constitutional provisions is shaped by evolving conceptions of morality and compassion in the dispensation of justice, was the basis for Brennan's unwavering insistence that capital punishment is categorically prohibited by the Eighth Amendment. The

---

706.   465 U.S. 37 (1984).

707.   *Id.* at 43-44.

708.   *Id.* at 60. The same year *Pulley* was decided, a study of eight states — Oklahoma, North Carolina, Mississippi, Virginia, Arkansas, Georgia, Florida, and Illinois — indicated persistence of racial discrimination and arbitrariness in capital sentencing. *See* Samuel R. Gross & Robert Mauro, *Patterns of Death: An Analysis of Racial Disparities in Capital Sentencing and Homicide Victimization,* 37 STAN. L. REV. 27 (1984).

709.   Gross & Mauro, *supra* note 708, at 64.

710.   *Id.*

only other member of the Court who completely embraced Brennan's position was Justice Thurgood Marshall.

V. Justice Marshall's Opinions on Capital Punishment

A. *Marshall's First Opinion on the Death Penalty:* Furman v. Georgia *(1972)*

Justice Marshall, who did not participate in any of the Warren Court decisions on the death penalty,[711] first communicated his categorical opposition to capital punishment by joining Brennan's *McGautha* opinion which expressed this sentiment.[712] Marshall's first, and most detailed, discussion of the death penalty appeared in his concurring opinion in *Furman v. Georgia.*[713] At the outset, Marshall pointed out that determining "with objectivity and a proper measure of self-restraint"[714] whether the death penalty was prohibited by the Eighth Amendment required careful examination of its original understanding, judicial precedents, and perception in contemporary society.

The prohibition of "cruel and unusual punishments," Marshall pointed out, "derive[d] from English law;"[715] however, prior to adoption of the Bill of Rights of 1689, barbaric forms of punishment, sometimes culminating in execution, were widespread.

---

711. Of six cases decided by the Warren Court (*see supra* text accompanying notes 236-64), Marshall had taken his seat prior to the adjudication of just two decisions — United States v. Jackson, 390 U.S. 570 (1968), and Witherspoon v. Illinois, 391 U.S. 510 (1968) — but did not participate.

712. McGautha v. California, 402 U.S. 183 (1971), *reh'g denied*, 406 U.S. 978 (1972), decided with Crampton v. Ohio, 402 U.S. 183 (1971), *vacated*, 408 U.S. 941 (1972) (Marshall, J., joining the dissent of Brennan, J.). *See supra* text accompanying notes 383-485.

713. 408 U.S. 238, *reh'g denied*, 409 U.S. 902 (1972). For the ruling and general sentiments of the Court, see *supra* text accompanying notes 276-84. Prior to *Furman*, Marshall had written just one opinion in a death penalty case. In Dutton v. Evans, 400 U.S. 74 (1970), the Court held that introduction by one of twenty witnesses for the prosecution in a capital trial of testimony concerning a statement allegedly made by the accused which conveyed an inference of guilt did not constitute hearsay evidence or an abridgment of the Sixth Amendment's command that a defendant have an opportunity "to be confronted with the witnesses against him." U.S. Const. amend. VI. The dissent written by Marshall focused on the meaning of the confrontation clause without addressing the constitutionality of capital punishment. 400 U.S. at 100-11 (Marshall, J., dissenting).

714. *Furman*, 408 U.S. at 316.

715. *Id.* at 317 n.7 (quoting 4 William Blackstone, Commentaries 376-77). For an overview of this period, see *supra* text accompanying notes 111-16. For Blackstone's comment on the widespread use of capital punishment, as well as his position on noncapital offenses, see *supra* note 129.

While acknowledging that the precise meaning of the prohibition against "cruel and unusual punishments" cannot be ascertained,[716] Marshall believed that the founding generation adopted this phrase from the Bill of Rights of 1689 "to outlaw torture and other cruel punishments."[717] He noted that a portion of the Virginia "Declaration of Rights" of 1776 contained "language . . . drawn verbatim from the English Bill of Rights of 1689,"[718] and that four other states adopted its phraseology.[719] Patrick Henry's comments at the Virginia ratifying convention,[720] as well as sentiments expressed in the First Congress,[721] convinced Marshall that "the history of the [cruel and unusual punishments] clause clearly establishe[d] that it was intended to prohibit cruel punishments."[722]

Turning to judicial precedents,[723] Marshall reasoned that punishments which involved "unnecessary cruelty"[724] and which were excessive in relation to the offense committed were proscribed by the Eighth Amendment. Two key components of the Court's jurisprudence are the concepts of proportionality, put forward in *Weems v. United States*,[725] and the notion that the degree and severity of punishment must evolve as perceptions of justice are redefined.[726] Based on prior rulings, Marshall put forward a set of principles, virtually identical to Brennan's,[727] by which punishments are to be reconciled with the Eighth Amendment. Guiding his formulation was the statement in *Trop v. Dulles*[728] — which Marshall said was "[p]erhaps the most important principle in analyzing 'cruel and unusual' punishment ques-

---

716. *Furman*, 408 U.S. at 319.

717. *Id.* For a discussion of views expressed in the First Congress, see *supra* text accompanying notes 121-23.

718. *Id.*

719. *Id.* n.16.

720. *Id.* at 320-21. Advocating inclusion of a bill of rights in the Constitution, Henry maintained that a clause prohibiting "cruel and unusual punishments" would prevent governmental attempts to "extort confession by torture, in order to punish with still more relentless severity." *Id.* at 321.

721. *See supra* text accompanying notes 121-22.

722. *Furman*, 408 U.S. at 322.

723. For a discussion of major Court rulings prior to *Furman*, see *supra* text accompanying notes 220-42.

724. *Furman*, 408 U.S. at 322.

725. 217 U.S. 349 (1910). For a discussion of this case, see *supra* text accompanying notes 226-32.

726. Trop v. Dulles, 356 U.S. 86 (1958). For a discussion of this case, see *supra* text accompanying notes 236-39.

727. *See supra* text accompanying notes 421-24. *Furman*, 408 U.S. at 271-79 (Brennan, J., concurring).

728. 356 U.S. 86 (1958).

tions"[729] — that the wording of the Eighth Amendment "'must draw its meaning from the evolving standards of decency that mark the progress of a maturing society.'"[730] With this pronouncement foremost in mind, Marshall put forward four criteria by which to assess whether punishment was cruel and unusual:

> First, there are certain punishments that inherently involve so much physical pain and suffering that civilized people cannot tolerate them. . . .[731]
>
> Second, there are punishments that are unusual, signifying that they were previously unknown as penalties for a given offense.[732]
>
> Third, a penalty may be cruel and unusual because it is excessive and serves no valid legislative purpose.[733]
>
> Fourth, where a punishment is not excessive and serves a valid legislative purpose, it still may be invalid if popular sentiment abhors it.[734]

Though he acknowledged the Court's support of the death penalty in the past,[735] Marshall maintained that this did not preclude reexamination of the issue. He pointed out that some forms of punishment — such as the rack and thumbscrew[736] — which were once practiced "have been barred since the adoption of the Bill of Rights."[737] Marshall also indicated that history and judicial precedents have not furnished a clear definition of the phrase "cruel and unusual," but believed that they pertain to the humaneness of punishment and the length of time it has existed.[738] Conceptions of proportionality, Marshall noted, also evolve over time, and a punishment deemed by contemporary society as excessive is invalid even though it may not have been considered unacceptably harsh in the past.[739] In addition, Mar-

---

729. *Furman*, 408 U.S. at 329.

730. *Trop*, 356 U.S. at 101.

731. *Furman*, 408 U.S. at 330.

732. *Id.* at 331.

733. *Id.*

734. *Id.* at 332.

735. Louisiana *ex rel.* Francis v. Resweber, 329 U.S. 459 (1947); *In re* Kemmler, 136 U.S. 436 (1890); Wilkerson v. Utah, 99 U.S. 130 (1879). *See supra* text accompanying notes 220-35.

736. *Furman*, 408 U.S. at 330.

737. *Id.*

738. *Id.* at 331.

739. *Id.* at 331-32.

shall maintained that a punishment "found . . . to be morally unacceptable"[740] is in violation of the Eighth Amendment.

Marshall's four criteria by which to assess capital punishment underscored that the Eighth Amendment mandated constant reevaluation of a principle intended to be aspirational. The authors of the Bill of Rights bequeathed to posterity not the practices of their generation but rather a vision of morality concerning the relationship between government and the citizenry which needed to be reexamined throughout history.

Marshall's examination of the death penalty, from its early history in England prior to Magna Carta, through the founding generation and up to the Civil War, and encompassing the evolution of the abolitionist movement during its periods of popularity and weakness up to the *Furman* decision,[741] pointed out that, in varying degrees of intensity, sentiment against capital punishment has always been expressed. In England, Marshall declared that the death penalty, probably originating as an act of "private vengeance" on the part of those seeking "violent retaliation by members of a tribe or group, or by the tribe or group itself, against persons committing hostile acts toward group members,"[742] became increasingly widespread from the 1100s onward, and, by the early 1800s, was statutorily authorized for more than 200 offenses.[743] In the American colonies, Marshall noted, capital punishment was prominent[744] but less widespread, and, as early as the 1600s, opposition to the death penalty was being expressed.[745] During the founding generation, abolitionist societies were conspicuous,[746] and, by the 1850s, movements to invalidate the death penalty had spread to a number of states.[747] Several states had abolished the death penalty in the generation following the Civil War,[748] and the movement, which "lost its

---

740. *Id.* at 332.

741. *Id.* at 333-42. For a discussion of the history of capital punishment from the period of Magna Carta up to the Civil War, see *supra* text accompanying notes 111-27. For an examination of abolitionist trends after 1865, see GORECKI, *supra* note 124, at 142-43; PATERNOSTER, *supra* note 116, at 8-15.

742. *Furman*, 408 U.S. at 333.

743. *Id.* at 334.

744. *See supra* text accompanying notes 117-20.

745. *Furman*, 408 U.S. at 335-36.

746. *Id.* at 336-37. For an examination of the abolitionist movements discussed by Marshall, see *supra* text accompanying notes 145-54.

747. GORECKI, *supra* note 124, at 142-43; PATERNOSTER, *supra* note 116, at 8-15.

748. *Id.*

vigor"[749] during the period between World Wars I and II, experienced "renewed interest"[750] in the years leading up to *Furman.* In addition, Marshall pointed out that the barbarity with which the death penalty had once been inflicted gradually abated as the twentieth century progressed.[751] This history, concluded Marshall, has indicated increasing uneasiness with retention of the death penalty.

Though he acknowledged that the abolitionist movement has been able to bring about repeal of the death penalty in "no more than one-quarter of the States . . . at any one time,"[752] Marshall inquired whether "American society has reached a point where abolition is not dependent on a successful grass roots movement in particular jurisdictions, but is demanded by the Eighth Amendment."[753] He proceeded to examine whether the reasons which have impelled states to adopt capital punishment are valid.

Retribution, Marshall pointed out, has stemmed from society's desire to punish those who have violated the law and, hopefully, rehabilitate offenders. Infliction of punishments for vengeance and retaliation, however, "have been roundly condemned as intolerable aspirations for a government in a free society,"[754] rejected "by scholars for centuries,"[755] and antithetical to the purpose of the Eighth Amendment.[756] Marshall did not elaborate on these assertions. The alleged justification of punishment has been extensively debated by proponents of utilitarianism and retributivism, and neither position can, in the abstract, be categorized as morally superior;[757] indeed, contrary to Marshall's position, a consensus on retribution, in theory and application, has never emerged, and there is no empirical evidence of its repudiation at any point in history.[758] Marshall cited *Weems v. United States,*[759] where the Court declared that sanctions must be proportionate to an offense,[760] to underscore his contention that "punishment for the sake of retribution was not per-

---

749. *Furman,* 408 U.S. at 340.
750. *Id.*
751. *Id.*
752. *Id.* at 341.
753. *Id.* at 341-42.
754. *Id.* at 343.
755. *Id.*
756. *Id.*
757. *See supra* text accompanying notes 175-82.
758. *Id.*
759. 217 U.S. 349 (1910).
760. *Id.* at 365-66. *See supra* text accompanying notes 226-32.

missible under the Eighth Amendment."[761] However, a punishment motivated by retribution may be proportionate to unlawful behavior. Would retribution be appropriate in this instance? There is no evidence that the Eighth Amendment was adopted to proscribe retribution; Marshall himself declared that its original understanding was "to outlaw torture and other cruel punishments,"[762] suggesting that the authors sought to address the degree of physical suffering inflicted on defendants rather than the motives of legislators for adopting a particular penalty. In short, Marshall did not substantiate his assertion that "retribution for its own sake"[763] violated the founders' perception of the Eighth Amendment.

Marshall also did not believe that deterrence was a valid justification for capital punishment. Relying primarily on the pioneering studies of Thorsten Sellin,[764] Marshall maintained that there is no evidence indicating that capital punishment is an effective deterrent to the commission of homicide.[765] He conceded that Sellin's findings may be inconclusive,[766] and that abolitionists "have not proved non-deterrence beyond a reasonable doubt;"[767] however, Marshall believed that there was "clear and convincing evidence that capital punishment is not necessary as a deterrent to crime in our society."[768] This, however, does not make it unconstitutional. Marshall did not explain why the failure of punishment to achieve a socially desirable objective rendered it "cruel and unusual." Marshall's other arguments against the death penalty — that the rate of recidivism by convicted murderers is not high;[769] that the ability of a state to obtain a confession by plea bargaining would not be impaired;[770] and that it is offensive for a state to seek to eliminate perceived undesirable

---

761. *Furman*, 408 U.S. at 344.

762. *Id.* at 319.

763. *Id.* at 345.

764. *See supra* text accompanying notes 157-61. At the time *Furman* was decided, not many studies on the alleged deterrent effect of capital punishment had been completed; however, there was some evidence, along with Sellin's findings, that the death penalty was not a statistically demonstrable method to prevent homicide, *id.*, that the prospect of execution affected the behavior of potential murderers. *See supra* text accompanying note 172.

765. *Furman*, 408 U.S. at 349-50.

766. *Id.* at 350-53. For a discussion of the debate between abolitionists and retentionists, see *supra* text accompanying notes 155-74.

767. *Furman*, 408 U.S. at 350.

768. *Id.* at 353. *See also* PATERNOSTER, *supra* note 116, at 217-46; *supra* text accompanying notes 189-90.

769. *Furman*, 408 U.S. at 355-56.

770. *Id.* at 356.

criminal offenders from society;[771] — may demonstrate lack of circumspection in formulating policy planning and poor fiscal judgment, but do not establish constitutional invalidity.

The central component of Marshall's jurisprudence on capital punishment was summarized in his statement that "the Eighth Amendment is our insulation from our baser selves."[772] In other words, the meaning of the Eighth Amendment is aspirational; it embodies a vision of morality which the citizenry seeks to achieve. Marshall's objective was not primarily to dictate policymaking priorities to states but rather to shape a psychological bond between government and the populace. In this regard, he contended that the death penalty "is an excessive and unnecessary punishment that violated the Eighth Amendment"[773] not because it was fiscally burdensome or unable to achieve social ends better than other forms of punishment but because it violated principles of justice which evolved with each generation. Enabling the citizenry to aspire to the vision and promise of the Eighth Amendment, contended Marshall, was the responsibility of the judiciary.

At some point, Marshall declared, it is necessary for the Court to ask itself whether "deference to the legislatures is tantamount to abdication of our judicial roles as factfinders, judges, and ultimate arbiters of the Constitution."[774] He wished to confer on the Court wide discretion to examine both the procedural and substantive components of legislation; it was necessary, Marshall declared, to determine "not whether the legislature acted wisely, but whether it had any rational basis whatsoever for acting."[775] This required the justices to formulate a perception of the moral underpinnings of constitutional provisions and assess whether legislation has fulfilled it. According to Marshall, striking down legislation — though enacted with majority support — which has undermined or contradicted the moral vision of a constitutional command was not a usurpation of judicial power but rather an appropriate expression of the Court's responsibility to elevate the citizenry to an enlightened conception of justice. Accordingly, he did not believe that adoption of capital punishment by a majority of the states established its constitutionality. He attributed widespread sanctioning of the death penalty to the ignorance of the citizenry regarding its costs, alleged deterrent

---

771. *Id.* at 356-57.
772. *Id.* at 345.
773. *Id.* at 358.
774. *Id.* at 359.
775. *Id.*

effect, and usefulness to society.[776] If individuals were factually informed about the death penalty, they would "find it shocking to [the] conscience and sense of justice."[777]

The uninformed citizenry, Marshall declared, does not realize that the death penalty has been arbitrarily inflicted. He cited statistics indicating that blacks "were executed far more often than whites in proportion to their percentage of the population,"[778] and that men have been executed far more frequently than women.[779] Also unknown to the public, according to Marshall, is that "the burden of capital punishment falls upon the poor, the ignorant, and the underprivileged members of society,"[780] and that efforts to prevent wrongful execution are "not fool-proof."[781] Though he conceded that it is "difficult to ascertain with certainty the degree to which the death penalty is discriminatorily imposed or the number of innocent persons sentenced to die,"[782] its mere possibility justified abolition.

Marshall did not discuss how revisions in penal codes might reduce the likelihood of discriminatory trial proceedings and erroneous convictions because he did not believe capital punishment could be legitimized with elaborate due process safeguards. The immorality of capital punishment, he concluded, was inconsistent with the Eighth Amendment's command to evolve progressively enlightened conceptions of justice between the government and the citizenry, and the Court's role was to enable the nation to transcend contemporary notions of punishment — which often stemmed from ignorance — and fulfill the aspirational tone of the prohibition against "cruel and unusual punishments." Marshall believed that his position was based not on a subjective value judgment but rather on views representative of the people who are not yet able to comprehend that abhorrence of the death penalty is their actual sentiment. Thus, while moral-

---

776. *Id.* at 362-63.

777. *Id.* at 369.

778. *Id.* at 364. Marshall pointed out that: "A total of 3,859 persons have been executed since 1930, of whom 1,751 were white and 2,066 were Negro. Of the executions, 3,334 were for murder; 1,664 of the executed murderers were white and 1,630 were Negro; 455 persons, including 48 whites and 405 Negroes, were executed for rape." *Id.* For an examination of a number of studies which confirmed Marshall's contention, up to the *Furman* decision, that the administration of capital punishment has been racially biased, see *supra* text accompanying notes 210-12, 217.

779. *Id.* at 365. Marshall declared that, "[o]nly 32 women have been executed since 1930, while 3,827 men have met a similar fate." *Id.*

780. *Id.* at 365-66.

781. *Id.* at 366.

782. *Id.* at 368.

ity played a large role in Marshall's concurrence, it was intended to vindicate the underlying objective of the Eighth Amendment. This sentiment guided Marshall as the Court considered a range of issues presented by capital punishment.

B.   Marshall Opposes Procedural Guidelines Put Forward by the Burger Court (1976-1986)

In the 1976 case of *Gregg v. Georgia*,[783] the Court, for the first time, explicitly acknowledged the constitutionality of the death penalty,[784] and, in companion cases,[785] discussed the type of discretion statutes needed to provide juries in trial proceedings.[786] Marshall, in dissent, reiterated his categorical opposition to capital punishment,[787] and explained why he believed statutory guidelines could not preclude arbitrariness in sentencing.

Relying on pronouncements in *Furman*, Marshall once again maintained that the death penalty is excessive in that it has not been shown to be a deterrent to the commission of homicide. Marshall examined studies by Isaac Ehrlich, published since the *Furman* decision, which suggested that capital punishment may have lowered the rate of murder,[788] as well as those seeking to discredit his position,[789] and concluded that Ehrlich's findings are "of little, if any, assistance in assessing the deterrent impact of the death penalty."[790] Marshall declared that his discussion in *Furman* denying a deterrent effect of capital punishment[791]

---

783.   428 U.S. 153, *reh'g denied*, 429 U.S. 875 (1976).

784.   *Id.* at 169.

785.   Jurek v. Texas, 428 U.S. 262, *reh'g denied*, 429 U.S. 875 (1976); Proffitt v. Florida, 428 U.S. 242, *reh'g denied*, 429 U.S. 875 (1976); Woodson v. North Carolina, 428 U.S. 280 (1976); Roberts v. Louisiana, 428 U.S. 325, *reh'g denied*, 429 U.S. 890 (1976).

786.   *See supra* text accompanying notes 287-305.

787.   *Gregg*, 428 U.S. at 231 (Marshall, J., dissenting). *See also*, Marshall's brief statement in *Woodson*, 428 U.S. at 306 (Marshall, J., concurring), and *Roberts*, 428 U.S. at 337 (Marshall, J., concurring).

788.   Isaac Ehrlich, *The Deterrent Effect of Capital Punishment: A Question of Life and Death*, 65 AM. ECON. REV. 397 (1975); ISSAC EHRLICH, THE DETERRENT EFFECT OF CAPITAL PUNISHMENT: A QUESTION OF LIFE AND DEATH, (National Bureau of Economic Research Working Paper No. 18, 1973) (cited by Marshall in *Gregg*, 428 U.S. at 234 n.4). For a discussion of Ehrlich's position, see *supra* text accompanying note 163.

789.   For an analysis of several studies in response to Ehrlich completed prior to *Gregg*, see *supra* note 164. These studies were cited by Marshall in *Gregg*, 428 U.S. at 235 n.8.

790.   *Gregg*, 428 U.S. at 236. For an analysis of arguments made by abolitionists and retentionists concerning the alleged deterrent effect of the death penalty, see *supra* text accompanying notes 155-74.

791.   *See supra* text accompanying notes 764-68.

"remains convincing,"[792] and that no new evidence refuting his position has emerged.

Marshall also left undisturbed his contention from *Furman* that the citizenry is not well-informed on the death penalty.[793] He noted in *Gregg* that thirty-five states (and the District of Columbia) have enacted new capital punishment statutes since the *Furman* decision,[794] but adhered to his position, "confirmed" by a study published in 1976,[795] that "the American people know

---

792. *Gregg*, 428 U.S. at 236.

793. *See supra* text accompanying notes 778-82.

794. *Gregg*, 428 U.S. at 232.

795. Austin Sarat & Neil Vidmar, *Public Opinion, the Death Penalty, and the Eighth Amendment: Testing the Marshall Hypothesis*, 1976 WIS. L. REV. 171 (1976). To test the accuracy of Marshall's contention that the public is not well informed on the death penalty, *Furman*, 408 U.S. at 362-63, Sarat and Vidmar randomly interviewed, during the spring and summer of 1975, 200 residents of Amherst, Massachusetts. Sarat & Vidmar, *id.* at 180. Nineteen of these interviews were unused, confining the sample to 181 individuals. *Id.* at 180-81. Based on a questionnaire containing 18 statements, the following responses were tabulated: "54 percent of our subjects favored the death penalty to some degree, 13 percent indicated that they were uncertain and 33 percent were opposed to it." *Id.* at 183. Concerning recent trends, "72 percent indicated that they knew that there are people currently awaiting execution in the United States; 29 percent indicated they knew that no one had actually been executed in the five years preceding the *Furman* decision." *Id.* at 185. With regard to the alleged racial and socioeconomic bias in capital sentencing, "almost 60 percent of the subjects of this study indicated that they also knew about these inequities in the application of the death penalty." *Id.* at 186. In addition, "52 percent of those favoring it did so even though they indicated that they knew that it has been imposed infrequently and disproportionately against poor people." *Id.* It was also found that "approximately one-third of our subjects indicated that they knew about the weight of evidence on the question of deterrence, and only 22 percent indicated that they knew that the murder rate does not generally fall in the weeks following a well publicized execution." *Id.* Thus, concerning Marshall's assertion on the public's ignorance about capital punishment, Sarat and Vidmar concluded that this position "needs some modification":

> People appear to know more about the way that capital punishment is applied, but are less well informed about its effects. In the strict sense that Justice Marshall meant when he used the term, however, few persons in our sample could be labelled 'informed' about the death penalty.

Id. at 187.

To test whether public attitudes had changed as information about the death penalty is furnished, the researchers prepared two 1500-word essays. The first dealt with "the 'Utilitarian' aspects of capital punishment and consisted of summaries of statistical studies, reports of personal experience and arguments about the psychology of deterrence as well as data on the recidivism rate among released murderers." *Id.* at 182. The second focused on the "'Humanitarian'" aspects of the death penalty: "first, the way capital punishment has typically been applied and administered and, second, the psychological and physical aspects of execution." *Id.* This material was then broken down into four cate-

little about the death penalty,"[796] and, had the citizenry been better informed, execution would not be acceptable.[797] More fundamentally, however, Marshall again insisted that the death penalty "is unconstitutional because it is excessive;"[798] it is a form of punishment which cannot be reconciled with deterrence — which is empirically unprovable —[799] or retribution, which is morally reprehensible.[800]

Marshall acknowledged that retribution exhibited a community's desire to encourage obedience to the law by imposing penalties on its transgressors, but added that the degree to which it may be expressed with particular offenses was limited. Punishment inflicted purely to exact retribution — irrespective of its proportionality to an offense and its likelihood to rehabilitate an offender — is impermissible. The death penalty, Marshall argued, satisfied neither of these objectives of punishment; it is disproportionate by denying "the wrongdoer's dignity and worth,"[801] and valueless as an educational remedy because an accused "concerned about conforming his conduct to what society says is 'right' and sentenced to life imprisonment "would [not] fail to realize that murder is 'wrong.'"[802] In other words, Mar-

---

gories — "(1) utilitarian information only, (2) humanitarian information only, (3) utilitarian and humanitarian information combined, and (4) a control condition consisting of an essay about law which was entirely unrelated to death penalty issues." *Id.* at 182-83. The researchers found that expression of support for the death penalty after reading the material declined from its initial level: in the group which read "utilitarian" perspectives (studies on the alleged deterrent effect of capital punishment), support declined from 51 to 38%; among those who read "humanitarian" material (concerning the humaneness and barbarity of capital punishment), support declined from 54 to 49%; after reading perspectives combining information on the utilitarian and humanitarian aspects, support for the death penalty declined from 62 to 42%; and the control group showed no change. *Id.* at 189-90.

Emphasizing that their findings "must be dealt with cautiously," Sarat and Vidmar concluded:

It was found that our subjects knew little about the death penalty, particularly its effectiveness. It was also found that when exposed to information about capital punishment, especially information regarding its utilitarian aspects, a substantial proportion of the subjects altered their opinions toward it.

Id. at 195.

796. *Gregg,* 428 U.S. at 232.
797. *Id.*
798. *Id.* at 233-36. *See also Furman,* 408 U.S. at 345, 358-69. *See supra* text accompanying notes 773-82.
799. *Gregg,* 428 U.S. at 233-36.
800. *Id.* at 236-37.
801. *Id.* at 241.
802. *Id.* at 238.

shall insisted that punishment must be meted out without disregarding the intrinsic humanity of an offender and in a manner which hopefully will communicate to the offender and the community at large that certain conduct is antithetical to the norms of social behavior. Capital punishment, Marshall claimed, was intended merely to unleash society's outrage in the form of vengeance toward the accused, rendering this penalty "unnecessary to promote the goal of deterrence or to further any legitimate notion of retribution,"[803] and an "excessive"[804] act prohibited by the Eighth and Fourteenth Amendments.

Marshall disagreed that the death penalty was an acceptable expression of society's moral outrage against a heinous offense. Proponents of capital punishment, he declared, seek to justify their position as "utilitarian" by "portray[ing] the death penalty as valuable because of its beneficial results."[805] However, absent evidence that capital punishment has achieved socially desirable ends, it must be categorized as an act of vengeance, and unacceptably retributive.[806] Moreover, Marshall maintained that even where a law has majority support it cannot be sustained merely to express "society's judgment that the murderer 'deserves' death."[807]

In *Gregg*, Marshall imposed his own perception of morality on the states. Retribution may be one of many factors which impelled a state to sanction capital punishment, and, depending on how meticulous a statute has enumerated aggravating and mitigating circumstances and compelled their consideration by jurors, this element may not be a substantial component of trial deliberations. Rather than focusing on procedural due process protections accorded a particular accused, Marshall categorically opposed enactment of capital punishment on an abstract belief that it inherently accentuated vindictive facets of human behavior. In devising penal codes, Marshall erected a threshold which states may not cross but did not explain why his understanding of morality, which viewed punishment in a rehabilitative context, was more compelling than a legislature's possible assumption that this objective was not the only justification for a severe penalty. Marshall expressed his position on the proper use of punishment in other death penalty cases which came to the Court after *Gregg*.

---

803. *Id.* at 241.
804. *Id.*
805. *Id.* at 239.
806. For a discussion of the concepts of utilitarianism and retributivism, see *supra* text accompanying notes 175-88.
807. *Gregg*, 428 U.S. at 240.

From 1977 to 1986, the last ten years of the Burger Court, Marshall wrote an opinion in fourteen capital punishment cases,[808] and added a brief concurring statement, similar to what Brennan had done on several occasions,[809] reiterating his unconditional opposition to the death penalty even when a conviction had been invalidated, in five others.[810] Three of Marshall's opinions dealt with the weighing by jurors of aggravating and mitigating circumstances,[811] and two others examined instructions to the jury in considering evidence;[812] four focused on the introduction of oral and written evidence into trial proceedings;[813] two examined the death penalty for particular types of offenders,[814] and three examined the filing of a petition for certiorari and habeas corpus.[815]

The Court's pronouncement in *Gregg* that jurors were required to weigh statutorily enumerated aggravating and mitigating circumstances before recommending sentence did not clearly articulate what factors needed to be examined and how much emphasis should be placed on the circumstances of an

---

808. Ford v. Wainwright, 477 U.S. 399 (1986) (Marshall, J., for the majority); Turner v. Murray, 476 U.S. 28 (1986) (Marshall, J., concurring in part and dissenting in part); Caldwell v. Mississippi, 472 U.S. 320 (1985) (Marshall, J., for the majority); Ake v. Oklahoma, 470 U.S. 68 (1985) (Marshall, J., for the majority); Strickland v. Washington, 466 U.S. 668, *reh'g denied*, 467 U.S. 1267 (1984) (Marshall, J., dissenting); Gray v. Lucas, 463 U.S. 1237 (1983) (Marshall, J., dissenting); Barefoot v. Estelle, 463 U.S. 880 (1983) (Marshall, J., dissenting); California v. Ramos, 463 U.S. 992 (1983) (Marshall, J., dissenting); Barclay v. Florida, 463 U.S. 939, *reh'g denied*, 464 U.S. 874 (1983) (Marshall, J., dissenting); Zant v. Stephens, 462 U.S. 862 (1983) (Marshall, J., dissenting); Coleman v. Balkcom, 451 U.S. 949 (1981) (Marshall, J., dissenting); Godfrey v. Georgia, 446 U.S. 420 (1980) (Marshall, J., concurring); Lockett v. Ohio, 438 U.S. 586 (1978) (Marshall, J., concurring); Gardner v. Florida, 430 U.S. 349 (1977).

809. *See supra* note 505.

810. Adams v. Texas, 448 U.S. 38, 51 (1980) (Marshall, J., concurring) (empaneling a jury); Beck v. Alabama, 447 U.S. 625, 646 (1980) (Marshall, J., concurring) (instructions to jury); Green v. Georgia, 442 U.S. 95, 98 (1979) (Marshall, J., concurring) (introduction of testimony); Bell v. Ohio, 438 U.S. 637, 643-44 (1978) (Marshall, J., concurring) (death penalty for accomplices); Coker v. Georgia, 433 U.S. 584, 600-01 (1977) (Marshall, J., concurring) (death penalty for rape).

811. *Zant*, 462 U.S. at 862; *Barclay*, 463 U.S. at 939; *Godfrey*, 446 U.S. at 420.

812. *Turner*, 476 U.S. at 28; *Ramos*, 463 U.S. at 992.

813. *Caldwell*, 472 U.S. at 320; *Ake*, 470 U.S. at 68; *Strickland*, 466 U.S. at 668; *Gardner*, 430 U.S. at 349.

814. *Ford*, 477 U.S. at 399 (mentally insane); *Lockett*, 438 U.S. at 586 (accomplices).

815. *Gray*, 463 U.S. at 1237 (certiorari); *Barefoot*, 463 U.S. at 880 (habeas corpus); *Balkcom*, 451 U.S. at 949 (certiorari).

offense and offender during trial deliberations, and, after 1976, the mode of proceeding by juries was litigated frequently.[816] Marshall addressed the wording of aggravating and mitigating circumstances in the 1980 case of *Godfrey v. Georgia*,[817] and in *Zant v. Stephens*[818] and *Barclay v. Florida*,[819] both decided in 1983.

The *Godfrey* case involved a statutory provision allowing the death penalty to be imposed in the second stage of a trial if sentencing authorities concluded that an offense "was outrageously or wantonly vile, horrible or inhuman in that it involved torture, depravity of mind, or an aggravated battery to the victim."[820] Though it held that the petitioner's homicide was no more atrocious than the circumstances of other murders, and that the statute was thus unconstitutionally applied to the accused,[821] the Court believed that the judge's instructions were sufficiently precise to channel the jury's discretion, and thus left the wording of this provision intact.

Marshall, in dissent, objected that this provision did not meet the requirement stipulated in *Gregg* that the discretion of sentencing authorities needed to be channeled to prevent arbitrariness. The wording of the aggravating circumstances is "hopelessly ambiguous and could be understood to apply to any murder," in effect conferring on the jury "unbridled discretion to impose the death penalty."[822] Thus, individualized consideration of the particular circumstances of an accused and alleged offense was precluded. Marshall did not believe, however, that aggravating and mitigating circumstances could ever be worded with sufficient precision to prevent arbitrariness in sentencing. The lingering and "disgraceful distorting effects of racial discrimination and poverty continue to be painfully visible in the imposition of death sentences,"[823] and their elimination was beyond the capability of the criminal justice system.[824] Marshall expressed hope that this realization would lead legislatures to conclude that "the effort to eliminate arbitrariness . . . is so plainly doomed to failure that . . . the death penalty [ ] must be abandoned alto-

---

816. *See supra* note 323.

817. 446 U.S. 420 (1980).

818. 462 U.S. 862 (1983).

819. 463 U.S. 939, *reh'g denied*, 464 U.S. 874 (1983).

820. 446 U.S. at 422.

821. *Id.* at 428-29.

822. *Id.* at 437.

823. *Id.* at 439.

824. *Id.* at 440.

gether."[825] Marshall reiterated this sentiment in *Zant*[826] and *Barclay*.[827]

Both of these cases examined whether a death sentence was invalid if a state supreme court had struck down one of the aggravating circumstances on which a jury based its verdict. The Court, in *Zant* and *Barclay*, refused to vacate a death sentence on the ground that a single aggravating circumstance is but one of many factors considered by a jury, and a verdict, based on assessment of evidence in the aggregate, is not diminished when one portion of an entire record is to be disregarded.[828]

Dissenting in *Zant*, Marshall declared that the trial judge was delinquent for submitting an invalidated aggravating circumstance to the jury, and it is uncertain whether the jury would have recommended a sentence of death if it had not been allowed to consider this provision.[829] Citing precedents, Marshall emphasized that the tone of the Court's Eighth Amendment jurisprudence has been that, to reduce the risk of arbitrariness, the sentencing discretion of juries must be confined so that factors unrelated to the circumstances of the accused may not be considered.[830] This, Marshall insisted, has not been observed. He condemned the majority's reliance on the "threshold theory" by which a jury may consider an unconfined range of aggravating and mitigating factors once it has determined that a particular defendant is statutorily eligible to receive the death penalty.[831] Enumeration of aggravating circumstances, Marshall declared, is intended to confine jurors' discretion at every stage of deliberations; if jurors were free to consider an unspecified array of potentially aggravating factors after having concluded that an accused was not precluded from receiving a capital sentence, there would be "no point in requiring state legislatures to identify specific aggravating circumstances."[832] In addition, Marshall believed that failure of the trial judge to explicitly inform jurors to weigh aggravating and mitigating evidence precluded judicial determination as to whether full assessment of the accused's individualized circumstances had been conducted.[833]

---

825. *Id.* at 442.

826. 462 U.S. at 862.

827. 463 U.S. at 939.

828. *Zant*, 462 U.S. at 879-80; *Barclay*, 463 U.S. at 949.

829. *Zant*, 462 U.S. at 916.

830. *Zant*, 462 U.S. at 907-10 (citing *Furman*, 408 U.S. at 238; *Gregg*, 428 U.S. at 153; *Jurek*, 428 U.S. at 262; *Proffitt*, 428 U.S. at 242; and *Godfrey*, 446 U.S. at 420).

831. *Zant*, 462 U.S. at 878.

832. *Id.* at 910.

833. *Id.* at 915.

Two weeks after *Zant* was decided, Marshall, dissenting in *Barclay*, objected that reliance by a trial judge, during pronouncement of sentence, on an aggravating circumstance not statutorily enumerated, also violated a central component of prior decisions which mandated channeling of discretion in trial proceedings. The *Barclay* case involved five black defendants who, motivated by racial animosity, killed a white youth. Prior to sentencing, the trial judge compared the racial motive of the accused's murder to what he personally witnessed at the opening of the Nazi concentration camps during World War II.[834] Marshall disagreed with the majority's position that, though the alleged racial motivations of an offense are not specifically designated as an aggravating factor, a judge may reflect on this implication to assess the magnitude of criminal action and determine whether the death penalty is warranted.[835] Such action, Marshall protested, enabled sentencing based on arbitrary considerations, and negated the Court's concern that the discretion of sentencing authorities be confined. If judges, contrary to express statutory provisions requiring examination of evidence against an accused to be confined only to those aggravating circumstances explicitly listed,[836] are permitted to make speculative extraneous observations, capital defendants may be sentenced on factors "randomly introduced."[837] This would preclude "consistency and fairness" in that "the fate of an individual defendant will inevitably depend on whether a given day his sentencer happened to respect the constraint imposed by . . . [state] law" or whether a judge "injects into the weighing process any number of nonstatutory factors in aggravation. . . ."[838]

Marshall's objection to the introduction at the time of sentencing of statements unspecified in statutory provisions underscored a deeper concern that capital proceedings could not unfold without injection of arbitrary sentiments. The Court, mindful of the enormity of the death penalty, has mandated that sentencing authorities give full consideration to the particular circumstances of the accused within the framework of carefully worded aggravating and mitigating factors. Both misinterpretation of statutory provisions and bias, among other factors, invariably tend to expand discretion, compelling lower judges and the Court, operating under these same limitations, to assess a sentence based on perceptions of fairness to the accused. The

---

834. *Barclay*, 463 U.S. at 948.
835. *Id.* at 949.
836. *Id.* at 985.
837. *Id.* at 986.
838. *Id.* at 986-87.

potential for arbitrariness, both at the trial and appellate levels, was addressed by Marshall as the Court examined different stages of trial proceedings. In the 1983 case of *California v. Ramos*,[839] and in *Caldwell v. Mississippi*,[840] decided two years later, Marshall examined guidelines concerning instructions to the jury.

The *Ramos* case considered a statutory requirement that a trial judge, in addition to communicating instructions on weighing aggravating and mitigating circumstances, inform jurors that a sentence of life imprisonment without parole may be commuted by the governor.[841] The majority did not believe that this introduced an impertinent factor which may divert the jury's attention from concentrating on aggravating and mitigating evidence or that jurors would perceive a diminished sense of importance concerning their pivotal role in trial deliberations. The Court believed that jurors, made aware that a defendant might not be indefinitely incarcerated, would more carefully weigh the individual circumstances of the accused when confronting the possibility that society may be penalized for inadequate consideration of all aggravating and mitigating factors. The majority also concluded that this instruction by the judge, encompassing but one of many components considered by the jury, did not undermine its ability to weigh aggravating and mitigating evidence in totality.

Marshall, in dissent, argued that communication of the possibility of gubernatorial commutation of a sentence "injects into the capital sentencing process a factor that bears no relation to the nature of the offense or the character of the offender."[842] He reminded the majority that jurors are required to examine the individual culpability of the accused, which has no relationship to the sentence ultimately imposed. A jury, told that a sentence of life imprisonment but not death may be commuted, "may impose the death sentence to prevent the Governor from exercising his power. . . ."[843] While this consideration may not necessarily be "more or less advantageous to defendants," it is "misleading"[844] by diverting the jury's attention away from the evidence presented and toward "ad hoc speculation about the likelihood of a release."[845] Without elaboration, Marshall also declared that commutation contradicted any professed goal of

---

839.   463 U.S. 992 (1983).
840.   472 U.S. 320 (1985).
841.   *Ramos*, 463 U.S. at 995.
842.   *Id.* at 1015.
843.   *Id.* at 1016.
844.   *Id.* at 1017.
845.   *Id.* at 1018.

retribution and deterrence to keep potentially dangerous individuals off the streets, and thus cannot be supported as justification of a state's adoption of capital punishment.[846]

The *Caldwell* case also examined whether comments to the
jury that its verdict would be reviewed by the state supreme court
diminished the members' sense of responsibility to carefully eval-
uate evidence. On behalf of the majority, Marshall declared that
this communication by the prosecutor unconstitutionally conveyed to the jury a perception that it was not ultimately responsible for the fate of the accused.[847] Marshall believed that this may
diminish a defendant's ability to have all evidence examined in
trial deliberations. Unlike jurors, who are present to "hear the
evidence and arguments and see the witnesses,"[848] an appellate
proceeding, which can only examine the written record, cannot
assess "intangibles a jury might consider in its sentencing determination."[849] Appellate courts, Marshall maintained, review sentencing decisions "with a presumption of correctness,"[850] and do
not take into account the individualized circumstances of the
accused.

Marshall speculated that communication to the jury that its
verdict may not be final would, in subtle ways, induce it to deliberate on factors unrelated to the accused and alleged offense. A
jury, made aware that its pronouncement would be reexamined,
may be coerced by a prosecutor's pressure to issue a verdict of
guilty and "'send a message' of extreme disapproval for the
defendant's acts."[851] In addition, some jurors, after being
informed that a sentence of life imprisonment "could not be
increased to a death sentence on appeal,"[852] may, given the
assurance that any errors they might have committed will be subsequently corrected, feel pressured to recommend execution.[853]
Marshall did not believe this possibility was remote; a jury, he

---

846. *Id.* at 1023.

847. *Caldwell,* 472 U.S. at 329-30.

848. *Id.* at 331.

849. *Id.* at 330. At the time of the *Caldwell* decision, several studies had
been published indicating that full examination of the accused's circumstances
had not been conducted in appellate proceedings and that arbitrariness had
entered this stage. *See* F. Patrick Hubbard, *'Reasonable Levels of Arbitrariness' in
Death Sentencing Patterns: A Tragic Perspective on Capital Punishment,* 18 U.C. DAVIS
L. REV. 1113 (1985); Ellen Liebman, *Appellate Review of Death Sentences: A Critique
of Proportionality Review,* 18 U.C. DAVIS L. REV. 1433 (1985).

850. *Caldwell,* 472 U.S. at 331.

851. *Id.* (quoting Maggio v. Williams, 464 U.S. 46, 54-55 (1983) (Stevens,
J., concurring)).

852. *Id.* at 332.

853. *Id.*

declared, "is made up of individuals placed in a very unfamiliar situation and called on to make a very difficult and uncomfortable choice,"[854] enhancing the possibility that it would engage in actions likely to involve ultimate participation by trained appellate judges. This type of coercion, Marshall concluded, is contrary to the tone of the Court's evolving position that sentence be based on the individualized circumstances of the accused.

Three years after the *Ramos* and *Caldwell* decisions, Marshall once again addressed introduction into trial proceedings of evidence which did not directly relate to the culpability of the accused. In *Turner v. Murray* (1986),[855] Marshall, in a brief statement concurring and dissenting in part, declared that a defendant, in an interracial crime, should not be prevented from inquiring into the possible racial bias of jurors.[856] Prevention of possible arbitrariness in deliberations was emphasized by Marshall in other stages of trial proceedings. In the 1977 case of *Gardner v. Florida,*[857] Marshall, writing in dissent, agreed with the majority's pronouncement that a state "must administer its capital-sentencing procedures with an even hand"[858] by making available to an accused a parole commission's presentence report, but expressed anger that the trial judge ignored the jury's recommendation and pronounced sentence with blatant disregard of a defendant's due process expectations.[859] The risk of arbitrariness in capital proceedings impelled Marshall to express doubt as to whether the Court had been improperly optimistic in believing that deliberations could be objectively conducted.[860] Seven years later, in the 1984 case of *Strickland v. Washington,*[861] Marshall again raised similar concerns.

In a strong dissent from the majority's willingness to allow states to gradually develop standards for assessing the quality of legal representation in capital proceedings,[862] Marshall insisted that, over time, defense attorneys will undermine due process

---

854. *Id.* at 333.
855. 476 U.S. 28 (1986).
856. *Id.* at 45 (Marshall, J., concurring in part and dissenting in part). For a discussion of this case, see *supra* text accompanying notes 599-600.
857. 430 U.S. 349 (1977).
858. *Id.* at 361.
859. *Id.* at 365.
860. *Id.* Marshall spoke at length on the failure to adhere to guidelines put forward in Proffitt v. Florida, 428 U.S. 242, *reh'g denied,* 429 U.S. 875 (1976). *Gardner,* 430 U.S. at 366-70. For a discussion of the Court's position in *Proffitt* and companion cases, see *supra* text accompanying notes 287-305.
861. 466 U.S. 668 (1984).
862. For a discussion of this case, see *supra* text accompanying notes 615-17.

safeguards. The quality of legal counsel, Marshall pointed out, has varied considerably from case to case, depending, in part, on the attorney's caseload and the ability of a defendant to afford representation.[863] In view of the enormity of capital proceedings, Marshall believed it was inappropriate for standards concerning competency of counsel to fluctuate in different localities; this, he argued, would reintroduce randomness in deliberations which had been deemed objectionable in evolving Eighth Amendment jurisprudence.[864] Marshall did not believe uniform guidelines to assess the performance of counsel could be articulated. It is "often very difficult to tell whether a defendant convicted after a trial in which he was ineffectively represented would have fared better if his lawyer had been competent,"[865] and compelling the defendant to demonstrate incompetence imposed a formidable burden.[866] Marshall insisted that evidence of inadequate legal representation required a retrial "regardless of whether the defendant suffered demonstrable prejudice. . . ."[867]

Marshall strongly objected to the majority's seeming unwillingness to demand stricter adherence to due process safeguards in capital as opposed to noncapital proceedings. The "severity and irrevocability of the sanction at stake" required that thoroughness of legal representation "be applied especially stringently in capital sentencing proceedings."[868] Marshall did not believe the defendant had been adequately represented in this case,[869] and his concern that arbitrariness would permeate capital proceedings made arguments in favor of abolition of the death penalty compelling. Marshall reiterated this sentiment in the 1985 case of *Ake v. Oklahoma*,[870] which also addressed procedural requirements concerning introduction of evidence.

The *Ake* case focused on the right of an indigent capital defendant to have a psychiatric examination conducted at state expense for use during trial deliberations. The accused, found by a psychiatrist to be incompetent to stand trial, was later declared by a mental hospital to be fit for courtroom delibera-

---

863. *Strickland*, 466 U.S. at 708.

864. *Id.* at 715.

865. *Id.* at 710.

866. *Id.* at 713. For a discussion of how the majority believed a defendant may prove ineffective counsel, see *supra* text accompanying note 616.

867. *Strickland*, 466 U.S. at 712.

868. *Id.* at 716.

869. *Id.* at 717-19.

870. 470 U.S. 68 (1985).

tions while under continued sedation.[871] The defense attorney's request for a psychiatric examination was denied, and, following the psychiatrist's comment at the guilt phase that the accused was a threat to the community, the jury, absent testimony on the defendant's competency at the time of the alleged offense, decided to convict.[872] Agreeing with the state's emphasis on the psychiatrist's assessment of the accused's perceived danger to society, a sentence of death was issued.[873]

On behalf of the majority, Marshall declared that the state is required to comply with an accused's request for psychiatric assistance during trial. Citing precedents in which the Court required right to counsel for indigents in noncapital proceedings,[874] Marshall insisted that a state's obligation "to assure that the defendant has a fair opportunity to present his defense"[875] is more compelling in capital trials. This, he claimed, is particularly apparent with regard to psychiatric assistance. Rejecting as "not substantial"[876] the state's argument that furnishing this assistance would be financially burdensome, Marshall emphasized that over forty states, as well as the Federal government, have statutorily recognized the pivotal role that psychiatry has come to play in criminal proceedings.[877] Professional examination of an accused's mental condition is of invaluable assistance in apprising sentencing authorities of an accused's blameworthiness, and, when a defendant "demonstrates to the trial judge that his sanity at the time of the offense is to be a significant factor at trial,"[878] the state must furnish psychiatric expertise. One year after the Ake decision, Marshall, on behalf of the majority in the 1986 case of Ford v. Wainwright,[879] ruled that executing the mentally insane was unconstitutional.

The prohibition against cruel and unusual punishment is intended not only to limit the kinds of penalties imposed but also to restrict their infliction to specific classes of offenders. While

---

871. Id. at 71-72.
872. Id. at 72-73.
873. Id. at 73.
874. See, e.g., Ake, 470 U.S. at 76 (citing Gideon v. Wainwright, 372 U.S. 335 (1963) and Douglas v. California, 372 U.S. 353 (1963)).
875. Ake, 470 U.S. at 76.
876. Id. at 79.
877. Id. at 83.
878. Id.
879. 477 U.S. 399 (1986). For an examination of the psychiatric analysis performed on the petitioner, as well as an account of judicial proceedings in the Ford case up through its appeal to the Court, see KENT S. MILLER & MICHAEL L. RADELET, EXECUTING THE MENTALLY ILL: THE CRIMINAL JUSTICE SYSTEM AND THE CASE OF ALVIN FORD (1993).

Marshall unwaveringly opposed capital punishment per se, he strongly insisted that those who did not commit murder[880] and who are incapable of comprehending the magnitude of their conduct[881] should not be subjected to the death penalty. In *Ford*, Marshall explained why he believed the Eighth Amendment proscribed the death penalty for the mentally insane.

Marshall explained that the prohibition against "cruel and unusual punishments" embodied an evolving attitude toward penalties whose origins are steeped in Anglo-American tradition. Dating back to the writings of Sir Edward Coke, British common law has opposed execution of the insane.[882] The language of the Eighth Amendment, Marshall declared, "embrace[d], at a minimum, those modes or acts of punishment that had been considered cruel and unusual at the time that the Bill of Rights was adopted;"[883] however, it also transcended "practices condemned by the common law in 1789"[884] and anticipated "'evolving standards of decency that mark the progress of a maturing society.'"[885] In the United States, Marshall noted that prohibition of the death penalty for the mentally insane was followed during the colonial period,[886] and that no state has sanctioned it in contemporary times.[887] He attributed this to an "intuition that such an execution simply offends humanity. . . ."[888]

---

880.   See Marshall's brief concurring statement in Lockett v. Ohio, 438 U.S. 586 (1978), which invalidated the death penalty for accomplices. *Id.* at 619-21. *See also*, Tison v. Arizona, 481 U.S. 137, *reh'g denied*, 482 U.S. 921 (1987) (Marshall, J., joining the dissenting opinion of Brennan, J.). For a discussion of the *Tison* ruling, see *supra* text accompanying notes 630-50.

881.   *See, e.g.*, Stanford v. Kentucky, 492 U.S. 361, decided together with Wilkins v. Missouri, 109 S. Ct. 2969 (1989) (death penalty for seventeen-year-olds) (Marshall, J., joining the dissenting opinion of Brennan, J.); Penry v. Lynaugh, 492 U.S. 302 (1989) (death penalty for the mentally retarded) (Marshall, J., joining the dissenting opinion of Brennan, J.). For a discussion of these cases, see *supra* text accompanying notes 652-58.

882.   *Ford*, 477 U.S. at 406-07. Marshall quoted Coke's statement that execution of "'a mad man'" was "'a miserable spectacle, both against Law, and of extream [sic] inhumanity and cruelty, and can be no example to others.'" *Ford*, 477 U.S. at 407 (quoting 3 EDWARD COKE, INSTITUTIONS 6 (1680). Marshall also pointed out that Blackstone categorized execution of the mentally insane as "'savage and inhuman.'" *Ford*, 477 U.S. at 406 (quoting WILLIAM BLACKSTONE, COMMENTARIES 24-25 (1769)).

883.   *Ford*, 477 U.S. at 405.

884.   *Id.* at 406.

885.   *Id.* (quoting Trop v. Dulles, 356 U.S. 86, 101 (1958) (concurring opinion)).

886.   *Id.* at 408. This attitude found its roots in several centuries of English common law. *Id.*

887.   *Id.* at 408-09.

888.   *Id.* at 409.

Marshall also pointed out that defendants who are to be examined by a psychiatrist are entitled to submit material which might affect assessment of their mental capacity or blameworthiness. To reduce the possibility of conviction based on an improper psychiatric diagnosis, sentencing authorities must confine their judgment to "'evidence offered by each party'"[889] in seeking to resolve differences of medical opinion on the mental state of the accused. In addition, an opportunity to challenge the findings of state appointed psychiatrists must be furnished.[890]

Marshall's insistence on adhering to meticulous due process safeguards underscored his concern that states not proceed against capital defendants arbitrarily. To ensure that sentences which may result in the penalty of death are based on full and unbiased consideration of the individualized circumstances of the accused, Marshall, like Brennan,[891] sought to maximize the opportunities of a defendant to challenge trial proceedings and decisions by petition for certiorari and habeas corpus.[892] In the 1980s he addressed this subject in three cases: *Coleman v. Balkcom*[893] and *Gray v. Lucas*,[894] both of which considered petitions for certiorari, and *Barefoot v. Estelle*,[895] which dealt with petition for habeas corpus.

Dissenting in both *Balkcom* and *Gray*, which denied petitions for certiorari,[896] Marshall emphasized that the need for appellate review is more compelling in capital proceedings. In *Balkcom* he noted that, "when the death penalty is in issue, the Constitution may impose unusual limitations on the States."[897] Marshall reiterated that: "If an individual is imprisoned for an offense he did not commit, the error can to some extent be rectified. But if he is executed, the wrong that has been done can never be corrected."[898] Believing that the state, in capital cases, "must survive close scrutiny on post-trial review,"[899] Marshall concluded that petitioner's claim to have been deprived of an opportunity,

---

889. *Id.* at 414 (quoting Ake v. Oklahoma, 470 U.S. 68, 81 (1985)).

890. *Id.* at 415.

891. *See supra* text accompanying notes 686-96.

892. For a discussion of these concepts, see *supra* text accompanying notes 674-96.

893. 451 U.S. 949 (1981).

894. 463 U.S. 1237 (1983).

895. 463 U.S. 880 (1983).

896. Gray v. Lucas, 463 U.S. 1237, 1240 (1983) (Marshall, J., dissenting); Coleman v. Balkcom, 451 U.S. 949, 953 (1981) (Marshall, J., dissenting).

897. *Balkcom*, 451 U.S. at 954.

898. *Id.* at 955.

899. *Id.*

under the Sixth Amendment,[900] to call witnesses,[901] merited review, and that the petition for certiorari should be granted.[902]

In *Gray*, Marshall believed that petitioner's challenge of a death sentence by exposure to cyanide gas[903] constituted prolonged and needless infliction of pain which violated judicial precedents.[904] This form of punishment, which involved "extreme pain over a span of 10 to 12 minutes,"[905] prolonged suffering longer than lethal injection, which has been perceived by state legislatures as a "more dignified way of administering the death penalty."[906] Based on evolving legislative trends which have rejected use of lethal gas, Marshall concluded that the petition for certiorari "raise[d] issues of sufficient import"[907] and should be granted. In *Barefoot*,[908] also decided in 1983, Marshall once again emphasized the importance of appellate review in capital cases.

Dissenting from the majority's upholding of a lower federal court decision to reject a petition for habeas corpus,[909] Marshall again urged that more careful scrutiny of trial proceedings take place where the penalty of death may be imposed. A defendant who, pursuant to congressional law, has obtained a certificate of probable cause to appeal denial of a petition for habeas corpus,[910] has already established that the grievance was not frivolous, and ought to be granted full review of the petition without risk that the lower courts may adopt "expedited procedures in resolving the merits of habeas appeals. . . ."[911] This alternative, Marshall objected, may result in denial of a petition for stay of execution without having considered the substantive grievances raised by a defendant; in effect, he maintained, a state could "execute the prisoner before his appeal is decided"[912] and render the appellate process "meaningless."[913] In view of "the

---

900. *See supra* text accompanying note 143.
901. *Id.* at 953-54.
902. *Id.* at 956.
903. *Gray*, 463 U.S. at 1240.
904. *Id.* at 1244-45 (quoting Gregg v. Georgia, 428 U.S. 153, 173, *reh'g denied*, 429 U.S. 875 (1976); Trop v. Dulles, 356 U.S. 86, 101 (1958); *In re* Kemmler, 136 U.S. 436, 447 (1890)).
905. *Id.* at 1245.
906. *Id.*
907. *Id.* at 1247.
908. Barefoot v. Estelle, 463 U.S. at 880 (1983).
909. *Id.* at 906 (Marshall, J., dissenting).
910. *Id.* at 906-07 n.1 (quoting 28 U.S.C. § 2253).
911. *Barefoot*, 463 U.S. at 894.
912. *Id.* at 910.
913. *Id.* at 907.

irreversible nature of the death penalty,"[914] Marshall concluded that it would be "grossly improper"[915] for an appellate court to rely on summary procedures in capital cases.

During the tenure of Chief Justice Burger, Marshall unwaveringly objected to the Court's perceived failure to preserve a full range of due process protections for capital defendants. He continued to express this concern after Justice William Rehnquist was elevated to the position of Chief Justice in 1986.

C. Objections to the Position of the Rehnquist Court (1986-   ) and an Emotional Dissent the Day Before Marshall's Retirement in 1991

In five years on the Rehnquist Court, Marshall wrote an opinion in eleven cases: five examined the weighing by jurors of aggravating and mitigating circumstances;[916] one reviewed the empaneling of jurors;[917] one dealt with a prosecutor's comments to the jury;[918] one focused on the withholding from defense counsel of a psychiatric report;[919] two considered standing to appeal capital convictions[920] and one focused on introduction of testimony describing the emotional effects of the victim's death on family members.[921]

Marshall continued to believe that arbitrariness had not been eliminated from capital proceedings and that the Court had not been consistent in its adjudication of cases on capital punishment.[922] With regard to the weighing of aggravating and mitigating factors, he maintained that the wording of statutory provisions did not confine jurors to the individualized circumstances of the accused. In the 1988 case of *Lowenfield v. Phelps*,[923] a judge, upon hearing of the jury's inability to agree upon a ver-

---

914. *Id.* at 913.
915. *Id.* at 915.
916. Shell v. Mississippi, 111 S. Ct. 313 (1990); McKoy v. North Carolina, 110 S. Ct. 1227 (1990); Boyde v. California, 110 S. Ct. 1190 (1990); Hildwin v. Florida, 109 S. Ct. 2055 (1989) (Marshall, J., dissenting) (brief statement expressing categorical opposition to capital punishment); Lowenfield v. Phelps, 108 S. Ct. 546 (1988).
917. Mu'Min v. Virginia, 111 S. Ct. 1899, *reh'g denied,* 112 S. Ct. 13 (1991).
918. Sawyer v. Smith, 110 S. Ct. 2822 (1990).
919. Satterwhite v. Texas, 108 S. Ct. 1792 (1988).
920. Whitmore v. Arkansas, 110 S. Ct. 1717 (1990); McCleskey v. Zant, 111 S. Ct. 1454, *reh'g denied,* 111 S. Ct. 2841 (1991).
921. Payne v. Tennessee, 111 S. Ct. 2597, *reh'g denied,* 112 S. Ct. 28 (1991).
922. For a discussion of the Rehnquist Court's position on the death penalty up to the time of Marshall's retirement in 1991, see *supra* text accompanying notes 337-64.
923. 108 S. Ct. 546.

dict, declared that a sentence of life imprisonment would be imposed if a unanimous recommendation was not forthcoming.[924] Shortly after this communication, a verdict of death was issued by the jury and adhered to in the sentence.[925] The Court upheld the judge's sentence of death, satisfied that the verdict was based not on intimidation but rather on full consideration of "the mitigating aspects of the crime and the unique characteristics of the perpetrator."[926]

Marshall, in dissent, believed that the judge's comments coerced the jury into reaching a verdict. Though compromise of jury objectivity is "difficult to discern in concrete situations,"[927] Marshall maintained that the enormity of the death penalty demanded stricter examination of jury deliberations than that conducted in noncapital proceedings, and that any doubt as to whether jurors were pressured to reach a verdict must be resolved by refusing to support a sentence of death. After examining the long hours of deliberation during which time a verdict could not be reached, and the relatively brief time which elapsed following the judge's communication and the announcement that jurors are in agreement,[928] as well as the tone of the judge's comments and manner in which the jury was addressed, Marshall concluded that the possibility of coercion was realistic.[929] In addition, he objected that the jury, basing its verdict on a single aggravating circumstance which essentially duplicated one of the defendant's allegations,[930] did not meet its burden of independently linking the nature and character of the accused and offense to a statutory provision. This, Marshall feared, might facilitate pronouncement of a death sentence without conducting a probing analysis into an accused's culpability.

Marshall again expressed disapproval with the manner in which jurors weighed aggravating and mitigating evidence in three 1990 cases: *Shell v. Mississippi*,[931] *Boyde v. California*,[932] and *McKoy v. North Carolina*.[933] In *Shell*, the Court, per curiam, declared that requiring the jury to assess whether a murder was "especially heinous, atrocious, or cruel"[934] insufficiently chan-

---

924. *Id.* at 549.
925. *Id.* at 549-50.
926. *Id.* at 555.
927. *Id.* at 556.
928. *Id.* at 557-58.
929. *Id.* at 557-59.
930. *Id.* at 560.
931. 111 S. Ct. 313.
932. 110 S. Ct. 1190.
933. 110 S. Ct. 1227.
934. 111 S. Ct. at 313.

neled its discretion.[935] Marshall, in a brief concurring statement, noted that even if the word "cruel" had been precisely defined, the statute would still contain "*two* constitutionally infirm"[936] guidelines, rendering the entire provision invalid. He spoke at greater length on the weighing by jurors of aggravating and mitigating circumstances in *Boyde* and *McKoy*.

Both of these cases dealt with consideration of mitigating evidence. In *Boyde*, the Court, citing precedents in *Lockett v. Ohio*[937] and *Penry v. Lynaugh*,[938] reiterated that a jury may consider any mitigating factors pertaining to the circumstances of the accused.[939] While uncertainty over the meaning of a judge's instructions on interpretation of aggravating and mitigating circumstances is not uncommon, the Court declared that proceedings needed to be examined in the aggregate to determine whether the jury has appeared to construe guidelines "in a way that prevents the consideration of constitutionally relevant evidence."[940] Formal exclusion of mitigating evidence from jury deliberations, however, violated these precedents; as the Court declared in *McKoy*, where a statute allowing consideration of only those mitigating circumstances unanimously found was held as an impermissible restriction on jurors' discretion.[941]

On behalf of the majority in *McKoy*, Marshall, relying on precedent established in *Mills v. Maryland*,[942] pointed out that any mitigating evidence introduced by the accused during proceedings must be assessed by jurors as an active and ongoing component of the accused's culpability. The unanimity requirement, however, would preclude this by enabling "one holdout juror to prevent the others from giving effect to evidence"[943] which may produce a verdict recommending a term of imprisonment. Marshall also expressed concern that this statutory provision would

---

935. *Id.* The Court based its ruling on the position taken in Godfrey v. Georgia, 446 U.S. 420 (1980). *See supra* text accompanying notes 821-23. *See also* Lewis v. Jeffers, 110 S. Ct. 3092, *reh'g denied*, 111 S. Ct. 14 (1990); Walton v. Arizona, 110 S. Ct. 3047, *reh'g denied*, 111 S. Ct. 14 (1990). In Gregg v. Georgia, 428 U.S. 153, *reh'g denied*, 429 U.S. 875 (1976), the Court held that a statutory aggravating circumstance referring to the heinous, vile, or inhuman nature of an offense is not unconstitutional on its face. *Id.* at 201. For a discussion of the *Gregg* decision, see *supra* text accompanying notes 287-305.

936. *Shell*, 111 S. Ct. at 314 (Marshall, J., concurring) (emphasis in original).

937. 438 U.S. 586 (1978). *See supra* text accompanying notes 306-11.

938. 109 S. Ct. 2934.

939. *Boyde*, 110 S. Ct. at 1196.

940. *Id.* at 1198.

941. 110 S. Ct. at 1234.

942. 108 S. Ct. 1860.

943. *McKoy*, 110 S. Ct. at 1231.

alter the tone of jury deliberations. During jury proceedings, various components of aggravating and mitigating evidence fluctuate in importance whereby, depending on the content of discussion, a factor initially considered substantial may later be deemed insignificant, and vice versa. Disallowing consideration of some mitigating evidence at the outset of deliberations unconstitutionally inhibited full examination of the entire character and background of the accused.[944] This risk of incomplete jury deliberations was also discussed by Marshall in *Boyde.*

Unlike the majority in *Boyde,* which believed that jurors are presumed to have fully discharged their responsibility absent evidence in the trial court's record indicating impropriety, Marshall insisted that, irrespective of actual performance, the potential, based on the content of instructions from a judge, for incomplete consideration of an accused's circumstances, presumed that "the jury's verdict *could* have rested on unconstitutional grounds,"[945] and rendered proceedings invalid. Prevention of arbitrary sentencing demanded more meticulous examination of due process protection accorded defendants in capital as opposed to noncapital proceedings, and allegations that a sentencing jury "reasonably could have believed that it could not consider [all] mitigating evidence regarding his character and background"[946] placed a burden on trial officials to prove that this had not transpired. The majority's unwillingness to make this inquiry, Marshall protested, stemmed from its "growing and unjustified hostility to claims of constitutional violation by capital defendants."[947] Marshall's concern that evidence of active consideration of the full range of a defendant's background and circumstances in courtroom deliberations be furnished was expressed with different stages of trial proceedings. In the 1991 case of *Mu'Min v. Virginia*[948] Marshall discussed enabling unbiased examination of an accused's situation in the manner prospective jurors are empaneled.

The *Mu'Min* case involved an extensively publicized murder where the trial judge refused to ask prospective jurors what they had read or heard about the alleged offense and defendant. Satisfied that the trial judge, who asked potential jurors who had been exposed to media reports whether they "had formed an opinion" and whether they could "determine petitioner's guilt or

---

944.   *Id.* at 1234.
945.   *Boyde,* 494 U.S. at 389 (emphasis in original).
946.   *Id.* at 387.
947.   *Id.* at 406.
948.   111 S. Ct. 1899, *reh'g denied,* 112 S. Ct. 13 (1991).

innocence based solely on the evidence presented at trial,"[949] took sufficient steps to empanel an unbiased jury, the Court ruled that the Sixth Amendment's guarantee of a trial "by an impartial jury"[950] had been met.

Marshall, in dissent, once again emphasized that the potential for bias, apart from its actual occurrence, compelled invalidation of proceedings where the trial judge had not taken sufficient steps to ensure objectivity by prospective jurors. Because "8 of the 12 jurors who ultimately convicted . . . [the accused] of murder and sentenced him to death admitted exposure to . . . [extensive pretrial] publicity,"[951] Marshall insisted that a majority of the jury may have begun deliberations with degrees of bias. To preclude this possibility, it is insufficient for the trial judge to merely ask potential jurors whether they could discharge their duty objectively; impartiality, he maintained, "cannot [be] realistically assess[ed] . . . without first establishing what the juror already has learned about the case."[952]

Interestingly, Marshall did not draw on recent precedents which appeared to corroborate his position. The majority's ruling was consistent with the Court's pronouncement in the 1968 case of *Witherspoon v. Illinois*,[953] which required a trial judge, irrespective of personal biases, to ensure that a potential juror could discharge an oath based on evidence presented.[954] In subsequent cases, however, the Court declared that it was permissible to question potential jurors on racial bias;[955] arguably, extensive pretrial publicity involving an alleged murder by an accused of Indian ancestry required comparable inquiry at the empaneling stage into possible ethnic bias. Though Marshall did not attempt to analogize this case with those involving potential bias stemming from interracial homicide,[956] his insistence on meticulous adherence to due process safeguards in capital proceedings was

---

949. *Id.* at 1901.

950. The Sixth Amendment in pertinent part states that: "In all criminal prosecutions, the accused shall enjoy the right to a speedy and public trial, by an impartial jury. . . ." U.S. CONST. amend. VI.

951. *Mu'Min*, 111 S. Ct. at 1909.

952. *Id.* at 1910.

953. 391 U.S. 510 (1968).

954. *Id.*

955. *See* Turner v. Murray, 476 U.S. 28 (1986); Wainwright v. Witt, 469 U.S. 412 (1985); Adams v. Texas, 448 U.S. 38 (1980). For a discussion of these rulings, see *supra* text accompanying notes 571-76, 579-86, 599-600.

956. The case of Wainwright v. Witt, 469 U.S. 412 (1985), was cited, but its pronouncements on the need to question jurors about possible racial biases were not relied on for comparison with Mu'Min's ethnicity. *Mu'Min*, 111 S. Ct. at 1913.

unabated. This was articulated by Marshall in the 1988 case of *Satterwhite v. Texas*,[957] which dealt with the withholding from defense counsel of a psychiatric report.

Agreeing with the majority's conclusion in *Satterwhite* that failure to provide defense counsel an opportunity to consult with the accused prior to the preparation of a psychiatric evaluation prohibited use of the psychiatrist's testimony at the sentencing stage,[958] Marshall, in a concurring opinion, emphasized that capital trials require more extensive due process protections than those followed in noncapital proceedings. Marshall declared that the majority's application to capital cases of the harmless error rule — which provides that, "if the prosecution can prove beyond a reasonable doubt that a constitutional error did not contribute to the verdict, the error is harmless and the verdict may stand"[959] — may qualitatively alter the tone of deliberations. A psychiatric evaluation, Marshall pointed out, "is clothed with a scientific authority that often carries great weight with lay juries,"[960] and the kind of preparation undertaken by a defense attorney "may be altered significantly"[961] if counsel is made aware of the state's intention to conduct such an analysis. The testimony of an accused, based on advice given by the defense attorney, would become part of a sentencing authority's "moral judgment involving a balancing of often tangible factors" as to whether "a defendant should live or die."[962] By failing to take this into account, Marshall believed that the majority undermined the manner in which a sentence in large part is based on evaluation of a number of factors which gradually unfold during a trial.

The basic principle which Marshall emphasized was that the trial judge must ensure that all aspects of the accused's character and background are being actively considered. Since a sentencing decision is based on cumulative evidence brought out in a trial, it is imperative, Marshall maintained, that an accused have an opportunity to challenge modes of proceeding at any stage of deliberations. In two cases decided in 1990 — *Sawyer v. Smith*[963] and *Whitmore v. Arkansas*[964] — as well as *McCleskey v. Zant*,[965] adju-

---

957. 486 U.S. 249 (1988).
958. 486 U.S. at 260.
959. *Id.* at 256.
960. *Id.* at 264.
961. *Id.*
962. *Id.*
963. 497 U.S. 227 (1990).
964. 495 U.S. 149 (1990).
965. 499 U.S. 467 (1991).

dicated one year later, Marshall insisted that this option is not diminished in appellate proceedings.

The enormity of a possible sentence of death, as well as concern that arbitrariness could occur at any stage in capital proceedings, impelled Marshall to support application of revised due process guidelines to those who have been sentenced without benefit of a new procedural interpretation, and to facilitate access to appellate courts for litigants wishing to challenge trial court pronouncements. In the 1989 case of *Teague v. Lane*,[966] the Court put forward a standard which a litigant had to meet for a new ruling to be applied retroactively; Marshall, dissenting in *Sawyer*, expressed his position on this issue.

An underlying principle of the Court's Eighth Amendment jurisprudence has been that execution, "qualitatively different . . . from all other punishments,"[967] compelled establishment of extensive due process protections, and opportunities for defendants to challenge perceived abridgment of explicit statutory provisions and trial proceedings which, in totality, enhanced "the *risk* that the death penalty would be imposed in an arbitrary or capricious manner."[968] Though he acknowledged that "recognition of a right under state law does not translate automatically into the existence of federal constitutional protection,"[969] Marshall added that state law has not "evolved independently of our Eighth Amendment decisions."[970] The commitment of states to "'a fair trial in the sentencing phase'"[971] established a right "cognizable under the Federal Constitution"[972] and subjected state practices to adjudication "informed by federal principles."[973] After indicating that retroactive application of rules "designed to promote the accuracy of criminal proceedings"[974] has been "routinely afforded defendants,"[975] Marshall emphasized that this policy is no less compelling with the commitment to "heightened

---

966.   489 U.S. 288, *reh'g denied*, 490 U.S. 1031 (1989). *See supra* text accompanying notes 680-83.

967.   *Sawyer*, 497 U.S. at 252.

968.   *Id.* (emphasis in original).

969.   *Id.* at 250.

970.   *Id.* at 251.

971.   *Id.* (quoting State v. Berry, 391 So.2d 406, 418 (La. 1980) (emphasis in original)).

972.   497 U.S. at 250.

973.   *Id.* at 251.

974.   *Id.* at 258.

975.   *Id.* (quoting Williams v. United States, 401 U.S. 646 (1971); and citing Stovall v. Denno, 388 U.S. 293 (1967), and Linkletter v. Walker, 381 U.S. 618 (1965)).

reliability in capital sentencing."[976] Denial of retroactive application of federal law to state proceedings constituted "an especially condescending federalism."[977] A state, he concluded, "undoubtedly possesse[d] a legitimate interest in the finality of its convictions;" however, when "the State itself undermine[d] the accuracy of a capital proceeding, that general interest must give way to the demands of justice."[978] Thus, Marshall believed that the position put forward by the Court in *Teague* concerning the retroactive application of new rules[979] is not to be followed in capital proceedings.

Marshall's position in *Sawyer* underscored his concern to make appellate review readily available to capital defendants. He further elaborated on this concept in *Whitmore* with regard to establishing standing for federal appellate review,[980] and in *McCleskey* concerning petition for habeas corpus.[981]

Disagreeing with the majority's ruling in *Whitmore* that an inmate lacked standing to appeal the death sentence of a defendant who, consistent with state law, waived the option to challenge the trial judge's pronouncement, Marshall, in dissent, declared that it was unconscionable to execute an individual without mandatory appellate review. Marshall did not attempt to directly refute the majority's position that the inmate failed to meet the requirements of Article III for securing a grant of jurisdiction from the federal courts;[982] rather, he declared that establishment of next-friend standing is not fixed in the Constitution but based on evolving principles of common law.[983] The Court, Marshall maintained, "certainly has the authority to expand or contract a common law doctrine where necessary to serve an important judicial or societal interest,"[984] and the majority's failure to acknowledge this indicated that its "desire to eliminate delays in executions exceed[ed] its solicitude for the Eighth Amendment."[985]

Marshall reiterated his concern that the risk of an erroneous capital conviction justified mandatory review of trial proceedings.

---

976.   497 U.S. at 246-47.

977.   *Id.* at 251.

978.   *Id.* at 259.

979.   *See supra* text accompanying notes 680-83.

980.   *See supra* text accompanying notes 676-79.

981.   *See supra* text accompanying note 675.

982.   For a discussion of the Court's position, see *supra* text accompanying notes 676-79.

983.   495 U.S. at 177.

984.   *Id.* at 177-78.

985.   *Id.* at 176.

Noting the relatively high rate of reversal of sentences of death in several state supreme courts,[986] Marshall emphasized that appellate examination "is an indispensable safeguard."[987] He did not believe that an individual's decision to waive appellate review outweighed a state's interest in dealing with defendants in a civilized manner. The Eighth Amendment's prohibition of "cruel and unusual punishments," Marshall maintained, envisioned moral conduct which required adherence "to our basic societal values and to the integrity of our system of justice."[988] Just as Marshall believed this command of the Eighth Amendment compelled mandatory appellate review, he no less fervently maintained, in the 1991 case of *McCleskey v. Zant*,[989] that restrictions on one's ability to challenge a sentence in capital proceedings by petition for a writ of habeas corpus were impermissible.

Examining the proper exercise of a habeas corpus petition in capital proceedings,[990] the Court in *McCleskey* held that one who failed to raise a legal claim in an initial petition must demonstrate, in a second or subsequent application seeking to refute the government's assertion that the writ has been abused, that "a fundamental miscarriage of justice would result from failure to entertain the claim."[991] Marshall, in dissent, believed that this standard presented a formidable obstacle to a defendant seeking to challenge a sentence. After examining applicable precedents,[992] Marshall declared that abuse of the writ occurred when a defendant intentionally sought to "achieve some end other than expeditious relief from unlawful confinement."[993] However, a litigant who, in an initial petition, made "a good-faith assessment of the claims available to him," or who has come

---

986. Marshall pointed out that "[s]ince 1983, the Arkansas Supreme Court, on direct review, has reversed in 8 out of 19 cases in which the death penalty had been imposed;" the "Florida Supreme Court set aside 47% of death sentences between 1972 and 1984;" the "Texas Court of Criminal Appeals reversed conviction or invalidated death sentence in 33% of cases between October 1975 and March 1979;" and that the "Georgia Supreme Court did same in 30% of capital cases between April 1974 and March 1979." *Whitmore*, 495 U.S. at 149.

987. *Whitmore*, 495 U.S. at 170.

988. *Id.* at 172.

989. 111 S. Ct. 1454, *reh'g denied*, 111 S. Ct. 2841 (1991).

990. *See supra* text accompanying note 675.

991. *McCleskey*, 111 S. Ct. at 1470.

992. *Id.* at 1477-79 (Marshall citing Murray v. Carrier, 477 U.S. 478 (1986); Smith v. Murray, 477 U.S. 527 (1986); Wainwright v. Sykes, 433 U.S. 72 (1977); Sanders v. United States, 373 U.S. 1 (1963); Price v. Johnston, 334 U.S. 266 (1948); and Wong Doo v. United States, 265 U.S. 239 (1924)).

993. *Id.* at 1478.

across "'new or additional information'[994] in support of a claim not previously raised,"[995] should not be required to "demonstrate any particular degree of prejudice"[996] before a second or subsequent petition is filed. If a defendant, Marshall maintained, "demonstrate[d] that his claim has merit, it is the State that must show that the resulting constitutional error was harmless beyond a reasonable doubt."[997] Marshall believed that an accused whose sentence may have been based on arbitrary factors should not be compelled to show that a lesser penalty would likely have been imposed had the alleged error not have been committed by the trial judge; this position, he concluded, placed a formidable obstacle on the accused, and may give a state reason to believe that there will be fewer occasions in which it has to justify its mode of proceeding leading to pronouncement of sentence.

In *Whitmore* and *McCleskey*, Marshall believed that the majority was more concerned with efficient administration of capital statutes than examining possibly protracted allegations of arbitrary trial proceedings. In the case of *Payne v. Tennessee*,[998] decided on the last day of the October, 1990 Term, Marshall expressed his strongest objection to the Court's perceived insensitiveness to a litigant's assertion of abridgment of due process protections.

The *Payne* case considered whether the introduction of statements from family members of the murdered individual concerning their emotional suffering unconstitutionally diverted the jury's attention from the circumstances of the accused and made possible a sentence based on factors unrelated to the defendant's culpability. Though the Court had previously disallowed such testimony due to its perceived likelihood of producing a verdict based on the jurors' emotions,[999] the majority in *Payne* believed that introduction of victim impact statements would enable jurors to more broadly weigh a range of factors connected to an offense and acquire a better insight into the character and circumstances of the accused.[1000] Prior rulings never held that "the defendant, entitled as he was to individualized consideration, was

---

994. Marshall quoting Price v. Johnston, 334 U.S. 266, 290 (1948).

995. *Id.* at 1479.

996. *Id.* at 1479.

997. *Id.* at 1479.

998. 111 S. Ct. 2597, *reh'g denied*, 112 S. Ct. 28 (1991).

999. *See* Booth v. Maryland, 482 U.S. 496, *reh'g denied*, 483 U.S. 1056 (1987), *overruled by* Payne v. Tennessee, 111 S. Ct. 2597 (1991); South Carolina v. Gathers, 490 U.S. 805, *reh'g denied*, 492 U.S. 938 (1989), *overruled by* Payne v. Tennessee, 111 S. Ct. 2597 (1991).

1000. *Payne*, 111 S. Ct. at 2607.

to receive that consideration wholly apart from the crime which he had committed,"[1001] and the Court, after indicating that states retained considerable discretion to formulate proceedings in trial deliberations,[1002] overruled precedent[1003] and concluded that the Eighth Amendment established "no per se bar"[1004] to the admission of victim impact evidence.

The dissenting opinion written by Marshall contained his most vitriolic statements on the majority's evolving Eighth Amendment jurisprudence. "Power, not reason," he declared at the outset, "is the new currency of this Court's decisionmaking."[1005] The majority's contention that "stare decisis is not an inexorable command,"[1006] and that the need to correct decisions which "are unworkable or are badly reasoned"[1007] is compelling when precedents are not old, was categorized by Marshall as a "staggering"[1008] position which "sends a clear signal that scores of established constitutional liberties are now ripe for reconsideration."[1009] Adherence to precedent, Marshall pointed out, furnished stability and continuity in the law, and its abandonment should not be undertaken without "'special justification.'"[1010] In the past several years, however, there have been no changes in legal or social developments to warrant a new constitutional interpretation. Marshall believed that the majority's pronouncement made a mockery of the Court's fundamental position to channel the discretion of sentencing authorities and confine examination of evidence to the individualized circumstances of the accused and offense. Sentencing decisions based on bias are now being sanctioned, and Marshall concluded with a pessimistic projection of future trends: "Cast aside today are those condemned to face society's ultimate penalty. Tomorrow's victims may be minorities, women, or the indigent."[1011]

On June 28, 1991, the day after the *Payne* decision was issued, Marshall, citing advancing age and declining health, announced his retirement.

1001. *Id.*
1002. *Id.* at 2608.
1003. *See supra* note 997.
1004. *Payne*, 111 S. Ct. at 2609.
1005. *Id.* at 2619.
1006. *Id.* at 2609.
1007. *Id.*
1008. *Id.* at 2619.
1009. *Id.*
1010. *Id.* at 2621 (quoting Arizona v. Rumsey, 467 U.S. 203, 212 (1984)).
1011. *Id.* at 2625.

VI.   A COMPARISON OF BRENNAN'S AND MARSHALL'S POSITIONS ON CAPITAL PUNISHMENT

The jurisprudence of Brennan and Marshall on the applicability of the Eighth Amendment's prohibition of "cruel and unusual punishments" to the death penalty is virtually identical. Categorical opposition to capital punishment was first expressed by both Justices in the 1972 case of *Furman v. Georgia*,[1012] essentially for similar reasons: the death penalty, a barbaric form of punishment which inflicts a great deal of pain, is offensive to human dignity; it is arbitrarily imposed and racially biased regarding the class of offenders sentenced to death; it is offensive to contemporary society; and it does not deter commission of homicide or serve any demonstrable purpose of punishment.[1013] Fundamentally, Brennan and Marshall fervently believed that the wording of the Eighth Amendment prohibited the death penalty, and both shared perceptions of judicial power which justified abolition notwithstanding widespread adoption of capital punishment at the state and federal levels.

Brennan and Marshall frequently expressed their views on the death penalty. In forty-two cases decided by the Burger Court (1969-1986), excluding petitions for certiorari and stays of execution decided without an opinion,[1014] Brennan wrote ten full opinions[1015] and a brief concurring statement[1016] in sixteen

---

1012.   408 U.S. 238, *reh'g denied*, 409 U.S. 902 (1972). *See also supra* text accompanying notes 404-85, 713-82.

1013.   For the position of Brennan, see *supra* text accompanying notes 421-24; for Marshall's pronouncements, see *supra* text accompanying notes 731-34.

1014.   *See supra* note 322; *see also*, Furman v. Georgia, 408 U.S. 238, *reh'g denied*, 409 U.S. 902 (1972); Jackson v. Georgia, 408 U.S. 238, *reh'g denied*, 409 U.S. 902 (1972); Branch v. Texas, 408 U.S. 238, *reh'g denied*, 409 U.S. 902 (1972); McGautha v. California, 402 U.S. 183 (1971), *reh'g denied*, 406 U.S. 978 (1972); Crampton v. Ohio, 402 U.S. 183 (1971), *vacated*, 408 U.S. 941 (1972). For an overview of the Burger Court's position on capital punishment, see *supra* text accompanying notes 265-336.

1015.   Glass v. Louisiana, 471 U.S. 1080 (1985) (Brennan, J., dissenting); Wainwright v. Witt, 469 U.S. 412 (1985) (Brennan, J., dissenting); Francis v. Franklin, 471 U.S. 307 (1985) (Brennan, J., for the majority); Strickland v. Washington, 466 U.S. 668, *reh'g denied*, 467 U.S. 1267 (1984) (Brennan, J., concurring in part and dissenting in part); Pulley v. Harris, 465 U.S. 37 (1984) (Brennan, J., dissenting); Maggio v. Williams, 464 U.S. 46 (1983) (Brennan, J., dissenting); Sandstrom v. Montana, 442 U.S. 510 (1979) (Brennan, J., for the majority); Gregg v. Georgia, 428 U.S. 153, *reh'g denied*, 429 U.S. 875 (1976) (Brennan, J., dissenting); Furman v. Georgia, 408 U.S. 238, *reh'g denied*, 409 U.S. 902 (1972) (Brennan, J., concurring); McGautha v. California, 402 U.S. 183 (1971), *reh'g denied*, 406 U.S. 978 (1972) (Brennan, J., dissenting).

1016.   *See supra* note 505.

others;[1017] Marshall wrote sixteen full opinions[1018] and added a brief statement reiterating his categorical opposition to the death penalty where the Court invalidated a sentence of death on ten occasions.[1019] The Rehnquist Court (1986-), up to Brennan's retirement in 1990, decided thirty-two opinions on capital pun-

---

1017. Turner v. Murray, 476 U.S. 28 (1986) (Brennan, J., concurring in part and dissenting in part); Cabana v. Bullock, 474 U.S. 376 (1986) (Brennan, J., dissenting); Campbell v. Washington, 103 Wash. 2d 1, 691 P.2d 929, *cert. denied,* 471 U.S. 1094 (1985) (Brennan, J., concurring); Baldwin v. Alabama, 472 U.S. 372 (1985) (Brennan, J., dissenting); Smith v. Kemp, 717 F.2d 1401 (11th Cir.), *cert. denied,* 464 U.S. 1032 (1983) (Brennan, J., concurring); Enmund v. Florida, 458 U.S. 782 (1982) (Brennan, J., concurring); Eddings v. Oklahoma, 455 U.S. 104 (1982) (Brennan, J., concurring); Estelle v. Smith, 451 U.S. 454 (1981) (Brennan, J., concurring); Adams v. Texas, 448 U.S. 38 (1980) (Brennan, J., concurring); Beck v. Alabama, 447 U.S. 625 (1980) (Brennan, J., concurring); Green v. Georgia, 442 U.S. 95 (1979) (Brennan, J., concurring); Coker v. Georgia, 433 U.S. 584 (1977) (Brennan, J., concurring); Dobbert v. Florida, 432 U.S. 282, *reh'g denied,* 434 U.S. 882 (1977) (Brennan, J., concurring); Gardner v. Florida, 430 U.S. 349 (1977) (Brennan, J., concurring); Roberts v. Louisiana, 428 U.S. 325, *reh'g denied,* 429 U.S. 890 (1976) (Brennan, J., concurring); Woodson v. North Carolina, 428 U.S. 280 (1976) (Brennan, J., concurring).

1018. Ford v. Wainwright, 477 U.S. 399 (1986) (Marshall, J., for the majority); Caldwell v. Mississippi, 472 U.S. 320 (1985) (Marshall, J., for the majority); Ake v. Oklahoma, 470 U.S. 68 (1985) (Marshall, J., for the majority); Strickland v. Washington, 466 U.S. 668, *reh'g denied,* 467 U.S. 1267 (1984) (Marshall, J., dissenting); Gray v. Lucas, 677 F.2d 1086 (5th Cir.), *cert. denied,* 463 U.S. 1237 (1983) (Marshall, J., dissenting); Barefoot v. Estelle, 463 U.S. 880 (1983) (Marshall, J., dissenting); Zant v. Stephens, 462 U.S. 862 (1983) (Marshall, J., dissenting); California v. Ramos, 463 U.S. 992 (1983) (Marshall, J., dissenting); Barclay v. Florida, 463 U.S. 939, *reh'g denied,* 464 U.S. 874 (1983) (Marshall, J., dissenting); Coleman v. Balkcom, 451 U.S. 949 (1981) (Marshall, J., dissenting); Godfrey v. Georgia, 446 U.S. 420 (1980) (Marshall, J., concurring); Lockett v. Ohio, 438 U.S. 586 (1978) (Marshall, J., concurring); Coker v. Georgia, 433 U.S. 584 (1977) (Marshall, J., concurring); Gardner v. Florida, 430 U.S. 349 (1977) (Marshall, J., concurring); Gregg v. Georgia, 428 U.S. 153, *reh'g denied,* 429 U.S. 875 (1976) (Marshall, J., dissenting); Furman v. Georgia, 408 U.S. 238, *reh'g denied,* 409 U.S. 902 (1972) (Marshall, J., concurring).

1019. Turner v. Murray, 476 U.S. 28 (1986) (Marshall, J., concurring in part and dissenting in part); Estelle v. Smith, 451 U.S. 454 (1981) (Marshall, J., concurring); Adams v. Texas, 448 U.S. 38 (1980) (Marshall, J., concurring); Beck v. Alabama, 447 U.S. 625 (1980) (Marshall, J., concurring); Green v. Georgia, 442 U.S. 95 (1979) (Marshall, J., concurring); Bell v. Ohio, 438 U.S. 637 (1978) (Marshall, J., concurring); Dobbert v. Florida, 432 U.S. 282, *reh'g denied,* 434 U.S. 882 (1977) (Marshall, J., concurring); Jurek v. Texas, 428 U.S. 262, *reh'g denied sub nom.* Gregg v. Georgia, 429 U.S. 875 (1976) (Marshall, J., dissenting); Woodson v. North Carolina, 428 U.S. 280 (1976) (Marshall, J., concurring); Roberts v. Louisiana, 428 U.S. 325, *reh'g denied,* 429 U.S. 890 (1976) (Marshall, J., concurring).

ishment;[1020] Brennan wrote ten full opinions[1021] and a brief statement in five others.[1022] During this period, Marshall wrote six full opinions[1023] and two brief concurring statements.[1024] In 1991, Marshall wrote an opinion in three[1025] of seven[1026] capital punishment cases decided by the Rehnquist Court. Brennan wrote just three[1027] majority opinions, and Marshall spoke for the

---

1020.   *See supra* notes 337-39. For an overview of the Rehnquist Court's position on capital punishment, see *supra* text accompanying notes 337-64.

1021.   Demosthenes v. Baal, 110 S. Ct. 2223 (1990) (Brennan, J., dissenting); Walton v. Arizona, 110 S. Ct. 3047, *reh'g denied*, 111 S. Ct. 14 (1990) (Brennan, J., dissenting; also applied to Lewis v. Jeffers, 110 S. Ct. 3092, *reh'g denied*, 111 S. Ct. 14 (1990); Blystone v. Pennsylvania, 110 S. Ct. 1078 (1990) (Brennan, J., dissenting); Saffle v. Parks, 110 S. Ct. 1257 (1990) (Brennan, J., dissenting); Stanford v. Kentucky, 492 U.S. 361, *reh'g denied*, 492 U.S. 937 (1989) (Brennan, J., dissenting); Penry v. Lynaugh, 492 U.S. 302 (1989) (Brennan, J., concurring in part and dissenting in part); South Carolina v. Gathers, 490 U.S. 805, *reh'g denied*, 492 U.S. 938 (1989) (Brennan, J., for the majority); McCleskey v. Kemp, 481 U.S. 279, *reh'g denied*, 482 U.S. 920 (1987) (Brennan, J., dissenting); California v. Brown, 479 U.S. 538 (1987) (Brennan, J., dissenting); Tison v. Arizona, 481 U.S. 137, *reh'g denied*, 482 U.S. 921 (1987) (Brennan, J., dissenting).

1022.   Clemons v. Mississippi, 494 U.S. 738 (1990) (Brennan, J., concurring in part and dissenting in part); Hildwin v. Florida, 490 U.S. 638, *reh'g denied*, 492 U.S. 927 (1989) (Brennan, J., dissenting); Mills v. Maryland, 486 U.S. 367 (1988) (Brennan, J., concurring); Johnson v. Mississippi, 486 U.S. 578 (1988) (Brennan, J., concurring); Maynard v. Cartwright, 486 U.S. 356 (1988) (Brennan, J., concurring).

1023.   McKoy v. North Carolina, 494 U.S. 433 (1990) (Marshall, J., for the majority); Whitmore v. Arkansas, 110 S. Ct. 1717 (1990) (Marshall, J., dissenting); Sawyer v. Smith, 110 S. Ct. 2822, *reh'g denied*, 111 S. Ct. 17 (1990) (Marshall, J., dissenting); Shell v. Mississippi, 111 S. Ct. 313 (1990) (Marshall, J., concurring); Lowenfield v. Phelps, 484 U.S. 231, *reh'g denied*, 485 U.S. 944 (1988) (Marshall, J., dissenting); Satterwhite v. Texas, 486 U.S. 249 (1988) (Marshall, J., concurring).

1024.   Boyde v. California, 494 U.S. 370, *reh'g denied*, 110 S. Ct. 1961 (1990) (Marshall, J., dissenting); Hildwin v. Florida, 490 U.S. 638, *reh'g denied*, 492 U.S. 927 (1989) (Marshall, J., dissenting).

1025.   Mu'Min v. Virginia, 111 S. Ct. 1899, *reh'g denied*, 112 S. Ct. 13 (1991) (Marshall, J., dissenting); McCleskey v. Zant, 111 S. Ct. 1454, *reh'g denied*, 111 S. Ct. 2841 (1991) (Marshall, J., dissenting); Payne v. Tennessee, 111 S. Ct. 2597, *reh'g denied*, 112 S. Ct. 28 (1991) (Marshall, J., dissenting).

1026.   Parker v. Dugger, 111 S. Ct. 731, *reh'g denied*, 111 S. Ct. 1340 (1991); McCleskey v. Zant, 111 S. Ct. 1454, *reh'g denied*, 111 S. Ct. 2841 (1991); Lankford v. Idaho, 111 S. Ct. 1723 (1991); Yates v. Evatt, 111 S. Ct. 1884 (1991); Mu'Min v. Virginia, 111 S. Ct. 1899, *reh'g denied*, 112 S. Ct. 13 (1991); Schad v. Arizona, 111 S. Ct. 2491, *reh'g denied*, 112 S. Ct. 28 (1991); Payne v. Tennessee, 111 S. Ct. 2597, *reh'g denied*, 112 S. Ct. 28 (1991).

1027.   South Carolina v. Gathers, 490 U.S. 805 (1989); Francis v. Franklin, 471 U.S. 307 (1985); Sandstrom v. Montana, 442 U.S. 510 (1979).

Court on four occasions.[1028] Except for one case — *Strickland v. Washington* (1984)[1029] — Brennan and Marshall always voted identically, and, in addition to this instance, they each wrote separate lengthy opinions in the same case on just one other occasion.[1030] Thus, from 1972 to 1990 (the year of Brennan's retirement), Brennan and Marshall took different perspectives in just two cases.[1031]

The central component of Brennan and Marshall's position on the death penalty was based on the Court's contention in *Trop v. Dulles* (1958)[1032] that the Eighth Amendment "must draw its meaning from the evolving standards of decency that mark the progress of a maturing society."[1033] Both believed that perceptions of unacceptable cruelty have evolved to a point where the death penalty is considered offensive to human dignity. This enlightened sense of justice, Brennan and Marshall maintained, also made evident that the death penalty is not a demonstrable deterrent to the commission of homicide and cannot be tolerated purely to inflict retribution on an alleged offender. Both Justices strongly believed that it was impossible to prevent arbitrariness and bias, in some degree, from entering into capital proceedings, and, given prejudice, ignorance, or lack of clarity concerning trial officials' scope of responsibility, wrongful conviction and sentence are unavoidable. Brennan and Marshall also maintained that it was appropriate to construe the Eighth Amendment in light of perceived changing attitudes and notions of justice; previous acceptance and infliction of the death penalty did not unwaveringly bind the Court to preserve its constitutionality intact.

In his Oliver Wendell Holmes, Jr. Lecture at Harvard University on September 5, 1986,[1034] Brennan, after summarizing the Court's Eighth Amendment jurisprudence,[1035] explained that, while the precise understanding of the Framers cannot be ascertained, the phrase "cruel and unusual punishments" indi-

---

1028.   McKoy v. North Carolina, 494 U.S. 433 (1990); Ford v. Wainwright, 477 U.S. 399 (1986); Caldwell v. Mississippi, 472 U.S. 320 (1985); Ake v. Oklahoma, 470 U.S. 68 (1985).

1029.   466 U.S. 668, *reh'g denied*, 467 U.S. 1267 (1984) (Brennan, J., concurring in part and dissenting in part) (Marshall, J., dissennting).

1030.   *Furman*, 408 U.S. 238 (1972) (Brennan, J., concurring) (Marshall, J., concurring). *See supra* text accompanying notes 404-85, 713-82.

1031.   *Strickland*, 466 U.S. 668 (1990); *Furman*, 408 U.S. 238 (1972).

1032.   356 U.S. 86 (1958).

1033.   *Id.* at 101.

1034.   William J. Brennan, Jr., *Constitutional Adjudication and the Death Penalty: A View From the Court*, 100 HARV. L. REV. 313 (1986).

1035.   *Id.* at 313-23.

cated an intention for a principle to endure. The Framers, Brennan pointed out, spoke unambiguously in certain provisions of the Constitution,[1036] and could have explicitly sanctioned the death penalty if this was desired. Instead, they adopted imprecise wording to convey to posterity an "understanding that this language ["cruel and unusual punishments"] was *not* specific and could be interpreted in any number of ways. . . ." The "best way to effectuate the intent of the Framers," Brennan declared, "is to allow the constitutional prohibition of cruel and unusual punishment to *breathe*, . . .[1037] by deriving and then applying the principles and values that underlie the clause."[1038] Since the Bill of Rights is intended to restrain legislative power, Brennan believed that ultimate responsibility for interpreting its provisions in light of contemporary values lies with the judiciary. This theme is similarly highlighted in Marshall's jurisprudence.

While the general tone of Brennan and Marshall's constitutional philosophy on capital punishment is evident with regard to their similarities, several subtle differences in perspective also emerge. Interestingly, Brennan expressed deeper sensitiveness to the alleged racially biased components of capital sentencing. To be sure, Marshall addressed this in *Furman*,[1039] *Godfrey*,[1040] and *Payne*,[1041] however, in *McCleskey v. Kemp* (1987),[1042] which, more than any other case, furnished an opportunity to elaborate on sentencing disparities between blacks and whites,[1043] he did not write a separate opinion.[1044] Brennan's opinions tended to accentuate the risk of arbitrary execution as a justification for abolition of the death penalty even where no discernible abridgment of due process protections had occurred in a particular case;[1045] Marshall, on the other hand, advocated abolition based on the perceived inability of trial officials and appellate proceed-

---

1036. *Id.* at 325. Brennan mentioned provisions concerning the minimum age to run for president, as well as the length of term for members of Congress. U.S. CONST. art. II, § 1, cl. 5; art. I, §§ 2, 3, cl. 1.

1037. Brennan, *supra* note 1034, at 325-26.

1038. *Id.* at 328.

1039. 408 U.S. 238. *See supra* text accompanying notes 778, 780.

1040. 446 U.S. 420. *See supra* text accompanying notes 823-25.

1041. 111 S. Ct. 2597. *See supra* text accompanying note 1009.

1042. 481 U.S. 279, *reh'g denied*, 482 U.S. 920 (1987).

1043. *See supra* text accompanying notes 507-17.

1044. *McCleskey*, 481 U.S. at 320 (Marshall, J., joining the dissenting opinion of Brennan, J.).

1045. *See, e.g., Blystone*, 494 U.S. at 299; *Saffle*, 494 U.S. at 484; *McCleskey*, 481 U.S. at 279; *Brown*, 479 U.S. at 538; *Gathers*, 490 U.S. at 805; *Turner*, 476 U.S. at 28; *Tison*, 481 U.S. at 137; *Francis*, 471 U.S. at 307; *Strickland*, 466 U.S. at 668; *Sandstrom*, 442 U.S. at 510. *See supra* text accompanying notes 506-650.

ings to accord full procedural safeguards to a litigant.[1046] Brennan tended to stress that the death penalty was antithetical to enlightened conceptions of human dignity,[1047] while Marshall focused on the inability of capital punishment to fulfill the legislative goal of deterrence.[1048] While both frequently objected that Court rulings are inconsistent with precedents,[1049] Brennan often cited the pronouncement in *Trop* that punishment is to be assessed in light of evolving conceptions of dignity,[1050] while Marshall emphasized the enormity and unique character of capital as opposed to noncapital offenses.[1051] Finally, Marshall's pronouncements in *Payne* revealed invective which did not appear in Brennan's opinions; however, this might be attributed to Marshall's frustration that his strongest judicial supporter was no longer on the bench.

VII. CONCLUSION

Few contemporary issues have brought forth a wider range of emotional feelings than the death penalty. Its statutorily widespread acceptance — only 13 states have refused to authorize capital punishment[1052] — makes the position of Brennan and Marshall, the only members who, up to the end of the October, 1992 Term, expressed unconditional opposition to the death

---

1046. *See, e.g., Caldwell*, 472 U.S. at 320; *Strickland*, 466 U.S. at 668; *Zant*, 462 U.S. at 862; *Barclay*, 463 U.S. at 939; *Ramos*, 463 U.S. at 992; *Godfrey*, 446 U.S. at 420. *See supra* text accompanying notes 818-69. For an elaboration of this position, see Thurgood Marshall, *Remarks on the Death Penalty Made at the Judicial Conference of the Second Circuit*, 86 COLUM. L. REV. 1 (1986).

1047. *See, e.g., Gregg*, 428 U.S. at 153; *Furman*, 408 U.S. at 238. *See supra* text accompanying notes 478-82, 491-97.

1048. For Marshall's most extensive comments on this subject, see *Gregg*, 428 U.S. at 153; *Furman*, 408 U.S. at 238. *See supra* text accompanying notes 789-93, 765-69; *see also, Ramos*, 463 U.S. at 992; *supra* text accompanying note 846.

1049. For Brennan's contention that the Court has not adhered to precedent, see generally, *Saffle*, 494 U.S. at 484; *Tison*, 481 U.S. at 137; *Brown*, 479 U.S. at 538; *McCleskey*, 481 U.S. at 279; and *Wainwright*, 469 U.S. at 412. For Marshall's objection that precedent has not been followed, see generally, *McKoy*, 110 S. Ct. at 1227; *Sawyer*, 110 S. Ct. at 2822; *Zant*, 462 U.S. at 862; *Caldwell*, 472 U.S. at 320; and *Ake*, 470 U.S. at 68. See, however, *Mu'Min*, 111 S. Ct. at 1899, and *supra* text accompanying notes 949-57.

1050. *See, e.g., Stanford*, 492 U.S. at 361; *Penry*, 492 U.S. at 302; *Glass*, 471 U.S. at 1080; *Gregg*, 428 U.S. at 153; *Furman*, 408 U.S. at 238.

1051. *See, e.g., Sawyer*, 497 U.S. at 227; *Whitmore*, 495 U.S. at 149; *Strickland*, 466 U.S. at 668; *Ake*, 470 U.S. at 68; *Barefoot*, 463 U.S. at 880; *Barclay*, 463 U.S. at 939; *Gregg*, 428 U.S. at 153; *Furman*, 408 U.S. at 238.

1052. The death penalty is prohibited in: Alaska, Hawaii, Iowa, Kansas, Maine, Massachusetts, Michigan, Minnesota, New York, North Dakota, Rhode Island, West Virginia, and Wisconsin. BUREAU OF JUSTICE STATISTICS, U.S. DEP'T OF JUSTICE, BULLETIN: CAPITAL PUNISHMENT, 1988 167 (1989).

penalty,[1053] dramatic. Though their views have never been adopted by a majority of the justices, Brennan and Marshall exerted an influence in shaping the direction of adjudication. On the Rehnquist Court, Brennan and Marshall provided a fourth and fifth vote to reverse seven capital convictions,[1054] and both were in the minority in all twelve rulings which upheld a sentence of death by a five-to-four vote.[1055] In 1991, following Brennan's retirement, Marshall contributed a fifth vote to reverse two capital sentences.[1056]

Perhaps Brennan and Marshall's position can best be challenged by pointing out that the penalty of death is recognized in the Fifth and Fourteenth Amendments,[1057] and that, while its manner of infliction may be regulated, adoption of capital punishment is not prohibited by the states. Brennan himself addressed this position, and denied that the death penalty is constitutionally sanctioned. He dismissed as "untenable" the contention "that the Constitution shows that the Framers *intended* that

---

1053. In *Furman*, 408 U.S. at 238, Justice Harry Blackmun conveyed the "depth of" his "distaste, antipathy, and, indeed, abhorrence, for the death penalty," and declared that, were he a legislator, he would vote against it. As a Justice, however, Blackmun felt obligated to support capital punishment. 408 U.S. at 405-06, 410-11 (Blackmun, J., dissenting). On February 22, 1994, Justice Blackmun announced that he would not longer support any death penalty convictions. Collins v. Collins, *cert. denied*, No. 93-7054. *See Blackmun: 'I . . . Concede That the Death Penalty Experiment Has Failed.'*, N.Y. TIMES, Feb. 23, 1994, at A10. Justice Arthur Goldberg, who sat on the Court from 1962-1965, expressed opposition to capital punishment after stepping down. *See* Arthur J. Goldberg, *The Death Penalty and the Supreme Court*, 15 ARIZ. L. REV. 355 (1973). Brennan intimated that he, along with Justices Goldberg and Douglas, was prepared to strike down the death penalty in the 1963 case of Rudolph v. Alabama, 375 U.S. at 889 (Goldberg, J., joined by Douglas, J., and Brennan, J., dissenting from denial of certiorari). Brennan, *supra* note 1034, at 315-16. For a discussion of *Rudolph*, see *supra* text accompanying notes 243-46.

1054. Murray v. Giarratano, 492 U.S. 1 (1989); *Gathers*, 490 U.S. at 805; Dugger v. Adams, 489 U.S. 401, *reh'g denied*, 490 U.S. 1031 (1989); Thompson v. Oklahoma, 487 U.S. 815 (1988); Mills v. Maryland, 486 U.S. 367 (1988); *Brown*, 479 U.S. at 538; Booth v. Maryland, 482 U.S. 496, *reh'g denied*, 483 U.S. 1056 (1987), *and overruled by* Payne v. Tennessee, 111 S. Ct. 2597 (1991).

1055. Lewis v. Jeffers, 497 U.S. 764 (1990), *reh'g denied*, 111 S. Ct. 14 (1990); Walton v. Arizona, 497 U.S. 639 (1990), *reh'g denied*, 497 U.S. 1050 (1990); *Sawyer*, 495 U.S. at 731; *Demosthenes*, 110 S. Ct. at 2223; *Clemons*, 494 U.S. at 738; *Saffle*, 110 S. Ct. at 1257; *Boyde*, 494 U.S. at 370; *Blystone*, 494 U.S. at 299; *Stanford*, 492 U.S. at 361; *Lowenfield*, 484 U.S. at 231; Burger v. Kemp, 482 U.S. 776, *reh'g denied*, 483 U.S. 1056 (1987); McCleskey v. Kemp, 481 U.S. 279 (1987); *Tison*, 481 U.S. at 137.

1056. Lankford v. Idaho, 111 S. Ct. 1723 (1991); Parker v. Dugger, 111 S. Ct. 731, *reh'g denied*, 111 S. Ct. 1340 (1991).

1057. *See supra* text accompanying notes 132, 133.

there be capital punishment;"[1058] rather, Brennan believed that the authors "sought to ensure that *if* there was capital punishment, the process by which the accused was to be convicted would be especially reliable."[1059] Regarding the wording of the Eighth Amendment, Brennan maintained that it does not categorize the death penalty "for all time as presumptively *not* cruel and unusual."[1060] In response, one may argue that the Constitution does not preclude states from adopting capital punishment and that the Court must abide by this decision while retaining power to prescribe its mode of infliction. Brennan and Marshall, however, maintained that the Court did have power to invalidate capital statutes even though they presumably had been enacted with majority support.

It is, arguably, difficult for a justice to separate perceptions of constitutionality from personal views of morality. The degree of deference to state policymaking choices or supervision of statutory provisions a justice chooses to follow is based, in part, on perceptions of dignity and humanity with which the citizenry is likely to be treated. This, in turn, may compel a justice to assess constitutionality in view of its perceived moral character. This was the perspective taken by Brennan and Marshall on capital punishment: it presented a constitutional question which could not be addressed without also examining its moral implications. Clearly, the position of Brennan and Marshall that a maximum sentence of life imprisonment is contemplated by the Eighth Amendment has not, any more than arguments put forward by retentionists, been shown to be a realistic deterrent to the commission of homicide, and their insistence, despite adoption of capital punishment by well over 50% of the states (and the District of Columbia), on categorically invalidating the death penalty, does not reflect support of majority rule or a policy preference representative of the people. Their opposition to the death penalty was based both on interpretation of the Eighth Amendment and their personal position on the taking by government of human life. In other words, they did not say that they personally did not object to capital punishment but, as Justices sworn by oath to interpret the Constitution, must oppose it; their opposition to the death penalty was substantially influenced by their perception of morality.

Fundamentally, Brennan and Marshall expressed a viewpoint on their understanding of the role of the Court in Ameri-

---

1058.   Brennan, *supra* note 1032, at 324 (emphasis in original).
1059.   *Id.* (emphasis in original).
1060.   *Id.* (emphasis in original).

can society. The Constitution, they believed, embodied moral principles which need to be reexamined by each generation, and the Court, in view of its pivotal responsibility to protect citizens from excessive and arbitrary governmental power, is obligated to reconcile the ongoing vision of the document with the perceived aspirations of the people. Thus, morality is an integral component of constitutional adjudication, and its expression by Brennan and Marshall has enriched our understanding of capital punishment.